THE TRINITY AND AN ENTANGLED WORLD

The Trinity and an Entangled World

Relationality in Physical Science and Theology

Edited by

John Polkinghorne

WILLIAM B. EERDMANS PUBLISHING COMPANY

GRAND RAPIDS, MICHIGAN / CAMBRIDGE, U.K.

© 2010 Wm. B. Eerdmans Publishing Co.

Published 2010 by
Wm. B. Eerdmans Publishing Co.
2140 Oak Industrial Drive N.E., Grand Rapids, Michigan 49505 /
P.O. Box 163, Cambridge CB3 9PU U.K.

Printed in the United States of America

16 15 14 13 12 11 10   7 6 5 4 3 2 1

Library of Congress Cataloging-in-Publication Data

The trinity and an entangled world: relationality in physical science and theology /
edited by John Polkinghorne.
p.   cm.
Includes bibliographical references.
ISBN 978-0-8028-6512-0 (pbk.: alk. paper)
1. Religion and science.
2. Physical sciences — Religious aspects — Christianity.
I. Polkinghorne, J. C., 1930-

BL240.3.T75   2010
261.5'5 — dc22

2010013889

www.eerdmans.com

Contents

Introduction   vii
John Polkinghorne

The Demise of Democritus   1
John Polkinghorne

The Entangled World: How Can It Be Like That?   15
Jeffrey Bub

Quantum Physics: Ontology or Epistemology?   32
Anton Zeilinger

A Self-Contained Universe?   41
Michael Heller

An Introduction to Relational Ontology   55
Wesley J. Wildman

Scientific Knowledge as a Bridge to the Mind of God   74
Panos A. Ligomenides

Relational Nature   93
Argyris Nicolaidis

Contents

The Holy Trinity: Model for Personhood-in-Relation   107
Kallistos Ware

(Mis)Adventures in Trinitarian Ontology   130
Lewis Ayres

Relational Ontology: Insights from Patristic Thought   146
John Zizioulas

Relation: Human and Divine   157
Michael Welker

A Relational Ontology Reviewed in Sociological Perspective   168
David Martin

Afterword: "Relational Ontology," Trinity, and Science   184
Sarah Coakley

Contributors   200

Index   205

Introduction

JOHN POLKINGHORNE

In its exploration of the physical world science has increasingly found that concepts of atomism and mechanism, useful though they undoubtedly are for some purposes, are nevertheless unable to express fully the character of physical reality. A methodological reductionism, decomposing complex entities into simpler constituent parts, has often proved an effective strategy for investigation in science, but this is by no means always the case. It seems that nature fights back against the supposition of the ontological adequacy of a purely atomistic point of view. The history of twentieth-century physics can be read as the story of the discovery of many levels of intrinsic relationality present in the structure of the universe.

In chapter 1, John Polkinghorne surveys the wide range of phenomena that have led to this recognition of holistic connectivity in the physical world. In chapters 2 and 3 respectively, Jeffrey Bub and Anton Zeilinger pay particular and detailed attention to one of the most remarkable phenomena of physical relationality, the property of quantum entanglement. In the subatomic world, interaction can bring about states that have to be considered as a single unified system, even though composed of constituents that may spatially be widely separated. Zeilinger emphasizes that in such entangled states, what is known with certainty is not the individual properties of constituents but the relationships existing between them.

In chapter 4, Michael Heller explores a new approach to cosmological theory that is based on the mathematics of noncommutative geometry. According to this view, at the deepest level of physical reality there are only global properties and our apparent experiences of localized space and time emerge as approximations to this more subtle physical reality.

These scientific insights and discoveries are of obvious relevance to metaphysical and theological accounts of reality. Yet one must recognize that there is no simple logical entailment between physics and metaphysics, or from science to theology. The discoveries of science constrain, but do not determine, the shape of more comprehensive thinking, rather as the foundations of a house constrain, but do not uniquely determine, the edifice to be built upon them. For instance, the nature of causality is a metaphysical issue not settled by physics alone, even if the latter's great explanatory success does not encourage the thought that all that is involved is a mysterious and inexplicable constant conjunction. The point is made clearly enough by the fact that there are both indeterministic and deterministic interpretations of quantum theory, both being of equal empirical adequacy. The choice between them has to be made on metascientific grounds, such as judgments of economy, elegance, and lack of contrivance. The relation between the physical insights presented in the first four chapters of this book and the discussions in the chapters that follow has to depend upon some form of alogical discernment of degrees of cousinly connection, of a kind that might be characterized by words such as "resonance," "consonance," "analogy," "mutual influence," and the like. Accordingly, this book offers a variety of options for how relational ontology may be understood when considered in the broadest context and the deepest manner.

In chapter 5, Wesley Wildman proposes to use a concept of causality as the common factor in considerations of relationality, though he admits that there are forms of relationship (value, conceptual, logical) that require elaborated argument under his rubric. Wildman identifies five metaphysical types of causal theory: participation (in which he locates Trinitarian theology); pratiya-samutpada (based on the Buddhist doctrine of anatta); process (following the thought of A. N. Whitehead); semiosis (derived from the thought of C. S. Peirce); and implicate-order (arising out of D. Bohm's deterministic interpretation of quantum theory). In chapter 7, Argyris Nicolaidis shows how a physicist finds the Peircean approach particularly illuminating.

In chapter 6, another scientist, Panos Ligomenides, explains that he finds most helpful the pantheistic concepts of Benedict Spinoza, identifying the divine with the deep structure of the universe *(deus sive natura)*. This kind of cosmic religion is quite common among scientists and it was embraced by Albert Einstein, who said that if he had a God it was indeed the God of Spinoza.

The next three chapters are concerned with the insights offered by Trinitarian theology, with its understanding of the triune God whose essential being is constituted by the perichoretic exchange of mutually interpenetrating love between the three divine Persons. In chapter 8, Timothy Ware offers a review of patristic Trinitarian theology. Contemporary assessments of this classic resource for Christian theology have recently produced a degree of revision in the judgments made. Earlier thinking had tended to draw a distinction between the theologies of the Eastern and Western churches, with the former being held to accord priority to the acknowledgment of the Three before moving to the discussion of the unity of the One, while the latter's thought was considered to move in the opposite direction from the One to the Three. It is now quite widely recognized that East and West are closer to each other than this approach suggests. Consequently a more balanced account is being proposed, giving precedence neither to relationality over being nor to being over relationality. Certainly a vigorous debate is in process on these issues, and chapters 9 and 10, by Lewis Ayres and John Zizioulas respectively, offer the reader access to this current discussion.

This volume deliberately concentrates its attention on the connection between thinking in the physical sciences and matters of wider interpretative concern, without in any way wishing to imply that important sources of insight are not to be found also in biology, anthropology, and sociology. The next two chapters endeavor to redress the balance of our book a little. In chapter 10, the systematic theologian Michael Welker draws on insights from child development studies to argue for a complex account of the nature of relationship, transcending simple notions of transactions between "two points of reference." In chapter 12, David Martin uses examples drawn from sociological studies to argue for a charismatic element in human relationships that will only find its complete fulfillment eschatologically.

In an Afterword, Sarah Coakley offers some reflections on Trinitarian relationality, and on the philosophical analysis of the concepts of relation and causation. These are offered partly as a contribution to carry the discussion further beyond the confines of the present book. Coakley discerns three phases in the twentieth-century development of Trinitarian theology. In the first (Lossky, Barth, Rahner) the focus was on opposing an Enlightenment dismissal of theological metaphysics. In the second phase (Zizioulas), it was atomistic individualism that had to be combated. The latter was a move that proved congenial to some scientists and it has served to encourage a positive interaction between science and theology. Many of the authors of this volume have been influenced by this development, but there has also been a third phase of reaction to it, which Coakley sees as represented in these pages by Ayres and, to a degree, by Ware. The conclusion of her theological analysis is that one can see "signals of the end of a mandatory Enlightenment clamp on speculative metaphysics about the divine," a judgment in which all the other authors of this volume will surely concur. Finally, Coakley emphasizes the complexity of philosophical debate about the concepts of relation and causality. Her final challenge is to ask the question, "Why three?"

A wide-ranging study of this kind faces terminological difficulties and conceptual problems. Fundamental to the discussion are terms such as "causality" and "relationality," which have a multivalent character, varying in their precise meanings according to the contexts in which they are being employed. Certainly there does not seem to be a simple univocal definition of these key words that would cover the whole range of the book. Instead, the authors access a portfolio of connected meanings, related to each other by something like a Wittgensteinian "family resemblance." For example, there are contexts in which the idea of causality involves a significant temporal element (cause preceding and bringing about an effect), which in other usages will be lacking (the Creator's causal sustaining of creation; the Trinitarian concept of the Father as the eternal fount of being of the Son and the Spirit). It is important to recognize this necessary semantic flexibility and not to insist on stipulating a single limited meaning. Similarly, the concept of relationship needs to be flexibly employed. Electrons as excitations in a common electron field; quantum entanglement; the gravitational interaction of Sun and planets; human kinship; Creator and creation; the Trinitarian mutuality of perichoresis — these are all properly to be thought of as forms of relationality, in a degree of mutual congruence with each other despite their obviously very different proper characters.

Finally, one might enquire what light one might reasonably expect physics to be able to shed on metaphysical or theological matters. We have already acknowledged that its influence will not be such as to determine finally the issues raised in that wider discourse. Instead, it can offer the possibility of a source of supportive consonance with more ambitious accounts of reality. Moreover, the practice of physics encourages the expectation that, just as physicists in their own domain have found relationality to be more extensive and more surprising in its character than prior expectation would have led them to anticipate, so philosophers and theologians should be open to the possibility of unexpected discovery and counterintuitive insight.

The papers that constitute the chapters of this book were presented and discussed at two conferences supported by the John Templeton Foundation. All the authors are grateful for this generosity and for the considerable assistance we have received from Dr. Mary Ann Meyers of the Foundation.

The Demise of Democritus

JOHN POLKINGHORNE

The minimal form of relationality is simple juxtaposition. Grains of sand simply lie beside each other on the seashore. Not much significance attaches to mere contiguity, though a pile of sand can acquire a relational property when its height reaches a tipping point, at which the addition of a few more grains will trigger a sand-slide. Chemists call mere aggregates "mixtures." Greater significance attaches to "compounds," where forces between the constituents bind them together in a union that endures unless some sufficient exterior influence breaks it apart. The dance of life in a biological cell involves a much more complex and dynamic relationality, sustained by continual interactions between enzymes and proteins in processes of great intricacy. Multicellular life exemplifies yet more complex relationships, as different kinds of cells perform different functions that are essential to the continued life of the organism. In higher animals, activities such as defense of the herd, grooming, and the sharing of food establish a kind of social relationality. Human persons are not simply individual egos, but they are partly constituted by a rich network of interpersonal relationships. Trinitarian theology speaks of Father, Son, and Holy Spirit united in one Godhead by the unique relationship of perichoresis, the mutual interpenetration and exchange of love between the divine Persons. Considerations of this kind suggest a metaphysical picture of reality as a Great Chain of Being, of which the successive links are levels of increasingly profound relationality, expressed in different ways according to the natures of the entities involved.

Developments that have taken place in physical science in the last century have strikingly confirmed this intuition of the fundamental character of relationality. The entities that physics investigates are much less complex than those that are the concern of biology and anthropology, let alone theology's concern with the infinite reality of God. Yet discoveries have been made and insights gained in physical science that have clearly indicated the need not to rely simply on atomistic accounts and reductive techniques of analysis, but to employ also a complementary approach characterized by holism and intrinsic relationality.

In the past, the methodology of physics was largely reductionist. Its motto was "Divide and rule." The motive for this strategy was the pragmatic pursuit of understanding sought in the most readily accessible way, since it is much easier to try to understand bits and pieces than it is to understand entities in their complex totalities. There is no doubt that much success has come to physics through following this approach. An elementary particle physicist like myself has to assert that the unveiling of the quark level in the structure of matter was an important advance, but this should not lead to the boastful claim, sometimes made by particle physicists, that constituent accounts of this kind are the true "Theory of Everything." Even within physics itself this is manifestly false. Using quantum chromodynamics (the theory of quarks) is not the way to tackle the task of understanding the turbulent motion of fluids. In the words of Philip Anderson, a Nobel Prize winner for his work in condensed matter physics, "More is different." Reductionist theories may be methodologically effective for some purposes, but they are far from being epistemologically or ontologically adequate.

The atomic approach fathered by Democritus might have seemed to have found its fullest expression in the eighteenth century, with the post-Newtonian conception of a mechanistic physics, picturing the world as made up of a collection of small particles colliding with each other as they moved in the container of space and in the course of the unfolding of universal time. Despite the mysterious interaction at a distance postulated for gravity, the dominant concept of interactive relationship held in the eighteenth century was through contact. Some pictured atoms as small balls with hooks attached, which might engage with other hooks on other atoms to form a linked system. This picture rose only slightly above the level of mere juxtaposition. Yet reality fights back against such reductive oversimplification. The conceptual world of modern physics is quite different, being altogether more interconnected and relational in its character. A number of developments have brought about the demise of a merely mechanical atomism.

Relationality in Modern Physics

Particles and Fields

Newton's concept of gravitational attraction at a distance, so successful in bringing interrelated order into an account of the solar system, had nevertheless been troubling to him. The character of gravity seemed mysterious, transcending anything capable of being conceived of in terms of contact forces between atoms. Some influence apparently pervaded space far beyond the bodies that were considered to be its source. In the nineteenth century, the development of electromagnetic field theory through the insights of Michael Faraday and James Clerk Maxwell led eventually to the idea of the ether as an all-pervading medium filling the "container" of space. This picture already represented a significant modification of the idea of physical reality as being composed of an assemblage of localized and isolatable units. However, classical fields, though they are spread out through space and vary in time, nevertheless are local entities in a causal sense. What happens in the neighborhood of a point can be altered without inducing immediate changes elsewhere, so even fields can be considered bit by bit. In classical physics, fields are fully determinate entities, described by partial differential equations whose solutions are as well defined as those of the ordinary differential equations that describe particles. Relativity theory abolished the idea of the ether as the carrier of the fields and concentrated on the fields themselves as being fully physical entities, possessing energy and momentum just as material particles do.

Quantum fields, whose properties were first discovered by Paul Dirac, exhibit both wavelike properties (because of their spacetime extension) and also particlelike properties (because their energy comes in discrete packets). Particles and fields are concepts that are fused in contemporary physics. Modern thinking pictures an entity such as an electron as being an excitation in the universal electron field, a concept that subtly modifies a purely atomized notion of electron nature. This field theory idea neatly explains why all electrons manifest exactly the same properties. They are related by their common origin in the electron field.

Quantum theory was also found to imply that collections of electrons are not simply ensembles of juxtaposed individuals, but the presence of many electrons imposes a restraint on the dynamical states available to each individual electron. This collective character of modern physical thinking is expressed in the concept of the "statistics" that govern the behavior of collections of identical particles. Two different kinds of constraint are possible. If the particles obey what is called fermi statistics, as is the case for electrons, then no two particles can ever occupy the same state of motion. The resulting "exclusion principle," implying that the presence of an electron in a state closes it to other electrons, lies at the basis of atomic structure and the form of the periodic table of chemistry, and so it plays a fundamental role in determining the structure of matter and enabling the processes of life. If the particles obey what is called bose statistics, then the reverse collective behavior applies. Bosons display a propensity to aggregate in the same state. Photons, the particles of light, are bosons and their consequent herd instinct is the basis of the laser. In the case of either form of statistics, the possible behavior of an individual particle is related to the state of its cousins.

Space and Time

Albert Einstein's great discoveries of special and general relativity abolished the Newtonian picture of the container nature of absolute space and the flow of an absolute time, totally distinct from each other and simply providing the setting for the motion of atoms. Relativity theory provided instead a consolidated account, intimately linking space, time, and matter in a single package-deal. Matter curves spacetime, and this curvature in its turn influences the paths of matter, in a way that produces the effect we call gravitation. Space and time are no longer the given setting, unchanging in its character, providing the stage on which the material actors of the cosmic drama perform their parts, but there is a dynamic and unfolding interaction between them all.

This integrated theory made it possible to attempt the construction of a model of the physical universe itself, providing the first opportunity for the formulation of a truly scientific cosmology. The intimate relational character of the universe thus constituted, constrained the nature of what could be supposed about its history and structure. In his initial attempt at a cosmology, Einstein, influenced by a preference as old as Aristotle for the concept of an everlasting universe, had thought it necessary to modify his equations in order to permit a static solution. He later described this as the greatest blunder of his life. He had missed the chance to find the time-varying solutions of the original equations, discovered independently by the Russian meteorologist Alexander Friedmann and the Belgian priest

Georges Lemaître, that described an expanding universe of the kind that the observations of Edwin Hubble would subsequently confirm to be the case.

Unified Theories

From one point of view, modern physics has been the tale of the search for ever greater unification of the fundamental properties of nature. The process started with Galileo's assertion, contrary to Aristotle, that terrestrial and celestial matter were the same. In the nineteenth century, the experimental discoveries of Hans Christian Oersted and Michael Faraday, and the deep theoretical insight of James Clerk Maxwell, led to the unification of what had seemed to be two quite different classes of phenomena, electricity and magnetism. In the 1960s, Steven Weinberg and Abdus Salam independently found a way to combine electromagnetism with the weak nuclear interactions responsible for radioactive phenomena such as β-decay, uniting them in a single account. This was a synthesis that on the face of it might have seemed highly unlikely, since the two interactions have very different strengths and the weak interactions display a chirality (a preference for left-handed configurations) that is not present in electromagnetism. Nevertheless it turned out that there was a deep relational structure that bound the two sets of phenomena together.

Since then there has been a vigorous quest for a way to draw the strong nuclear forces and gravity into the greater synthesis of a Grand Unified Theory (GUT), a search that has been encouraged by the way in which the extrapolation of present effects into the realms of ultra-high energy that would have been operative at the epoch immediately following the big bang seems to indicate that all these forces would then have been of comparable strengths. So far, speculative ideas of this kind have not proved wholly successful, or commanded universal acceptance, though many regard superstring theory as a promising contemporary candidate for this unificatory role. Whatever reservations some physicists may have about particular proposals, most nevertheless entertain the expectation that there is indeed some form of GUT underlying the superficial diversity of the forces of nature, a hope that may be seen as expressing a deep intuitive conviction that there is a coherent unified structure expressed in the relationships of the physical world.

Nonlocalizability

Einstein had been one of the grandfathers of quantum theory, but he had come to detest his grandchild. He felt that its cloudy fitfulness threatened the reality of the physical world, in whose character he wanted there to be an unproblematic objectivity. Consequently he sought to discover properties of quantum theory that, he believed, would demonstrate its incompleteness. As part of this program Einstein, together with two young collaborators, Boris Podolsky and Nathan Rosen, showed that once two quantum entities had interacted with each other, the theory implied that they remained coupled together to the extent that a measurement made on one of them would have immediate consequences for the other, however far it had moved away since the interaction. In other words, quantum theory implied nonlocality, a togetherness-in-separation, of a counterintuitive kind. Einstein himself felt that this effect was so "spooky" that it showed there must be something in need of correction in quantum thinking. Yet, long after Einstein's death there came ample experimental confirmation of the mutual entanglement present in quantum processes (the "EPR effect").[1] Quantum entities can be found in states where effectively they behave as a single system, so that acting on one has an instantaneous effect on the others (see the contributions of Jeffrey Bub and Anton Zeilinger). Physical reality fights back against a crass reductionism. It is not possible to describe the world of subatomic physics atomistically! Nature is intrinsically relational.

Two comments need to be made on this remarkable phenomenon. The first is to emphasize that its character is ontological and not merely epistemological. There is, of course, nothing surprising in the fact that knowledge acquired here can also have implications for some distant state of affairs. If an urn contains two balls, one white and one black, and we both take out a ball in our clenched fists, if subsequently I open my hand and see the white ball, then I immediately know that you have the black ball, even if you are now miles away. This was always the case and all that has happened is that I am now aware that it is so. The EPR effect is different. Whatever is measured here has an immediate causal effect, bringing about a new state of affairs elsewhere. It is as if, were I to find a red ball, then you would find you have a blue one, but if I had found a green ball, then your ball would have

---

1. See, for example, John Polkinghorne, *Quantum Theory: A Very Short Introduction* (Oxford: Oxford University Press, 2002), pp. 77-81.

become yellow. The second point is that this EPR effect, though it acts instantaneously, does not violate special relativity. The latter forbids the communication of information faster than the velocity of light, but analysis shows that the EPR process cannot be used for the immediate transmission of the details of the state of affairs from one point to another point. Quantum entanglement is a subtle form of interrelationality.

Modern physics has also discovered limitations on the isolatability previously assumed to be present at the macroscopic level in classical Newtonian physics. These restrictions arise in a way quite different to the case of quantum theory. The systems described by chaos theory display an extreme sensitivity to the minutest detail of their circumstance, and this implies such a degree of vulnerability to external disturbance that they cannot properly be considered in isolation from their environment. The so-called "butterfly effect" gives vivid expression to this insight. When the Earth's weather system is in a chaotic mode, a butterfly stirring the air with its wings in the African jungle today could cause a disturbance capable of growing exponentially till it resulted in a storm over Europe in three to four weeks time. Not only is detailed long-term weather forecasting never going to be possible, but it is clear that the interrelationship of meteorological events is subtle and extensive.

Thus the separability of entities from each other that seems to be so apparent a part of our everyday experience, and which is needed by science for the possibility of successfully contained experimentation (since otherwise one would have to take everything into account before being able to investigate anything), is far from being unproblematic. The older style of scientific thinking started with isolated systems and then asked how they might be conceived to interact with each other. We now see that this is too simplified an account, which needs supplementation by an adequate recognition that holistic effects are also active in the physical world. What all this implies for physics and for metaphysics is still far from being well worked out, but it is clear that atomism has to give way to some intrinsically more relational form of the structure of physical reality.

Causal Structure

For physics, one of the most important relationships is causal connection. However, we shall see that physics by itself is not sufficient to determine its character unambiguously.

The post-Newton generations, greatly influenced by the apparently clear and deterministic character of classical physics, inclined to think that a mechanical model provided the best way to think about causal character, even writing books with titles such as "Man the Machine" (de la Mettrie). It has become clear, however, that a more subtle and supple account is called for. The picture of the universe as a gigantic piece of cosmic clockwork has had to be replaced by thinking that draws on organismic notions as well as those of mere mechanism, perhaps not an altogether surprising conclusion since we ourselves are part of that universe and we are not inclined to act as though we thought we were elaborate automata.

The twentieth century saw the discovery of intrinsic unpredictabilities present in nature, first discerned at the atomic level through the discoveries of quantum theory, and then at the macroscopic level through the recognition of chaos theory. Unpredictability is an epistemological property and there is no direct entailment from epistemology to ontology. It requires an act of metaphysical decision to determine what relationship should be postulated. This leaves it open to those of a realist cast of mind, for whom what we know and what is the case are considered to be closely aligned, to give unpredictability an ontological interpretation as the sign of the presence of a degree of openness in causal structure. Such an interpretation has been widely accepted in the case of quantum theory, where Heisenberg's uncertainty principle, discovered as an epistemological limitation on what can be measured, has almost universally been interpreted as a principle of actual indeterminacy rather than merely a principle of ignorance. However, the same strategy has proved more controversial in the case of chaos theory. It might seem tempting to try to solve the problem by a judicious combination of quantum theory and chaos theory, since the behavior of chaotic systems soon comes to depend upon fine details of circumstance to which the uncertainty principle forbids access. Yet this attempt is frustrated by the fact that, as they stand, these two physical theories are mutually incompatible, since quantum theory has a scale (set by Planck's constant), while the fractal character of chaotic dynamics means that it is scale-free. The fact of the matter is that the physicists' account of causal process is patchy, excellent within certain defined domains but with the connections between these domains often not properly understood. (Consider the unsolved measurement problem in quantum theory, essentially concerned with how the quantum domain and the classical domain relate to each other. We do not understand how it is that cloudy and fitful quantum entities yield definite answers on each occasion that they are experimentally interrogated by reliable classical measuring apparatus.)

Ultimately, questions concerning the nature of causality, though constrained by physics, have to be settled by metaphysical decision. For example, there are in fact both indeterministic and deterministic interpretations of quantum theory, each with the same empirical consequences. The choice between them has to be made on metascientific grounds, such as judgments of economy and naturalness of explanation.[2]

In the case of chaos theory, it is possible to exercise this power of metaphysical decision in a way that envisages a degree of openness being present in the "bottom-up," constituent picture of physical process, in a manner that leaves room for the operation of further causal principles of a "top-down" kind, corresponding to the influence of the whole on the behavior of the parts.[3] Top-down causality of this sort would not only seem to bear a correspondence to the basic human experience of the personal exercise of conscious agency mediated through the actions of our bodies, but it could also gain support from the nascent scientific study of the behavior of (moderately) complex systems. Both in the case of computer emulations of logical networks, and also in the study of physical dissipative systems held far from equilibrium through the continuous exchange of energy and entropy with their environment, it is found that complex systems display quite astonishing self-organizing powers, being able to generate spontaneously large-scale patterns of ordered behavior, of a kind that one would never have guessed from considering a purely constituent approach.[4] No general theory is yet known that covers these remarkable phenomena, but it seems entirely reasonable to suppose that eventually science will need to complement its traditional account of causality framed in terms of the exchange of energy between constituents, with a holistic, top-down account framed in terms of the pattern-forming operations of what one might come to call the causal principle of "active information."

2. Polkinghorne, *Quantum Theory,* pp. 53-56.

3. John Polkinghorne, *Belief in God in an Age of Science* (New Haven: Yale University Press, 1998), pp. 48-75.

4. Stuart Kauffman, *At Home in the Universe* (New York: Oxford University Press, 1995); Ilya Prigogine and Isabelle Stengers, *Order Out of Chaos* (London: Heinemann, 1984). The computer models are based on deterministic bottom-up causality, but this need not be the case for the physical models.

Emergence

Cosmic history has been characterized by the appearance of qualitatively novel consequences of the evolutionary exploration of the deep potentiality with which the universe has been endowed.[5] The emergence of terrestrial life is one example. The appearance of organisms possessing consciousness would be another. The third example is perhaps the most remarkable of all, for it is the emergence of that particular reflective awareness and ability to project thought into the past and future that human beings possess and which we call self-consciousness. In the genus homo the universe became aware of itself, perhaps the most dramatic moment in its long history so far. As an eventual by-product of this development, science became possible and understanding was gained of the processes that over almost fourteen billion years had brought humanity to birth. Blaise Pascal, while reflecting on human insignificance on the cosmic scale (mere "reeds"), nevertheless asserted humans to be greater than all the stars, since we know them and ourselves and they know nothing (we are "thinking reeds"). The fruitful history that is punctuated by these emergences is a story of unfolding complexity and ever-enhancing relationality. The human brain, with its 10^{11} neurons and the 10^{14} connections between them, is far and away the most intricately interrelated entity that scientists have ever encountered in their exploration of the universe. It seems clear that the development of ever-increasing relational subtlety and intricacy, both internally constituted and externally shared, has been one of the engines driving the fertile history of emergence.

Cosmic Effects

About one hundred years ago, the philosopher-physicist Ernst Mach pointed out that the inertial frames that define dynamical properties in our terrestrial environment are at rest, or in a state of uniform motion, with respect to the fixed stars. In other words, local physics here on Earth has a character that is related to the overall distribution of matter in the universe. Interest in "Mach's principle" has fluctuated in the physics community, but it is surely necessary to take some account of an intriguing pointer to yet another form of relationality apparently present in the physical world, con-

---

5. See Philip Clayton, *Mind and Emergence* (Oxford: Oxford University Press, 2004).

necting the local to its cosmic context. One may also note that, although relativity theory abolished the Newtonian idea of a universal "now," the effectively homogeneous character of our particular universe considered on the largest scales allows the definition of a cosmic frame of reference (at rest with respect to the background radiation), which cosmologists use in their definition of the overall age of the universe. One might even speculate that there might be some connection between that cosmic "now" and our human perception of the present moment, a fundamental experience that finds no representation in the reductionist equations of physics, which assign no special significance to any particular value of t. In more general terms, one can say that we have motivation to believe that local particularity may relate in subtle ways to the character of the cosmic whole.

This brief survey of a number of modern physical insights illustrates the way in which exploration of the physical world has revealed the presence in it of a remarkable degree of intrinsic relationality. Democritan atomism is definitely dead. Some possible implications this might have for theology need finally to be considered.

Theological Reflections

There is, of course, no simplistic way in which to translate science's discoveries about the character of the physical universe into implications for an understanding of the infinite reality of God. It would be absurd to argue that the EPR effect demonstrated the truth of Trinitarian theology. Yet a cautiously expressed theology of nature might be expected to offer some insight into the manner in which the divine creation reflects, however palely, the character of its Creator. The classic New Testament endorsement of such an expectation was given by Paul when he wrote to the Romans (1:20), "Ever since the creation of the world, [God's] invisible nature, namely his eternal power and deity, has been clearly perceived in the things that have been made." Our survey in this chapter of science's account of "the things that have been made" has shown many of the forms in which the fundamental significance of relationality is manifested in the physical universe. The invisible nature of the Creator might surely be expected to manifest something not totally dissimilar.

Theology has often to proceed by careful appeal to analogy, making use of, and seeking to extend, concepts formed in the course of human experience, in order to guide and control its attempts to use finite human language to speak of the infinite reality of God. What is being suggested here about hints of the Creator discerned in the form of creation encourages the belief that human descriptive language is not totally powerless to convey something of the nature of God. Images drawn from science, such as mutual entanglement, may provide a modest analogical resource, however pale they may be in comparison with the brightness of divine reality. The discourse will be qualified by the warnings of apophatic theology concerning the inaccessible mystery of the divine, but surely something must be said, even if human language is necessarily being used in some open and "stretched" sense when it is applied to God.

The interconnected integrity of the physical universe can be understood theologically as reflecting the status of the world as a divine creation whose intrinsic relationality has been conferred on it through its origin in the will of the triune God. The language of science and the language of theology are not connected by bonds of logical necessity, but by an alogical relation of consonance, a degree of conceptual congruity that makes it mutually illuminating to consider together science's picture of the relational nature of the physical world and theological belief in the Trinitarian nature of God. Involved is an appeal to what Aquinas called the analogy of attributes. In this modest manner, the context of understanding is enhanced and deepened.

For the Christian, the true "Theory of Everything" is Trinitarian theology. Acknowledging the Creator not only provides an explanation of the deep intelligibility of the universe when its order is conceived as having originated in the mind of God, together with an understanding of the fruitfulness of cosmic history when it is seen as an expression of the divine creative purpose, but it also leads to seeing the ethical dimension of reality as arising from intuitions of God's good and perfect will, and human aesthetic experience as being a creaturely sharing in the Creator's joy in creation. The universe is deeply relational in its character and unified in its structure, because it is the creation of the one true God, Father, Son, and Holy Spirit.

Christian theology speaks of God as the One whose eternal being is constituted by the perichoretic exchange of love between the three divine Persons. Thus the deepest reality is relational, and this will surely be the character of all that originates from that divine source. John Zizioulas writes of Trinitarian theology under the rubric "Being as Communion."[6] The physicist can see science's parallel discovery in its own domain that

6. John Zizioulas, *Being as Communion* (Crestwood, NY: St. Vladimir's Seminary Press, 1993).

"Reality Is Relational," as being a faint but distinct echo of the triune character of the Creator of the universe.[7]

Orthodox Trinitarian thinking is bounded on either side by two heresies that the Church rejected. Modalism, with its concept of Father, Son, and Spirit as simply labeling three different forms of encounter with a single divine reality, was found not to do justice to the distinctive characters of the divine Persons, as manifested, for example, in the account of the baptism of Jesus. On the other hand, a view of the Persons so differentiated that it amounted to a crude tritheism was also rejected, because the Church held on to the conviction that it had inherited from Judaism, that "the Lord our God is one Lord." There is a single divine will and purpose at work in creation. The early Fathers of the Church, in their attempts to articulate an intermediate position between these two unacceptable extremes, made use of ideas such as the perichoretic exchange that constitutes the uniquely intimate union of the life of the Godhead, and the Western idea of appropriation that licensed speech about the way the Persons are associated with different roles in the external revelatory events of the divine economy, so that we associate creation with the Father, salvation with the Son, and sanctification with the Spirit, while recognizing that these are all acts of the one true God.

Science today faces a problem not totally dissimilar to that addressed by those early Trinitarian theologians. The physical world is not so atomized that we can understand it fully by an examination conducted constituent piece by constituent piece. Nor is it so inextricably relationally integrated that until one is able to comprehend the totality, one cannot understand anything at all. Physical science needs to wrestle with the issue of how it may both acknowledge the substantial degree of relationality manifested in phenomena such as quantum entanglement and the mutuality of space, time, and matter, while at the same time being able to do justice to our everyday experience of a significant degree of separability between objects in the macroscopic world. Like theology in its different sphere, science has to struggle with the problem of reconciling unity with diversity. In fact, all theoretical engagement with issues of relationality has to find some way of combining connection with separation, since it is only to the extent that one can recognize a distinction between two entities that one can also speak of their being in mutual relationship.

---

7. For a fuller discussion, see J. C. Polkinghorne, *Science and the Trinity* (London: SPCK; New Haven: Yale University Press, 2004); *Exploring Reality* (London: SPCK; New Haven: Yale University Press, 2005), chap. 5.

BIBLIOGRAPHY

Clayton, Philip. *Mind and Emergence.* Oxford: Oxford University Press, 2004.

Coveney, P., and R. Highfield. *Frontiers of Complexity.* London: Faber & Faber, 1995.

Kauffman, S. *At Home in the Universe.* New York: Oxford University Press, 1995.

Polkinghorne, John. *Belief in God in an Age of Science.* New Haven: Yale University Press, 1998.

Polkinghorne, John. *Quantum Theory: A Very Short Introduction.* Oxford: Oxford University Press, 2002.

Polkinghorne, John. *Science and the Trinity.* London: SPCK; New Haven: Yale University Press, 2004.

Polkinghorne, John. *Exploring Reality.* London: SPCK; New Haven: Yale University Press, 2005.

Prigogine, Ilya, and Isabelle Stengers. *Order Out of Chaos.* London: Heinemann, 1984.

Zizioulas, J. *Being as Communion.* Crestwood, NY: St. Vladimir's Seminary Press, 1993.

The Entangled World: How Can It Be Like That?

Jeffrey Bub

Einstein and Bohr were famously at odds over the interpretation of quantum mechanics. The central issue in the debate after 1935 was how to make sense of the peculiar non-classical correlations exhibited by quantum systems in so-called "entangled" states, characterized by Schrödinger (Schrödinger, 1935, p. 555) as "*the* characteristic trait of quantum mechanics, the one that enforces its entire departure from classical lines of thought." Einstein defended what Pauli (Pauli, 1994, p. 60) identified as a core principle of classical physics: "the ideal of the detached observer," and argued for an interpretation of quantum mechanics as incomplete.

Here I provide an accessible account of entanglement and show how the concept of information, in the physical sense, is the critical organizing and illuminating principle underlying a conception of the entangled quantum world as necessarily excluding a "detached observer" description.

The Ideal of the "Detached Observer"

Richard Feynman (Feynman, 1967, p. 129) is often quoted as saying that nobody understands quantum mechanics:

> There was a time when the newspapers said that only twelve men understood the theory of relativity. I do not believe there ever was such a time. . . . On the other hand, I think I can safely say that nobody understands quantum mechanics. . . . Do not keep saying to yourself, if you can possibly avoid it, "But how can it be like that?" because you will get

"down the drain," into a blind alley from which nobody has yet escaped. Nobody knows how it can be like that.

What is it about quantum mechanics, as opposed to the theory of relativity, that raises a special problem of intelligibility?

In classical (Newtonian) mechanics, the state of a system is defined by a list of the system's properties, or a specification of a set of parameters from which the list of properties can be reconstructed. The dynamics specify how properties change in terms of a law of evolution for the state. The special theory of relativity adds two principles or constraints to this theoretical framework: roughly, as Hermann Bondi (1980) put it, "velocity doesn't matter" — more precisely, the equivalence of inertial frames for physical laws covering mechanical as well as electromagnetic phenomena, and "no overtaking of light by light," the constancy of the velocity of light in vacuo for all inertial frames.[1] These principles are irreconcilable in the geometry of Newtonian spacetime, where inertial frames moving relative to each other are related by Galilean transformations (so that, e.g., the velocity of a person walking on a moving walkway in an airport terminal, relative to the terminal, is simply the sum of the velocity of the person relative to the walkway and the velocity of the walkway relative to the terminal). The required revision yields Minkowski spacetime, where inertial frames are related by Lorentz transformations (so velocities are not merely additive but involve the speed of light in a particular way).

A consequence of these relativistic principles is that space and time cannot be the sort of thing Newton thought it was. Specifically, simultaneity turns out to be relative to an inertial frame. Yet, in a fundamental sense, the classical mode of description of being and change in terms of systems with separable properties that exist independently of the physical process of observation is unchanged in the theory of relativity. Pauli (Pauli, 1994, p. 60) characterized this feature of classical physics as a "detached observer" idealization, at the heart of Einstein's dispute with Bohr over the interpretation of quantum mechanics.

. . . it seems to me quite appropriate to call the conceptual description of nature in classical physics, which Einstein so emphatically wishes to re-

1. A Newtonian inertial frame is a reference frame for spatial and temporal coordinates relative to which Newton's three laws of motion hold: bodies not under the action of forces move uniformly in straight lines, bodies under the action of forces accelerate by an amount proportional to and in the direction of the forces, and forces evoke equal and opposite reactions.

tain, "the ideal of the detached observer." To put it drastically the observer has according to this ideal to disappear entirely in a discrete [sic] manner as hidden spectator, never as actor, nature being left alone in a predetermined course of events, independent of the way in which phenomena are observed. "Like the moon has a definite position," Einstein said to me last winter, "whether or not we look at the moon, the same must also hold for the atomic objects, as there are no sharp distinctions between these and macroscopic objects. Observation cannot *create* an element of reality like a position, there must be something contained in the complete description of physical reality which corresponds to the *possibility* of observing a position, already before the observation has been actually made."

Bohr's interpretation of quantum mechanics, which he termed "complementarity," eventually became entrenched as the orthodox Copenhagen interpretation, a loosely connected set of ideas incorporating formulations of Bohr's view by Heisenberg, Pauli, and others. On the Copenhagen interpretation, the quantum state of a system is understood as specifying probabilities for the outcomes of possible measurements on the system, rather than a list of properties. Einstein rejected this view, perhaps because of its instrumentalist[2] flavor, and took the position that the quantum state is simply an incomplete characterization of a physical system.

Pauli expressed the Copenhagen position this way (Pauli, 1994, pp. 260-61):

Now there is a big difference between the observers, or instruments of observation, which must be taken into consideration by modern microphysics, and the detached observer of classical physics.[3] By the lat-

2. Instrumentalism is the view that a scientific theory should be regarded as nothing more than an instrument for prediction. So, on this view, theoretical terms do not correspond to real properties or relations in the world, and the content of theoretical statements is exhausted by their empirical consequences. The classic statement of instrumentalism is Osiander's preface to Copernicus' *De Revolutionibus Orbium Coelestium.* Osiander argued that Copernicus' heliocentric theory should not be literally construed as placing the sun at the center of the universe and the earth in motion, but that the theory should rather be understood as a simpler and more accurate instrument than the Ptolemaic geocentric theory for predicting the motions of the planets.

3. Note that what is meant by an "observer" here — as is apparent from Pauli's reference to "instruments of observation" — is a measuring instrument: a macroscopic physical system that can enter a range of possible states as the possible outcomes of a suitable inter-

ter I mean one who is not necessarily without effect on the system observed but whose influence can always be eliminated by determinable corrections. In microphysics, however, the natural laws are of such a kind that every bit of knowledge gained from a measurement must be paid for by the loss of other, complementary items of knowledge. Every observation, therefore, interferes on an indeterminable scale both with the instruments of observation and with the system observed and interrupts the causal connection of the phenomena preceding it with those following it. This uncontrollable interaction between observer and system observed, taking place in every process of measurement, invalidates the deterministic conception of the phenomena assumed in classical physics: the series of events taking place according to pre-determined rules is interrupted, after a free choice has been made by the beholder between mutually exclusive experimental arrangements, by the selective observation which, as an essentially non-automatic occurrence (Geschehen), may be compared to a creation in the microcosm or even to a transmutation (Wandlung) the results of which are, however, unpredictable and beyond human control.

The core of the debate between Einstein and Bohr over the interpretation of quantum mechanics was about whether the transition from classical to quantum mechanics requires giving up "the ideal of the detached observer," and how then to understand the nature of theoretical physics.

Entanglement

The culmination of Einstein's challenge to the Copenhagen interpretation was the joint publication with Boris Podolsky and Nathan Rosen in 1935 of an argument for the incompleteness of quantum mechanics. Note that Einstein's notion of a complete theory did not include the requirement of determinism. Rather, Einstein proposed certain conditions of separability and locality for composite systems consisting of separated component systems: each component system separately should be characterized by its own properties (even if these properties manifest themselves probabilistically), and it should be impossible to alter the properties of a remote system instantaneously (or the probabilities of these properties) by acting on a local system.

---

action with the observed system, which can be interpreted as stable records or irreversible registrations of different possible states of the observed microsystem.

The Einstein-Podolsky-Rosen (EPR) argument (Einstein, Podolsky, and Rosen, 1935) considers two particles that are prepared from a source in a certain quantum state and then move apart. There are "matching" correlations between both the positions of the two particles and their momenta: a measurement of either position (x) or momentum (p) on particle 2, say, will allow the prediction, with certainty, of the outcome of a position measurement or momentum measurement, respectively, on particle 1. These measurements are mutually exclusive: either a position measurement can be performed, or a momentum measurement, but not both simultaneously. Either correlation can be observed, but the subsequent measurement of momentum, say, after establishing a position correlation, will no longer yield any correlation in the momenta of the two particles. It is as if the position measurement disturbs the correlation between the momentum values.

Here is how Schrödinger put the puzzle in the first part of a two-part commentary (Schrödinger, 1935, 1936) on the EPR argument (Schrödinger, 1935, p. 559):

> Yet since I can predict *either* x_1 or p_1 without interfering with the system No. 1 and since system No. 1, like a scholar in an examination, cannot possibly know which of the two questions I am going to ask first: it so seems that our scholar is prepared to give the right answer to the *first* question he is asked, *anyhow*. Therefore he must know both answers; which is an amazing knowledge; quite irrespective of the fact that after having given his first answer our scholar is invariably so disconcerted or tired out, that all the following answers are *wrong*.

It is an "amazing knowledge" because the quantum state of the particle pair, which is supposed to be a *complete* specification of the physical condition of the particles, does not contain the answers to both questions (and is precluded from containing both answers by the structure of the quantum state space). EPR concluded that the quantum state was an incomplete description of the physical state of a system.

Schrödinger coined the term "entanglement" to describe this peculiar connection between quantum systems (Schrödinger, 1935, p. 555):

> When two systems, of which we know the states by their respective representatives, enter into temporary physical interaction due to known forces between them, and when after a time of mutual influence the sys-

tems separate again, then they can no longer be described in the same way as before, viz. by endowing each of them with a representative of its own. I would not call that *one* but rather *the* characteristic trait of quantum mechanics, the one that enforces its entire departure from classical lines of thought. By the interaction the two representatives [the quantum states] have become entangled.

In the second part of his two-part paper on the EPR argument (Schrödinger, 1936), Schrödinger showed that an experimenter can, by a suitable choice of operations carried out on one system, "steer" the second system into any chosen "mixture" of quantum states.[4] "It is rather discomforting," he remarked (Schrödinger, 1935, p. 555), "that the theory should allow a system to be steered or piloted into one or the other type of state at the experimenter's mercy in spite of his having no access to it." Schrödinger regarded this as a "sinister" consequence of entanglement (Schrödinger, 1935, p. 555), a feature he found so unsettling that he speculated (wrongly, as it turned out) that when two entangled systems separate, the entanglement itself decays, leaving the pair in a mixture that still embodies some correlations, but not of the "sinister" sort: they would be classical correlations that would not allow for "remote steering."

Most physicists attributed the counterintuitive features of entangled quantum states to the inappropriateness of a "detached observer" idealization for quantum systems, and regarded Bohr's reply to the EPR argument (Bohr, 1935) as vindicating the Copenhagen interpretation. The issue languished until John Bell's reconsideration and extension of the EPR argument about thirty years later (Bell, 1964, 1987). Bell looked at entanglement in simpler systems than the EPR case: matching correlations between two-valued dynamical quantities, such as polarization or spin, of two separated systems in an entangled state. What Bell showed was that the statistical correlations between the measurement outcomes of suitably chosen different quantities on the two systems are inconsistent with an inequality derivable from Einstein's separability and locality assumptions — in effect from the assumption that the correlations have a common cause.

Bell's investigation generated an ongoing debate on the foundations

---

4. The second system cannot be steered into any particular state at the whim of the experimenter, but the experimenter can constrain the state into which the second system evolves to lie in any chosen set of states, with a probability distribution fixed by the entangled state.

of quantum mechanics. In the 1980s, confirmation that entanglement persists over long distances (see Aspect, 1981, 1982), falsifying Schrödinger's supposition that entanglement would decay spontaneously as two entangled particles separated, was followed by the realization that the non-local correlations of entangled quantum states could be exploited as a new kind of non-classical information resource. This has led to an explosive surge of research among physicists and computer scientists on the application of information-theoretic ideas to quantum computation (which exploits entanglement in the design of a quantum computer, so as to enable the performance of certain computational tasks exponentially faster than any known algorithm on a classical machine), to quantum communication (new forms of "entanglement-assisted" communication, such as quantum teleportation), and to quantum cryptography (the identification of cryptographic protocols that are guaranteed to be unconditionally secure against eavesdropping or cheating, by the laws of quantum mechanics, even if all parties have access to quantum computers).

The non-classical features of entangled states are nicely illustrated by the Greenberger-Horne-Zeilinger (GHZ) experiment (Greenberger, Horne, and Zeilinger, 1989). Three particles,[5] labeled 1, 2, 3 (e.g., three photons), are emitted from a source in a certain entangled quantum state and move away from the source symmetrically. (The numbering is introduced simply for reference. There is no distinction between the particles: they behave identically.)

Measurements of two different physical quantities, labeled X and Y (e.g., the polarization of a photon in two different directions), can be made on each of the three particles: X_1, Y_1 for particle 1; X_2, Y_2 for particle 2; X_3, Y_3 for particle 3. Each quantity, X or Y, can take one of two possible values, ± 1, for each of the three particles.

Note that X and Y cannot be measured simultaneously on the same particle (one can first measure X and then Y, or first measure Y and then X), and once a measurement has been made, the three particles are no longer in the same quantum state as before the measurement. (Of course, X and Y can be measured simultaneously on different particles.)

The crucial point is this: the initial state is so constituted — as an essentially relational entity, in which no one of the three particles has a sepa-

---

5. The version of the experiment discussed here is due to Mermin (Mermin, 1990). The original experiment involved four entangled particles.

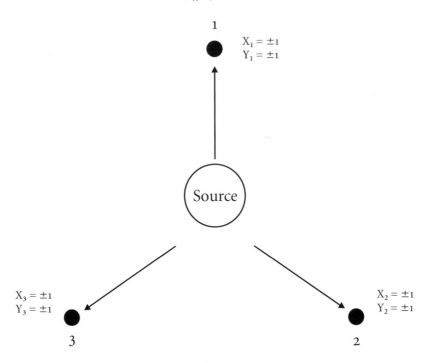

rate identity — that the following constraints relate the outcomes of any triple of measurements on the particles:

$$X_1 \cdot Y_2 \cdot Y_3 = 1$$
$$Y_1 \cdot X_2 \cdot Y_3 = 1$$
$$Y_1 \cdot Y_2 \cdot X_3 = 1$$
$$X_1 \cdot X_2 \cdot X_3 = -1 \qquad (1)$$

The first three constraints say that the product of the outcomes of an X-measurement on one particle and Y-measurements on the other two particles is 1. The fourth constraint says that the product of the outcomes of an X-measurement on all three particles is -1.

Now, it is logically impossible to satisfy these four constraints. That is, no combination of +1 and -1 for $X_1, Y_1; X_2, Y_2; X_3, Y_3$ can satisfy these constraints (where the X's and Y's here refer to the outcomes of X or Y measurements on the different particles).

For example: suppose $X_1 = 1$, $Y_2 = 1$, $Y_3 = 1$. This satisfies the first constraint. Suppose $Y_1 = 1$. Then, since the second constraint requires that $Y_1 \cdot X_2 \cdot Y_3 = 1$, we must have $X_2 = 1$ also, since we already have $Y_3 = 1$.[6] So now we have:

$$X_1 = 1 \quad X_2 = 1$$
$$Y_1 = 1 \quad Y_2 = 1 \quad Y_3 = 1$$

The third constraint requires that $X_3 = 1$. But this contradicts the fourth constraint, which requires that $X_3 = -1$, since $X_1 = X_2 = 1$ and the product $X_1 \cdot X_2 \cdot X_3$ is -1.

The proof that it is impossible to satisfy the constraints is elementary. Simply multiply the left-hand sides of the equations in (1) together. Notice that each quantity

$$X_1, Y_1, X_2, Y_2, X_3, Y_3$$

appears exactly twice in this product:

$$(X_1 \cdot Y_2 \cdot Y_3) \cdot (Y_1 \cdot X_2 \cdot Y_3) \cdot (Y_1 \cdot Y_2 \cdot X_3) \cdot (X_1 \cdot X_2 \cdot X_3) =$$
$$(X_1 \cdot X_1) \cdot (Y_1 \cdot Y_1) \cdot (X_2 \cdot X_2) \cdot (Y_2 \cdot Y_2) \cdot (X_3 \cdot X_3) \cdot (Y_3 \cdot Y_3) \quad (2)$$

(The parentheses are introduced simply for ease in reading the expression.) So whether a particular quantity is +1 or -1, the product of the left-hand sides of (1) is +1. Now the product of the left-hand sides of (1) must equal the product of the right-hand sides. But the product of the right-hand sides is: $1 \cdot 1 \cdot 1 \cdot -1 = -1$!

The amazing thing is that a triple of particles in this state always produces outcomes, +1 or -1, that do satisfy the constraints. But no prior "conspiracy" or "agreement" among the particles in a triple with respect to measurement outcomes — no prior assignment of +1 and -1 to X and Y for each particle — will produce outcomes that satisfy the constraints, for any possible combination of X and Y measurements we can perform on the particles. Recall that we can measure only one quantity, X or Y, on each particle in a single measurement operation. If we measure X on a particle, we cannot experimentally check a proposed answer to the counterfactual question: "What would the outcome have been if we had instead measured

---

6. Note the implicit locality assumption here: that $Y_3 = 1$ — particle 3 is so constituted as to yield the outcome 1 when probed by a Y-measurement — independently of what measurements are performed on the other two distant particles.

Y?" There can be no answer to this question that satisfies the constraints. *So it seems that the particularity of each particle — the way it answers the question: "What is your X-value?" or "What is your Y-value?" — is constituted by its relationality to the other particles. It is impossible to reconstruct this phenomenon (the satisfaction of the constraints) by particles that separately and independently are assigned X and Y values prior to the measurements.*

To use the terminology of apophatic theology, one might say that a particle's response to a measurement — e.g., that the outcome of an X-measurement on particle 1 is +1 (denoted by $X_1 = +1$) — is a particular "hypostasis" of the particle in the initial entangled relational state of the three-as-one. This suggests a relational ontology for which the "view from nowhere" of Pauli's detached observer is inapplicable, except in an ideal or approximate sense.

Information

To repeat Feynman's question: But how can it be like that?

A particularly counterintuitive feature of entanglement is the possibility of "remote steering" that Schrödinger demonstrated. This has an even more dramatic consequence than Schrödinger pointed out. Suppose Alice and Bob share an entangled state of the sort considered by Bell, say two photons in an entangled state of polarization. That is, Alice has in her possession one of the entangled photons, and Bob the other. Suppose that Alice has an additional photon in an unknown state of polarization, p. It is possible for Alice to perform an operation on the two photons in her possession that will transform the state of Bob's photon into one of four states, depending on the four possible (random) outcomes of Alice's operation: either the state p, or a state that is related to p in a definite way. Alice's operation entangles the two photons in her possession, and disentangles Bob's photon, steering it into a state p'. After Alice communicates the outcome of her operation to Bob, Bob knows either that p' = p, or how to transform p' to p by a local operation. This phenomenon is known as "quantum teleportation" and has been experimentally confirmed (see Bouwmeester, Pan, Mattle, Eible, Weinfurter, and Zeilinger, 1997; Boschi, Branca, Martini, Hardy, and Popescu, 1998).

What is extraordinary about quantum teleportation is that Alice and Bob have managed to use their shared entangled state as a quantum communication channel to destroy the state p of a photon in Alice's part of the universe and re-create it in Bob's part of the universe. Since the polarization state of a photon requires specifying a direction in space (essentially the value of an angle that can vary continuously), without a shared entangled state Alice would have to convey an infinite amount of information to Bob for Bob to be able to reconstruct the state p precisely.

To see why this is so, consider that the decimal expansion of an angle variable represented by a real number is represented by a potentially infinite sequence of digits between 0 and 9. The binary expansion is represented by a potentially infinite sequence of 0's and 1's. The notion of "information" here is the standard physical notion of information first formulated by Shannon (Shannon, 1948). In Shannon's theory, information is a quantifiable resource associated with a stochastic source that produces a probability distribution of output states, where the physical nature of the systems embodying these output states is irrelevant to the amount of information associated with the source. The amount of information associated with an information source that produces two distinguishable states, represented as 0 or 1, where each of the two states has probability 1/2, is conventionally taken as one "bit." So to specify the value of an arbitrary angle variable requires an infinite number of bits. To specify the outcome of Alice's operation, which has four possible outcomes, with equal probabilities of 1/4, requires two bits of information. Remarkably, Bob can reconstruct the state p on the basis of just two bits of information communicated by Alice, by exploiting the entangled state as a quantum communication channel to transfer the remaining information.

This is so because quantum information, a physical resource stored in the quantum states of physical systems, is radically different from classical information. The unit of quantum information is the "qubit," representing the amount of quantum information that can be stored in the state of the simplest quantum system, for example, the polarization state of a photon. Essentially, the difference between classical and quantum information has to do with the different distinguishability properties of classical and quantum states: in general, two quantum states of a system — which specify probabilities for the outcomes of possible measurements on the system — cannot be reliably distinguished. Classical information is understood as that sort of information represented in a probability distribution over distinguishable states, and so can be regarded as a subcategory of quantum information, where the states may or may not be distinguishable.

It would be incorrect, however, to think of quantum information as a sort of "fuzzy" version of classical information. As we have seen, an arbitrarily large amount of classical information can be encoded in a qubit. This information can be processed and communicated (e.g., as in the phenomenon of quantum teleportation) but, because of the peculiarities of quantum measurement, it turns out that at most one bit can be accessed. It is this partial "inaccessibility" of quantum information that underlies the possibility of non-local correlations that have no classical counterpart.

To see this, suppose that Bob were able, via some measurement, to identify the quantum state in his possession immediately after Alice's measurement in a teleportation experiment, without the additional two bits of classical information supplied by Alice. In that case, the information about the outcome of Alice's measurement operation — one of four possibilities — would be instantaneously transmitted to Bob. This would violate a "no signaling" constraint satisfied by both classical and quantum theories: whether or not a measurement has been performed at location A, or what kind of measurement has been performed, cannot change the probabilities of measurement outcomes at another location B. If Alice could change the probabilities of Bob's measurement outcomes merely by making a measurement on particles in her possession (without communicating the outcome of the measurement to Bob), then Alice would be able to signal superluminally to Bob, in violation of the theory of special relativity. So the partial inaccessibility of quantum information is precisely what allows the non-classical, non-local correlations of entangled quantum states, without violating the "no signaling" constraint.

Does the concept of information (in the physical sense of Shannon's theory) provide new insight into the puzzling features of quantum phenomena and suggest a way of answering Feynman's question?

It is instructive here to compare relativity theory with quantum mechanics. The principle for quantum mechanics that plays an analogous role to the light postulate in relativity is "no cloning." That is, it is impossible to copy the information in an unknown quantum state. More precisely, there is a restriction on copying. It is possible to construct a copying device that could copy any state in a set of distinguishable quantum states — e.g., the quantum states corresponding to the values of a single observable — but not the states corresponding to the values of an "incompatible" observable (an observable that cannot be measured simultaneously with the first observable): that would require a different copying device. From this perspective, classical information is a special case of quantum information applicable to sets of states for which a copying device is physically possible.

Once the light postulate is added to classical physics, space and time cannot be the sort of thing we thought it was before. That is, given the light postulate, what we mean by a spatial and temporal interval, and the measurement of such intervals (how a value gets to be assigned to an interval), requires an analysis. It is a consequence of this analysis that simultaneity is relative to an inertial frame — that the old notion of space and time as absolute properties has to be given up. Similarly, in quantum mechanics, once it is accepted that cloning is restricted, what we mean by a measurement can't be the sort of thing it is in classical theories: essentially a copying of information about one system onto another system. That is, the operations we call measurements can't be measurements in the sense of revealing "absolute" or pre-existent properties that are there prior to the measurement and merely copied by the measurement. The world we live in is not *the sort of world* in which there are properties that are there in an absolute sense to be revealed by measurement as a copying operation, just as the world we live in is not the sort of world in which there are absolute temporal and spatial intervals. So what we now mean by measurement requires an analysis, similar to the analysis of space and time in relativity.

It is a consequence of this analysis that a dynamical account of measurement, which is possible in a classical theory, is impossible in quantum mechanics. Furthermore, any theory that takes quantum mechanics as incomplete and introduces additional structure over and above the algebra of observables and states of quantum theory to "solve the measurement problem" (i.e., to provide a dynamical account of measurement) will have to introduce some mechanism to hide this additional structure at the empirical level. That is, in any such "hidden variable" theory (e.g., Bohm's theory; see Goldstein, 2001), the additional structure must be idle at the empirical level: the hidden variables must remain hidden if quantum mechanics is strictly true. (For a discussion, see Bub, 2004, 2005.)

From this perspective, the choice — once "no cloning" is accepted as a principle characterizing our world — is between (I) thinking of the world as the sort of world in which cloning is in principle possible in an unrestricted way, and what prevents cloning is a restriction on the dynamics (as in a hidden variable theory), and (II) thinking of the world *as just not the sort of world in which unrestricted cloning is in principle possible*. Position I corresponds in relativity theory to Lorentz's position (Lorentz, 1909), where a dynamical account is provided for length contraction and time dilation, and hence for the invariance of the velocity of light with respect to different inertial frames, and in quantum mechanics to Einstein's position

Jeffrey Bub

or Bohm's position. Just as Lorentz's theory is an attempt to provide a dynamical explanation of the constancy of the velocity of light for all inertial observers, via a dynamical account of length contraction and time dilation, so Bohm's theory is an attempt to provide a dynamical explanation of why cloning is impossible. Position II corresponds to Einstein's position in relativity, and in quantum mechanics to an information-theoretic interpretation (with some loose affinity to Bohr's complementarity interpretation and the Copenhagen interpretation).

Rejecting a dynamical account of measurement in a "no cloning" world amounts to the assertion that the ultimate measuring instrument in any application of quantum mechanics is simply a source of classical information in Shannon's sense, i.e., it plays the role of a "black box" that produces a probability distribution over a range of outcomes, and how these outcomes "come about" is not further analyzed in terms of the dynamics of the theory. Note that this is a consequence of accepting "no cloning" as a fundamental principle about our world. Of course, one could analyze the functioning of this measuring instrument dynamically in terms of the theory, but then there will be some other system that plays the role of the ultimate measuring instrument in this application of the theory, that is not analyzed dynamically. (In the terminology of the Copenhagen interpretation, the "cut" between measuring instrument and system measured can be shifted arbitrarily.)

In the case of relativity, once an inertial frame is fixed, space and time are classical, i.e., Euclidean. It is only when the relation between different frames is considered that the effect of space-time being relativistic — the effect of the constancy of the velocity of light — becomes apparent. In the case of quantum mechanics, fixing an observable of a system fixes an orthogonal basis or frame in Hilbert space, the representation space for the states of a quantum system. With respect to such a frame, the probabilities represent classical information. It is only when measurements in different frames are considered that the effect of "no cloning" becomes apparent. In a relational quantum world, the analogue of a classical state, which specifies a complete list of a system's properties (inapplicable in a quantum world), is the quantum state, which specifies an equally objective feature of a quantum system: the probabilistic relations between different frames.

One might ask how classical information can arise in a quantum world characterized by "no cloning." Granted, it is part of the information-theoretic view expressed here that the *individual occurrence of a measurement outcome* in a quantum measurement process does not require a dynamical explanation — that this would be like giving a Lorentzian explanation of length contraction — but it is still legitimate to ask for a quantum mechanical account of the possibility of classical information sources. Here we need to consider the phenomenon of decoherence: an extremely fast process that occurs in the spontaneous interaction between a macrosystem and its environment that leads to the virtually instantaneous suppression of entanglement in a certain sense. What happens, roughly, is that a macrosystem, like the macroscopic measuring instrument for measuring the polarization of a photon in the GHZ experiment, typically becomes correlated with the environment — an enormous number of stray dust particles, air molecules, photons, background radiation, etc. — in an entangled state that takes a certain form with respect to a preferred set of states that very rapidly approach orthogonality as the interaction develops and includes more and more particles. It is as if the environment is "monitoring" the system via a measurement of the observable associated with the preferred states. The stability or robustness of the preferred states allows one to identify certain emergent structures in the overall pattern of correlations — such as macroscopic pointers and information-gatherers in general — as classical-like: the correlational information required to reveal the difference between a mixture that embodies classical correlations (such as the correlation between a polarization state, the instrument pointer state, and the state of the experimenter reading the instrument) and the "sinister" correlations of entanglement for these structures is effectively lost in the environment. So it appears that an information-theoretic view is consistent with both (i) the conditions for the existence of measuring instruments as sources of classical information, and (ii) the existence of information-gatherers with the ability to use measuring instruments to apply and test quantum mechanics, given a characterization of part of the overall system as the environment. In this sense, we can account for the emergence of our familiar classical world, in an approximate sense.

The usual objection to decoherence solutions to the measurement problem is that, while decoherence can underwrite the emergence of a classical probability distribution in quantum measurement process, it cannot deliver a particular event. But here we are setting aside the measurement problem as like the problem of giving a dynamical account of length contraction in relativity, so all that we require of decoherence is an explanation of how a classical probability distribution arises in a measurement process, and this is what decoherence provides.

To sum up: once we accept "no cloning" as a fundamental principle of physics (comparable to the light postulate — "no overtaking of light by light," or the thermodynamic principle — "no perpetual motion machines"), and we take this principle as the statement that we live in the sort of world in which unrestricted cloning is not possible (as opposed to accepting this principle in the sense that the sort of world we live in is just a classical world in which cloning is in principle possible, but what prevents unrestricted cloning as a contingent matter is a restriction on the dynamics), then we are in effect accepting an information-theoretic interpretation of quantum mechanics. That is, the sort of world in which cloning is not possible is the sort of world in which the probabilities associated with measurement outcomes are "irreducible" and cannot be further analyzed in terms of the dynamics by which these outcomes are produced. This is not, of course, to say that there are no genuine measurement outcomes, or that nothing actually happens. Rather, the process by which measurement events happen is not susceptible to a dynamical analysis — more precisely, there will have to be some ultimate measurement events that are not analyzed dynamically. It follows that the structure of probabilities takes a non-classical form that reflects the structural feature of the world manifested in the "no cloning" principle. But this is just to say that quantum mechanics is a non-classical theory of information, and that in taking quantum mechanics as our fundamental theory of being and change, we are committed to grasping our entangled world via a theory about the representation, manipulation, and communication of information.

BIBLIOGRAPHY

Aspect, Alain, Philippe Grangier, and G. Roger. "Experimental Tests of Realistic Local Theories via Bell's Theorem." *Physical Review Letters* 47 (1981): 460-77.

Aspect, Alain, Philippe Grangier, and G. Roger. "Experimental Realization of EPR Gedankenexperiment: A New Violation of Bell's Inequalities." *Physical Review Letters* 49 (1982): 91-94.

Bell, John Stuart. "On the Einstein-Podolsky-Rosen Paradox." *Physics* 1 (1964): 195-200. Reprinted in John Stuart Bell, *Speakable and Unspeakable in Quantum Mechanics*. Cambridge: Cambridge University Press, 1989.

Bell, John Stuart. "The Theory of Local Beables." In John Stuart Bell, *Speakable and Unspeakable in Quantum Mechanics*, pp. 52-62. Cambridge: Cambridge University Press, 1989.

Bohr, Niels. "Can Quantum-Mechanical Description of Physical Reality Be Considered Complete?" *Physical Review* 48 (1935): 696-702.

Bondi, Hermann. *Relativity and Common Sense*. New York: Dover Publications, 1980.

Boschi, D., S. Branca, Francesco De Martini, Lucien Hardy, and Sandu Popescu. "Experimental Realization of Teleporting an Unknown Pure Quantum State via Dual Classical and Einstein-Podolsky-Rosen Channels." *Physical Review Letters* 80 (1998): 1121-25.

Bouwmeester, Dirk, Jian-Wei Pan, K. Mattle, Manfred Eible, Harald Weinfurter, and Anton Zeilinger. "Experimental Quantum Teleportation." *Nature* 390 (1997): 575-79.

Bub, Jeffrey. "Why the Quantum?" *Studies in History and Philosophy of Modern Physics* 35B (2004): 241-66.

Bub, Jeffrey. "Quantum Mechanics Is about Quantum Information." *Foundations of Physics* 34 (2005): 541-60.

Einstein, Albert, Boris Podolsky, and Nathan Rosen. "Can Quantum-mechanical Description of Physical Reality Be Considered Complete?" *Physical Review* 47 (1935): 777-80.

Feynman, Richard P. *The Character of Physical Law.* Cambridge, MA: MIT Press, 1967. First published in 1965 by the British Broadcasting Corporation.

Goldstein, Sheldon. "Bohmian Mechanics." In *The Stanford Encyclopedia of Philosophy*, 2001, ed. E. N. Zalta; http://plato.stanford.edu/entries/qm-bohm.

Greenberger, Daniel M., Michael A. Horne, and Anton Zeilinger. "Going Beyond Bell's Theorem." In *Bell's Theory, Quantum Theory and Conceptions of the Universe*, ed. M. Kafatos, pp. 69-72. Dordrecht: Kluwer, 1989.

Lorentz, H. A. *The Theory of Electrons.* New York: Columbia University Press, 1909.

Mermin, N. David. "Quantum Mysteries Revisited." *American Journal of Physics* 58 (1990): 731-34.

Milburn, Gerard J. *Schrödinger's Machines.* New York: W. H. Freeman, 1997.

Milburn, Gerard J. *The Feynman Processor.* Cambridge, MA: Perseus Books, 1998.

Pauli, Wolfgang. *Writings on Physics and Philosophy.* Edited by Charles Paul Enz and Karl von Meyenn. Translated by Robert Schlapp. Cambridge: Springer-Verlag, 1994.

Schrödinger, Erwin. "Discussion of Probability Relations Between Separated Systems." *Proceedings of the Cambridge Philosophical Society* 31 (1935): 555-63.

Schrödinger, Erwin. "Probability Relations Between Separated Systems." *Proceedings of the Cambridge Philosophical Society* 32 (1936): 446-52.

Shannon, Claude E. "A Mathematical Theory of Communication." *Bell System Technical Journal* 27 (1948): 379-423, 623-56.

Quantum Physics: Ontology or Epistemology?

Anton Zeilinger

The year 2005 was declared by the United Nations General Assembly as the "World Year of Physics" in celebration of the centenary of Albert Einstein's *annus mirabilis,* his miraculous year of 1905. Einstein had published five groundbreaking papers in this year, including his theory of relativity and the most famous equation in physics: $E = mc^2$.

The first paper to be published that year, "Über einen die Erzeugung und Verwandlung des Lichts betreffenden heuristischen Gesichtspunkt" ("On a Heuristic Viewpoint Concerning the Production and Transformation of Light"), was concerned with Einstein's proposal that light consists of quanta. Although the title conveys a tone of cautiousness, the content itself was bold, suggesting that real light particles existed, moving around and behaving in a manner similar to that of gas particles. It is apparent that Einstein did have some insight into the revolutionary nature of the papers. In correspondence with his friend Habicht, in the same year the papers were published, Einstein wrote in anticipation of their very important nature, referring to the first paper as "truly revolutionary." It has been suggested that this is the only paper Einstein ever called revolutionary, and it therefore seems fitting that it is for this work that he received the Nobel Prize, rather than for his theory of relativity.

Einstein's particles of light are today called photons, coined by the American chemist Gilbert N. Lewis. It has become commonplace in many laboratories around the world to experiment with individual photons and with many different kinds of more complex varieties of photon states. It is unsurprising, therefore, that the concept of photons has been experimentally verified with extremely high precision.

Regardless of this level of experimentation and precision, a unique discussion within the history of science continues to this day, and can be simply reduced to the question of "What is light?" — a question that even Einstein was unable to unravel within his lifetime. In a deeper sense the question is concerned with how quantum mechanics should be interpreted; this is a contentious issue and one on which there is still an ongoing debate.

We should remark here that, like most physical theories, there are at least two levels of interpretation of quantum mechanics. The first, lower level of interpretation deals with the question of how the constituent parts of a theory translate into experimental observation. This is by no means a simple and obvious question. On the contrary, relating a mathematical theory to experimentation at best involves large sets of explicit and implicit (although sometimes implicit alone) assumptions, agreements, procedures, and rules, concerning what an experimenter must do to establish a link between observations and theoretical prediction. For example, the simple symbol x usually refers to position. For the experimenter, it is not enough to realize that an object sits at position $x;$ he/she must also ensure that measurements are made of that position. This requires at least two factors. First, a definition of scale is needed, and second, the position of the object can only be defined relative to positions of other objects. The definition scale for distance, as it is currently understood, is directly connected to the definition of time, since distances are only defined through time and the velocity of light. More interesting in terms of the present discussion, however, is the second observation: that any given position is only defined in *relation* to the position of other objects in the universe. Following this line of reasoning, position per se does not make any sense at all. In fact, this can be taken even further; making the assumption that a single object existing in an otherwise empty universe has a position, is a concept devoid of meaning. One consequence of this, according to Mach's principle, is that all dynamics must be explicable in terms of the relative positions of objects and any changes to these relative positions. For example, when a pail full of water is rotated the centrifugal force observed is the result of the pail moving relative to the fixed stars. To return to the interpretation of quantum mechanics, while there are certainly complicated rules on this lower level, there also appears to be general agreement among physicists about what the symbols of quantum mechanics mean. Ultimately, the quantum state gives the probability of observing a certain predicted result, where the registered result is simply some property of the classical apparatus used.

Beyond this primary level of interpretation there is a secondary level, which might be called a metalevel. On this level, it is not satisfactory merely to connect the constituent parts of our theory with the results obtained from observation. Rather, we want to understand what the meaning of the theory is: what it tells us about the inner structure of the world, our position in the world, and whether we play any significant role in it. It is clear that within the twentieth century some of these questions have been considered as unanswerable and have therefore fallen into neglect, but that is not to say that humanity has ceased to ask deep questions about meaning and its role in the universe.

For most participants in the debate, this interpretational question does not represent a criticism of quantum physics. Such a position would be rather difficult to maintain in view of the immense accuracy of quantum mechanics. The debate, however, focuses essentially on questions about the deeper meaning of the theory, specifically, the consequences that quantum theory has on our worldview.

An alternative stance would be to take the view that, at present, the conceptual foundations of quantum mechanics have not been settled. This does not imply that the mathematical axioms normally put forward are incorrect. Rather, it raises the question of the exact nature of the general underlying physical principles upon which quantum theory is built. Such underlying principles are known to form the foundations both of special and of general relativity theory; namely the relativity principle stating that all laws of physics must be the same for all inertial observers, and the equivalence principle of general relativity theory.

This chapter suggests that the foundational debate in quantum physics might gain new momentum by having its basis in real experimentation. While gedanken experiments have been very instrumental to the early debate, many of the community at large today fail to notice the incredible detail in which it is possible to perform experiments with individual quantum systems. These experiments have not only confirmed all predictions of quantum mechanics, but they have opened doors for new technologies — for example, new quantum information technology, including concepts like quantum teleportation and the quantum computer.

The nature of the reality to which quantum mechanics refers is one question that must be addressed, and to which a broad spectrum of responses have been given. At one end of this spectrum lies the assumption that quantum physics refers to a reality whose existence is independent, prior to observation of any of its observed aspects. This position, for ex-

ample, was upheld by Albert Einstein. It is found in its most succinct formulation in the desideratum expressed in the celebrated Einstein-
Podolsky-Rosen paper; namely, that every element of physical reality must
have a counterpart in a complete physical theory. Exploring the EPR-
definition of elements of reality led to the development of theorems by
John Bell as well as Kochen and Specker, asserting that the assumption of
the existence of such elements of reality, independent of observation, is in
contradiction to quantum mechanics.

At the other end of the spectrum is the position held by Niels Bohr, according to which the equations of quantum physics do not describe reality
per se, but only what we can know about the world. According to this position, the concern of quantum mechanics is epistemological. The ontological question then arises: What is the object of this epistemology? What is *it*
that we know something about?

It is interesting to note that in some recent experiments using quantum entanglement in general, but particularly in those specifically concerned with quantum teleportation, these questions have had direct experimental relevance. For example, why is it that systems can perfectly
correlate with each other over large distances, yet it is wrong to assume
that this correlation is due to the individual properties of the system?

We shall briefly discuss the situation of entanglement using a rather
simple futuristic "example." Consider a pair of entangled "quantum dice."
These quantum dice, which might become a favorite Christmas present for
children at some time far in the future, behave as follows: If we throw the
two dice, they will always show the same number. Unpack the next pair of
dice, throw them — again they will each show the same number. This
number might vary from one pair of dice to the next, but for each pair, the
first throw always specifies what that number will be.

Next, we might ask ourselves if this magic connection, which Albert
Einstein calls "spooky," continues to exist over large distances. To investigate this, we might take our pair of dice, throw one here and the other at
some far-off distance. We will find that we observe the same result: the two
dice continue to show the same number. There are various possibilities to
explain why this happens. One way might be to assume that the pair of dice
are loaded so that they have some internal property that determines what
number will appear when they are thrown. This explanation can be easily
excluded by throwing the same pair of dice more than once. We might find
that each one independently shows a random sequence of numbers, but
that the number is always the same for both dice on the first throw.

Another possibility would be to assume that the two pairs of dice some-how manage to "talk" to each other when they are thrown. In other words, perhaps there is transfer of information from A to B, whereby the behavior of one die is influenced by the behavior of the other. Any information trans-fer from one die to the other can be ruled out as an explanation because the two dice instantly "know" to show the same face on the first throw.

The idea that each die has its own internal properties, and that B can only be influenced by the state of A if there is a transfer of information from A to B maximally at the speed of light, is called local realism. It is a very interesting consequence of twentieth-century physics that we now know that such a worldview is not tenable. It has been shown by John Bell that predictions of local realism contradict the predictions of quantum mechanics for certain experiments on entangled particles. Increasing ex-perimental evidence clearly confirms the predictions of quantum mechan-ics and thus disproves local realism.

It is now important to address what this means from a conceptual viewpoint. A simple consequence is that we cannot assume that entangled particles possess their individual properties before they are measured. When one particle is measured, it assumes a given property in a random manner. In the case of the dice, the die randomly decides "which number to show," and the same holds for the second particle; it also randomly de-cides "which number to show." Both dice, however, show the same result, which begs the question, "How can two random events give the same re-sult without there being any connection between them?" This mystery is the reason why Erwin Schrödinger called entanglement *the* essential fea-ture of quantum mechanics, the issue that forces us to abandon all our cherished views about how the world works.

From a more in-depth perspective, we notice something remarkable here. While the properties of the individual system (for example, the num-ber that a die will show) are completely undefined, and the observed result is random in an absolute way, the relation between the two sides is fully de-fined. They both have to show the same result. *Therefore, it is impossible to build an ontology of the individuals, but it is possible to build an ontology of relations.* The relation between two objects is well defined and can be pre-dicted with certainty. That is, we can predict with certainty that the two dice will show the same number, even though the properties of the individuals are completely undefined. We therefore conclude that one consequence of entanglement is that relations are more important than individuals.

In quantum teleportation, very deep philosophical issues have been raised concerning what constitutes the identity of a system. In such experiments the quantum state, which is the representation of all information carried by a system, is transferred completely from one system to another. This is not copying, however, because the original loses its individual characteristics. The question arises: Is the new system the original or not? Let us briefly analyze again what has happened. The original has lost all its properties, and a new original has come into existence that has exactly the same properties as the first.

In teleportation, matter is not transferred; it is only the features, the information carried by a system, that are. The original system becomes a system without properties (something never encountered in everyday life or in classical physics) and the new system becomes identical to the original. It turns out that the question of identity cannot be answered from an ontological point of view without making additional assumptions, which might be unwarranted in a quantum context. If one adopts an operational approach, however, then the answer has to be a positive one because no possible operation can distinguish the new original from the old. Such an approach seems to suggest that a criterion of operational decidability is important for the concept of identity.

Most interestingly, in some experiments one can have individual quantum events (registrations of individual particles), which can be brought about at some earlier time but whose meaning is disclosed later — not only is this disclosed at a later time, but the experimenter also has the choice to define later their meaning. For example, a later measurement can decide whether the data on the system already observed can be understood as implying entanglement with another system or not. Again, these experiments tell us that there is no meaning attached to individuals. The result from the individual measurement previously obtained has no meaning in itself; it cannot be understood on its own. The only way to understand it is in *relation* to other events that will happen in the *future*. We note that actually there might be a long chain from past to future where meaning may slowly be built up.

This means that we are faced with a very interesting situation. While the events themselves exist with no need of interpretation, the connections between them and the meaning that we give them are not absolute but depend on the acts of the observer. Furthermore, the individual events in quantum physics are random in an irreducible way. This objective randomness is probably the strongest indication there is a world existing independently to us.

Anton Zeilinger

The quantum state gives us probabilities of future events. In my view, however, it would be going too far to assume that it describes reality directly. Rather, it is the representation of our knowledge of the situation that allows us to make predictions about the probability of future events. To assume that the quantum state describes anything like reality between these events is not necessary, and appealing to Ockham's razor is one way to suggest its redundancy.

It immediately follows that if one assumes that the quantum state is simply a device to yield probabilities of future events, then all the well-known puzzles and paradoxes of quantum physics disappear. The photon does not go through both slits at the same time in a double-slit experiment; it is just the objective observer's independent lack of information regarding which slit the photon passes through that makes the interference pattern possible. Schrödinger's cat is not both alive and dead at the same time.

Such a position should not be confused with the assumption that reality does not exist unless it is observed. It suffices to say that quantum physics does not make any statements about an unobserved reality. It simply tells us what we can know should we decide to perform a certain experiment.

It should also be noted that the experimenter plays a very important role in quantum physics that goes beyond that of classical physics. This new role is related to the notion of quantum complementarity; that two (or more) concepts may be mutually exclusive. For position and momentum this is expressed quantitatively in the Heisenberg uncertainty relations. The important point here is that the experimenter has a choice of which quantity to measure, position or momentum. Once the choice is made, for example a measurement of position, that quantity will be what emerges as a result of conducting the experiment. The other quantity, momentum, is not only unknown, but the quantum system does not possess a definite value for that quantity. It is the choice of experimental setup, therefore, that determines which physical quality becomes reality. This means that the nature of existing reality is not independent of human action, yet the answer Nature gives us as the result of the individual measurement is random. The result is beyond our control, which indicates an independent physical reality.

In conclusion, it is argued that one should adopt a middle ground that is neither purely ontological nor purely epistemological. Instead, quantum physics may suggest to us that a separation between reality and information, between existing and being known, and in other words between ontology and epistemology, should be abandoned. What are the practical implications of this view? It is important to bear in mind that, when considering what existence might mean, we are simply reflecting on the information we have gathered so far about what exists. Our knowledge that we have acquired of the experimental results is what we are really talking about. Being, therefore, without also being known, makes no sense at all.

In a similar manner to Berkeley's "esse est percipi," information itself is a concept that has no meaning unless it refers to something else. Information always refers to existence and, therefore, always has a referent. In physics we have learned to abandon distinctions that cannot be operationally verified. For example, a huge progression within the discipline occurred when Newton realized that the distinction between the motion of heavenly bodies and the motion of objects on Earth had to be abandoned. He proposed that the same law of gravity governs the motion of planets around the sun, as it governs the motion of an apple falling from a tree. The history of physics is full of such unifications. What we are discussing here is something very similar. We propose that the distinction between reality and information should be abandoned, and that the two concepts should be considered as two sides of the same coin. From that point of view, it does not make sense to make an ontological statement without at the same time admitting that one speaks only about information. Information in this sense stands in relation to the observer — the person who takes note of the information and has the potential to take action as a consequence of it.

If the position outlined above is correct, then ultimately what can be said about the world must define or at least restrict what can exist. Thus, one might gain some understanding of the physics used in making a careful analysis, and in doing so realize what it means to make statements about the world. If we accept such a position, we immediately realize that there are certain inherent structures that follow. For example, we can make one, two, or three statements about the world, but not 1.3 statements. Making statements, therefore, is a quantized procedure by its nature. Furthermore, it has been suggested that the principle of quantization in physics follows from the fact that information itself is quantized.

The ideas outlined in this chapter also have practical implications, and they have been actualized in an interesting research program. In the group for which I work, it has been possible to generate a new understanding of entanglement in this manner, to give a reason for the randomness of individual events using this principle, and also to understand quantum complementarity in a more fundamental way. In summary, quantum physics, from the point of view outlined within this paper, is both a science of information and also a science of what can exist, because of the impossibility of separating epistemology and ontology.

A Self-Contained Universe?

MICHAEL HELLER

Introduction

Disputes between adherents of relational ontologies and defenders of absolutist views had begun much earlier than the polemic between Newton and Leibniz on the nature of space and time gave them new momentum. Newton defended the view that space and time are like objects that exist independently of "anything else"; Leibniz argued that space and time are but a network of ordering relations that cannot exist without events between which the relations hold. Proponents of the "relational world" usually had better marks in the history of philosophy — they seemed to leave fewer things unexplained — but physical sciences always tended to support absolutist views. Such was the case with Newton, who proposed better physics, and Leibniz, who preached a more attractive philosophy. The recent history of the so-called Mach's Principle (MP) is also a good illustration of this regularity. This history started with Einstein's claim that the local inertial mass is fully determined by the global mass distribution in the universe, but it soon assumed strong accents of the "relational versus absolute" dispute. There is a general feeling that a good cosmological theory should not only be *self-consistent,* i.e., logically coherent and at least not contradicting experimental data, but also *self-contained,* i.e., nothing should be put by hand into such a theory, and everything "inside the theory" should be implied by everything. In other words, the universe should be a self-explaining structure. In practice, the tendency to produce a self-contained theory of the universe amounts to reducing or eliminating arbitrary parameters or initial conditions. But in physics nothing comes of nothing. Even the most fundamental principles do not come for free. This is why the idea of a self-contained universe remains vague, and our struggle to implement it in a solid physical theory seems to be never ending.

It seemed that MP made precise this rather vague postulate with respect to at least one of the world's properties, namely its inertial mass. According to MP, mass is not *a priori* given to a considered body, but is "induced" to it by other masses present in the universe. However, it soon turned out that MP is not as precise as it seemed to be, and that there are serious problems with implementing it in a physical theory. Discussions around MP, and a growing number of its formulations, became a modern version of the "relational versus absolute" struggle, and revived the problem of whether the universe can explain itself.

In the recent history of cosmology several strategies were elaborated to implement the goal of a self-explaining universe, such as: perpetually oscillating worlds or worlds with closed histories, the steady state cosmology, quantum creation models, the multiverse idea. They have certainly helped us to understand that the "problem of the universe" is deep and many-faced, but they leave us with our most disturbing questions unanswered.[1] Moreover, there are strong suggestions coming from theorems of Gödel, Church, Turing, Tarski, and others on the incompleteness of logical systems that our program to fully understand the universe could forever remain an unfulfilled dream: If in arithmetic there are improvable truths, could we expect to prove everything about the universe?[2]

In this essay, I focus on only one aspect of these ambitious questions having direct connection to the main theme of the present volume — relational ontologies. In the recent history of cosmology "relational tendencies" surfaced in a guise of various formulations of MP and discussions around them. In the next two sections, I briefly recall the story of MP in relativistic physics and of its opposite doctrine, the so-called geometrodynamics. I then present some key ideas of noncommutative geometry and its application to fundamental physics that seem to throw a new light onto these time-honored questions. Finally, I collect some conclusions and add some methodological and philosophical questions.

---

1. See my paper "Can the Universe Explain Itself?" in *Wissen und Glauben,* ed. W. Löffler and P. Weingartner (Wien: ÖBV & HPT, 2004).

2. John D. Barrow, *Theories of Everything* (Oxford: Clarendon Press, 1991), especially the last chapter.

Spacetime from Matter

Mach's philosophy of physics[3] strongly influenced thinking about physics at the turn of the nineteenth and twentieth centuries. His speculations on the origin of inertia taken up by Einstein, who coined the name "Mach's Principle," played an important role in the origin of general relativity and relativistic cosmology,[4] and later on became the subject-matter of incessant discussions on the foundations of physics.[5]

The diversity of MP formulations[6] have a "common philosophical denominator" that was correctly captured by Julian Barbour:

Cosmology is a unique subject and, perhaps more than any other, forces us to consider the question of foundations. The viewpoint that Mach expressed so cogently and influentially was that there are in fact no external foundations. There can be no foundation on which the world rests. The observed world must itself supply the terms of its own description. It must be conceived to reside and unfold self-referentially in nothing.[7]

This rather vague idea can be made more concrete in manifold ways. For instance, we could postulate that any cosmological theory, besides being *self-consistent*, i.e., logically coherent and at least non-conflicting with observational data, should also be *self-contained*, i.e., requiring no initial or boundary conditions that would have to be imposed by hand.[8] When I throw a stone, its motion is determined by Newtonian law, but it is my hand that imposes onto this law the initial conditions (the starting place and velocity) that select a concrete trajectory from the infinite number of possible trajectories. Such a procedure in cosmology would contradict the assumption that "there is nothing outside the universe." Therefore, in cos-

---

3. Ernst Mach, *The Science of Mechanics* (Chicago and London: Open Court, 1974).

4. Julian B. Barbour, "The Part Played by Mach's Principle in the Genesis of Relativistic Cosmology," in *Modern Cosmology in Retrospect*, ed. B. Bertotti, R. Balbinot, R. Bergia, and A. Messina (Cambridge: Cambridge University Press, 1990), pp. 47-66.

5. Julian B. Barbour and Herbert Pfister, eds., *Mach's Principle: From Newton's Bucket to Quantum Gravity* (Boston, Basel, and Berlin: Birkhäuser, 1995).

6. In my paper "Mach's Principle and Differentiable Manifolds" (*Acta Physica Polonica* B1 [1970]: 131-38), I have collected nearly twenty various formulations of MP.

7. Barbour, "The Part Played by Mach's Principle," p. 47.

8. Zhong Chao Wu, *No-boundary Universe* (Changsha: Hunan Science and Technology Press, 1993), p. 67.

mology we seem to be constrained to look for world models that would either make any initial or boundary conditions superfluous, or provide them themselves without any outside help.

In his first cosmological work,[9] Einstein decided to get rid of boundary conditions. He wrote:

> For if it were possible to regard the universe as a continuum which is finite (closed) with respect to its spatial dimensions, we should have no need at all of any such boundary conditions.

Indeed, since in the Einsteinian closed universe there are no space boundaries, there is no place for boundary conditions. And what about the initial conditions? Of course, to identify Einstein's static solution in the family of other solutions of this class some initial conditions are indispensable, but Einstein's universe lasts from minus time infinity, and the initial conditions are not truly "initial." They are a purely "computational device" and can be chosen at any instant of time. It is interesting to notice that the possibility of an "infinite history" has been achieved by adding to the equations the famous cosmological constant. Its primary goal was to stabilize the equations, but it turned out that without the delicate balance between attractive gravity and repulsive cosmological constant there would have been no "eternal world."

Einstein learned yet another lesson from reading Mach. He formulated it in the following way:

> In the consistent theory of relativity there can be no inertia relatively to "space," but only an inertia of masses relatively to one another.[10]

There is a positivist touch in this doctrine. The only real things in the universe are bodies, and their masses constitute a universal backdrop against which local inertial properties should be measured. Local inertial properties should not be merely influenced by the distribution of distant bodies but entirely determined by it. Since field equations establish a correspondence between matter distribution and spacetime geometry, the latter should be entirely determined by its material content.

In spite of its philosophical attractiveness, MP strongly resisted its full

9. Albert Einstein, "Kosmologische Betrachtungen zur allgemeinen Relativitätstheorie," *Königlich preussische Akademie der Wissenschaften (Berlin), Sitzungsberichte* 1 (1917): 142-52.

10. Einstein, "Kosmologische Betrachtungen."

implementation in general relativity. It was de Sitter's cosmological model that, in the early years of general relativity, played the role of a principal argument against MP. Einstein, motivated by his belief in MP, supposed that his field equations had only one cosmological solution (found by him in 1917) and, in particular, had no solution for the vanishing density of matter (no matter, no spacetime). However, in the same year Willem de Sitter provided another cosmological solution to Einstein's field equations with the zero matter density.[11] In the de Sitter universe there was no matter, but spacetime had very well-determined geometric structure. It became clear that general relativity does not fully satisfy Machian requirements.

On the other hand, there was an effect, calculated in 1918 by Josef Lense and Hans Thirring,[12] indicating that distribution of matter influences (at least partially) the behavior of the local reference frame. The Lense-Thirring effect was, in fact, an implementation of the famous Newton's bucket experiment in the relativistic context. It turned out that Mach was, at least partially, right when he claimed that "if the sides of the vessel increased in thickness and mass till they are ultimately several leagues thick,"[13] then the surface of the water in the vessel could change under the influence of the nearby agglomeration of matter. Lense and Thirring's calculations showed that something very similar indeed obtains in general relativity, and recent satellite experiments have beautifully confirmed this prediction.[14]

It became gradually more and more clear that the "Machian ideology" is only partially implemented in general relativity: the global distribution of matter influences the local properties of spacetime, but it does not determine them fully. In particular, there could exist solutions with well-determined spacetime structure but with no matter in it (de Sitter's solution is only one example). In spite of these theoretical facts, MP, in a variety of its incarnations, continued to be attractive for many researchers. It seemed to be a natural extension of the relativity principle. Refer-

11. Willem de Sitter, "On the Relativity of Inertia: Remarks Concerning Einstein's Latest Hypothesis," *Proceedings of the Koninklijke Nederlandse Akademie van Wetenschappen, Amsterdam* 19 (1917): 1217-25.

12. Josef Lense and Hans Thirring, "Über den Einfluss der Eigenrotation der Zentralkörper auf die Bewegung der Planeten und Monde nach der Einsteinschen Gravitationstheorie," *Physikalische Zeitschrift* 19 (1918): 156-63.

13. Mach, *The Science of Mechanics*, p. 284.

14. Lorenzo Iorio, "A Critical Analysis of the Recent Test of the Thirring-Lense Effect with the LAGEOS Satellites," arXiv: gr-qc/0412057.

ence frames are always connected with physical bodies. It seemed natural to postulate that anything measurable should acquire its meaning by reference to all bodies present in the universe rather than to an abstract space. In spite of many failures to fully incorporate MP into general relativity, innumerable attempts were undertaken to ensure its implementation in a physical theory. Roughly speaking, there were two strategies: either to change general relativity or to weaken Machian postulates. Neither of them gave lasting results. Such a situation persists, more or less, up to the present day.[15]

Matter from Spacetime

Difficulties connected with the implementation of MP in a physical theory led to another conception (which initially was not seen as a concurrence to MP): if spacetime cannot be produced out of matter, let us try the reverse and produce matter out of spacetime. This program was proposed by John Archibald Wheeler under the name of *geometrodynamics*.[16] The idea was to obtain the entire physics (the full theory of elementary particles included) as a geometry of various spacetime configurations. Soon it became clear that in pursuing this program one must take into account quantum "spacetime fluctuations," and consequently geometrodynamics on the fundamental level should change into quantum geometrodynamics.[17] Unfortunately, the program broke down when Wheeler realized that there was no place within the usual geometrical setting for spin 1/2 particles. To save the program Wheeler claimed that it is a "pre-geometry" rather than geometry that constitutes the building block of everything.[18] The concept of pre-geometry was vague — "a combination of hope and need, of philosophy and physics and mathematics and

15. Barbour and Pfister, *Mach's Principle*.

16. John Archibald Wheeler, "Geometrodynamics and the Issue of the Final State," in *Relativity, Groups and Topology*, ed. Cécile M. deWitt and Bryce S. DeWitt (New York: Gordon & Breach, 1964), pp. 315-20; John Archibald Wheeler, "Superspace and the Nature of Quantum Geometrodynamics," in *Battelle Rencontres: 1967 Lectures in Mathematics and Physics*, ed. Cécile M. deWitt and John Archibald Wheeler (New York and Amsterdam: Benjamin, 1968), pp. 242-307.

17. Wheeler, "Superspace," in *Battelle Rencontres*.

18. John Archibald Wheeler, "Pregeometry: Motivations and Prospects," in *Quantum Theory and Gravitation*, ed. A. R. Marlow (New York: Academic Press, 1980), pp. 1-11.

logic."[19] Wheeler made several proposals to make it more concrete. Among others, he explored the idea of propositional logic or elementary bits of information as fundamental building blocks of physical reality (Wheeler's famous saying: "every *it* from a *bit*"). A common denominator of all these proposals was that the usual spacetime geometry had to be an approximation of pre-geometry whatever its nature.[20]

All these conceptions appear now rarely in scientific papers, but a lesson that could be learned from them still motivates many researches, and the lesson is this: on the fundamental level of physics (also called the Planck level) the usual spacetime dissolves into something more fundamental; pointlike events lose their meaning and, consequently, the usual interplay between "local" and "global" should be replaced by a new structural pattern. To go beyond philosophical intuitions one should look for a mathematical structure that would make them physically workable. One of the possible candidates is noncommutative geometry.

Noncommutative Spaces

Noncommutative geometry is a rapidly developing field of mathematical research with a growing number of applications to physics.[21] Among these applications there are many related to the final unification of physics, in particular to the unification of general relativity with quantum theory.[22] It turns out that if we assume that the idea of pre-geometry is concretized as a sort of "noncommutative regime," we obtain interesting results referring to the main topic of the present essay. Although the following discussion is

19. Charles W. Misner, Kip S. Thorne, and John Archibald Wheeler, *Gravitation* (San Francisco: Freeman & Co., 1973), p. 1203.

20. For more about various concepts of pre-geometry, see Jacques Demaret, Michael Heller, and Dominique Lambert, "Local and Global Properties of the World," *Foundations of Science* 2 (1997): 137-76.

21. Some basic references are: A. Connes, *Noncommutative Geometry* (New York and London: Academic Press, 1994); José M. Gracia-Bondía, Joseph C. Várilly, and Héctor Figueroa, *Elements of Noncommutative Geometry* (Boston, Basel, and Berlin: Birkhäuser, 2001); Giovanni Landi, *An Introduction to Noncommutative Spaces and Their Geometries* (Berlin and Heidelberg: Springer-Verlag, 1997); John Madore, *An Introduction to Noncommutative Differential Geometry and Its Physical Applications* (Cambridge: Cambridge University Press, 1999).

22. I restrain myself from quoting any works. Any sample of them would be an unfair sample. Some references could be found in the books quoted in the preceding note.

based on my own works in this field,[23] the results I am going to present are general enough to be valid in the majority of noncommutative models referring to the fundamental level of physics.

In modern differential geometry, one considers spaces called *differential manifolds*. A differential manifold is a space with minimum structure yet geometrically tractable. One can define a differential manifold with the help of two different methods. The first method consists in equipping a set *M* of points with local coordinate systems, essentially a device allowing one to localize individual points (i.e., ascribing to them numbers as their coordinates), and a rule on how to change from one coordinate system to another coordinate system. The second method consists in defining a family of functions (having some simple properties) on this set of points *M*, called *smooth functions* on *M*. Both methods are equivalent, but the first method, as easier in computations, is used more often. On the other hand, the second method is mathematically more elegant, and more suitable for further generalizations. In the following we shall focus on it.

Let us consider a set of points *M*, and let us denote the family of smooth functions on *M* by $C^\infty(M)$. This family has nice addition and multiplication properties owing to which it is qualified as an *algebra*. Let *f* and *g* be functions belonging to $C^\infty(M)$. We can multiply them, and the result of this multiplication does not depend on the order of factors, i.e.,

$$f \cdot g = g \cdot f.$$

We say that the algebra $C^\infty(M)$ is a *commutative* algebra. If an algebra fails to satisfy this condition, it is said to be a *noncommutative* algebra. The property of commutativity is crucial. All spaces investigated in traditional geometry owe to it many of their fundamental properties. This is why it is now called *commutative* geometry. The concept of *noncommutative geometry* was born when a few courageous people decided to assume that

23. Michael Heller, Zdzisław Odrzygóźdź, Leszek Pysiak, and Wiesław Sasin, "Noncommutative Unification of General Relativity and Quantum Mechanics: A Finite Model," *General Relativity and Gravitation* 36 (2004): 111-26; Michael Heller, Leszek Pysiak, and Wiesław Sasin, "Noncommutative Dynamics of Random Operators," *International Journal of Theoretical Physics* 44 (2005): 619-28; Leszek Pysiak, Michael Heller, and Wiesław Sasin, "Observables in a Noncommutative Approach to the Unification of Quanta and Gravity," *General Relativity and Gravitation* 37 (2005): 541-55; Michael Heller, Leszek Pysiak, and Wiesław Sasin, "Noncommutative Unification of General Relativity and Quantum Mechanics," *Journal of Mathematical Physics* 46 (2005): 122501-515.

noncommutative algebras also define some "spaces," in spite of the fact that nobody had the slightest idea what such spaces could look like. Such a way of proceeding is not new in the history of mathematics. For instance, the discovery of complex numbers was the consequence of treating the equation $x^2 = -1$ "as if it had a solution." Similarly, if A is a noncommutative algebra, we treat it as if it were an algebra of functions on a certain "virtual" space. This is a noncommutative space. And then we try to develop geometry on this space in terms of the algebra A in an analogous manner to what one usually does in the case of commutative geometry. In this way, we obtain a powerful generalization of the usual (commutative) geometry. Many spaces that do not surrender to the standard methods can be effectively investigated within the framework of noncommutative geometry. No wonder that noncommutative spaces exhibit many properties unexpected from the classical point of view.

We are accustomed to think about spaces as sets of points. It is rather obvious that each point p of a commutative space M can be identified with all functions of $C^\infty(M)$ that vanish at p. In the algebraic language we say that all such functions form a *maximal ideal* of the algebra $C^\infty(M)$. The crucial fact is that noncommutative algebras, in general, have no maximal ideals! Consequently, in noncommutative geometry the concept of point is (in general) meaningless. This is only one, perhaps the most conspicuous, fact distinguishing noncommutative spaces from commutative ones. Noncommutative spaces are non-local entities. In general, no local properties have any meaning in them.

Of course, these mathematical facts have important consequences when noncommutative spaces are used to model the fundamental level of physics. First of all, in the noncommutative regime there is no space and time in their usual sense, as consisting of points and pointlike time instances, respectively. In such a situation, we can truly speak of a pregeometry out of which the usual space and time will emerge only when one goes beyond the Planck threshold.

Another interesting property of the noncommutative regime is that some concepts, so far independent of each other, are unified in the noncommutative setting — for instance, the concepts of dynamics and probability. In classical physics, dynamics is deterministic: knowing the initial conditions, we are able to predict, with certainty, the future (and the past) states of the system. In quantum physics, dynamics is probabilistic: the future outcomes of an experiment can be predicted only with certain probabilities. And there is practically one probability concept. In the noncommutative regime, things change radically. Let us consider the pair (A, ϕ) where A is a noncommutative algebra satisfying certain additional conditions that qualify it as a *von Neumann algebra,* and ϕ is a *state* on this algebra. From the physical point of view, ϕ describes the state of the considered system.[24] Let us notice that the concept of state is non-local: the entire system can find itself in this or in the other state. Therefore, it is a legitimate concept in "noncommutative physics." And now, a surprise. One can prove that the same pair (A, ϕ) is both a "dynamic object" and a "probabilistic object."[25] In other words, probability and dynamics coincide. Let us contemplate this surprise for a while.

First, the pair (A, ϕ) is a "dynamical object." There is a theorem, due to Tomita and Takesaki, stating that if a state ϕ associated with the von Neumann algebra A satisfies certain conditions,[26] then there is a family of transformations of this algebra that can be numbered in a continuous way with the help of real numbers.[27] In other words, real numbers serve as a parameter that "parametrizes" this family of transformations, and exactly this parameter can be used as a substitute of the usual time. There is a prejudice that dynamics require time: a system evolves if it changes in time. Although in a noncommutative regime there is no usual time, it turns out that it is enough to use the parameter of the Tomita-Takesaki theorem to write the dynamical equation. In contrast with the usual dynamics, the noncommutative dynamics depends on the state ϕ. If the state changes, for instance from ϕ to ψ, one must switch to another dynamical equation.[28] And one must remember that one is in the "noncommutative environment": the state-dependent dynamics does not imply a change "from place to place," but rather . . . well, our imagination does not work in a noncommutative way; it is much better to say that this means simply a transition to another dynamical equation.

Second, the pair (A, ϕ) is a "probabilistic object." It is less known that even the standard probability theory is intimately connected with (com-

24. Mathematically, state is a functional on A; in principle, many such states can be defined on a given algebra.

25. Heller, Pysiak, and Sasin, "Noncommutative Dynamics of Random Operators."

26. The state ϕ must be normal and faithful.

27. These transformations (automorphisms of the algebra A) form a one-parameter group called a modular group.

28. If the von Neumann algebra A satisfies conditions of the Connes-Nicodym-Radon theorem, one can get rid of the dependence on ϕ, but these conditions are not easily satisfied.

mutative) von Neumann algebras.[29] This fact was a starting point for a series of works by Dan V. Voiculescu, out of which a new generalized probability theory has emerged. It is now called free probability theory.[30] The idea was to ascribe to noncommutative von Neumann algebras an analogous role to that played by commutative von Neumann algebras in the usual theory of probability. In consequence, Voiculescu defined a "noncommutative probability space" as a pair (A, ϕ) where A is a (not necessarily commutative) von Neumann algebra, and ϕ a state associated with it. The state ϕ is a generalization of what mathematicians call the probability measure. In contrast with the usual probability theory, there are many such probability measures.[31] If the state ϕ changes to a state ψ, say, one must switch to another "theory of probability."

The surprise consists in the fact that in free probability theory the state ϕ must satisfy essentially the same conditions as are required by the Tomita-Takesaki theorem. We see that in the noncommutative setting dynamics and probability are unified in the sense that both are represented by the same mathematical structure. If we change to another dynamical regime (by changing from the state ϕ to another state ψ, say), we automatically change to another "theory of probability." There are sound reasons to believe that the probabilistic evolution in quantum physics is but a trace of the original unified probability and dynamics.[32]

Interplay Between Local and Global

I do not claim that the model presented in the preceding section is the correct model of the fundamental physical level. It is not mature enough, and it has at least several better-elaborated and more popular rivals (superstrings, M-theory, Ashtekar loop quantum gravity, and others). On the other hand, the possibility that the model (perhaps in its more advanced version) could be incorporated into one of these more developed theories should not be

29. Bounded measurable functions (modulo equality almost everywhere) on the interval are naturally isomorphic with a (commutative) von Neumann algebra.

30. See, for instance, Dan V. Voiculescu, Kenneth J. Dykema, and Alexandru M. Nica, *Free Random Variables* (Providence, RI: American Mathematical Society, 1992).

31. In the standard probability theory there is essentially one probability measure, the so-called Lebesgue measure.

32. For more, see Heller, Pysiak, and Sasin, "Noncommutative Dynamics of Random Operators."

rejected out of hand. We also should remember that it is experiment that has to decide which of them (if any) is the correct one. But so far no such experiment is in sight, and many exploratory paths should be followed. Moreover, I think there is a sense in which our noncommutative model is important from the philosophical point of view.

We are looking for a fully relational ontology — a world that would be woven out of a network of relations between everything and everything. All "things" in such a world would be but knots of various relations. This is a very attractive ideology favored by many philosophers and philosophical systems. Verbal descriptions of such a world are always possible, and they abound (perhaps the most popular among them is Whitehead's process ontology). But human language is elastic, and we do not know whether a given description is free of contradictions as long as we do not have a logical or mathematical model of what this description is about. As far as I am aware, neither in logic, nor in mathematics is there available a fully relational, or fully self-referential, system that would not contain at least some absolute (non-relational) elements. I do not know either of any proof, general enough, that such a system is impossible. It is therefore important to construct logical or mathematical models that would show what is possible and what is impossible in the field of relational ontologies. Let us look, from this point of view, at our noncommutative model.

A noncommutative approach to fundamental physics has clear references to the Machian ideology. As we have seen, all MP formulations postulate a connection between a certain local property and a certain global aspect of the world structure (the former should be somehow determined by the latter). In fact, one of the most maximalistic formulations of MP states that *all* local properties of spacetime should be *fully* determined by the global structure of spacetime. This postulate has clear affinity with the ideal of a fully relational ontology: in the fully relational world all localities are made out of the net of relations between everything and everything in this world. However, it was noticed long ago that such a maximalistic postulate cannot be implemented in the standard geometric setting. Indeed, the local structure, around any point p of any space (differential manifold) considered in the usual differential geometry, is at least partially determined by the structure of the flat tangent space to that space at the point p, independently of what happens at large distances.[33] The strict analogy is that the Earth surface seems to be always locally flat in spite of the fact that it is

---

33. Heller, "Mach's Principle and Differentiable Manifolds."

curved at larger distances. In the noncommutative regime this situation changes radically. Local properties simply do not exist. All localities are totally engulfed by the global structure. If the fundamental level of physics is indeed governed by such a regime, it is fully Machian, in the sense that the whole of physics is entirely determined by the global world structure.

This Machian character of the noncommutative regime has yet another aspect, namely an unexpected interplay of concepts. As we have seen, on this level dynamics and probability are fully unified. We could guess that the same is true as far as other key physical concepts are concerned. Perhaps our present non-Machian physics is but the result of the first ever symmetry breaking in the history of the universe: the transition from the noncommutative era to our era of space, time, and multiplicity. But these are mere epiphenomena that exist only because they are rooted in the fully Machian, and therefore fully relational, fundamental level. Our world is but a shadow of a noncommutative reality.[34]

A struggle to implement Machian ideology in a concrete mathematical structure reflects a tendency inherent in the scientific method to produce a self-contained world model. The postulate to produce such a model should be regarded as a methodological postulate, a directive that requires minimizing the number of independent assumptions. It is true that often behind this methodological postulate an ontological belief is hidden that the universe is indeed a self-contained structure. As we have seen in the present paper, attempts to implement this postulate in a physical theory meet serious difficulties; nevertheless it is firmly rooted in philosophical reflections surrounding scientific progress. As it is well known, Einstein's idea that the universe had to be spatially closed was inspired by Spinoza's pantheism: the geometric self-closedness of the world model was intended to be a scientific counterpart of the Spinozan ontological self-containedness of the God-Universe.

Ontological connotations of the "self-containedness principle" seem to be also consonant with the doctrine of panentheism. This doctrine goes beyond pantheism in claiming that the world "is contained" in God who, however, infinitely transcends the world. According to more refined versions of panentheism, the world is not included in God dualistically, as a part contained in the totality, but rather monistically, as an aspect of the whole. In the latter case, panentheism could also be interpreted "in the Einstein style" by asserting that the mathematical structure of the world is

---

34. This expression is borrowed from the title of the paper by M. Dubois-Violette, J. Madore, and R. Kerner, "Shadow of Noncommutativity," arXiv:q-alg/9702030.

but an aspect of the "mind of God," and as such it should be self-contained in the ontological sense.

The above ideas are only metaphysical reflections "around science." Within the sciences themselves the postulate of self-containedness functions as a methodological postulate steering scientific progress towards less-assuming theories. Suppose that one day we have a final physical theory. Will it be really final, or rather a step towards even more distant horizons? Could the limitations coming from the theorems of Gödel, Church, Turing, Tarski, and others be overcome in physics and cosmology? Even if so, this would not mean that metaphysics will be eliminated. Big philosophical questions are always imminent. Why this mathematical structure rather than the other? Why mathematics at all? Why does anything exist rather than nothing?

BIBLIOGRAPHY

Barbour, J. B. "The Part Played by Mach's Principle in the Genesis of Relativistic Cosmology." In *Modern Cosmology in Retrospect*, ed. B. Bertotti, R. Balbinot, S. Bergia, and A. Messina. Cambridge: Cambridge University Press, 1990.

Barbour, J. B., and H. Pfister, eds. *Mach's Principle: From Newton's Bucket to Quantum Gravity*. Boston, Basel, and Berlin: Birkhäuser, 1995.

Chamseddine, A. H., G. Felder, and J. Fröhlich. "Gravity in Noncommutative Geometry." *Communications in Mathematical Physics* 155 (1993): 205-17.

Connes, A. *Noncommutative Geometry*. New York and London: Academic Press, 1994.

Connes, A. "Noncommutative Geometry and Reality." *Journal of Mathematical Physics* 36 (1995): 6194-6231.

Demaret, Jacques, Michael Heller, and Dominique Lambert. "Local and Global Properties of the World." *Foundations of Science* 2 (1997): 137-76.

Gracia-Bondía, José M., Joseph C. Várilly, and Héctor Figueroa. *Elements of Noncommutative Geometry*. Boston, Basel, and Berlin: Birkhäuser, 2001.

Heller, Michael, Zdzisław Odrzygóźdź, Leszek Pysiak, and Wiesław Sasin. "Noncommutative Unification of General Relativity and Quantum Mechanics: A Finite Model." *General Relativity and Gravitation* 36 (2004): 111-26.

Heller, Michael, Leszek Pysiak, and Wiesław Sasin. "Noncommutative Unification of General Relativity and Quantum Mechanics." *Journal of Mathematical Physics* 46 (2005): 122501-515.

Landi, Giovanni. *An Introduction to Noncommutative Spaces and Their Geometries*. Berlin and Heidelberg: Springer, 1997.

Madore, John. *An Introduction to Noncommutative Differential Geometry and Its Physical Applications*. Cambridge: Cambridge University Press, 1999.

Wu, Zhong Chao. *No-boundary Universe*. Changsha: Hunan Science and Technology Press, 1993.

An Introduction to Relational Ontology

Wesley J. Wildman

Relational ontology is a hot topic these days. It appears in theology, philosophy, psychology, political theory, educational theory, and even information science. The basic contention of relational ontology is simply that the relations between entities are ontologically more fundamental than the entities themselves. This contrasts with substantivist ontology in which entities are ontologically primary and relations ontologically derivative. Unfortunately, there is persistent confusion in almost all literature about relational ontology because the key idea of *relation* remains unclear. If we know what relations are, and indeed what entities are, we can responsibly decide what we must mean, or what we meaningfully can intend, by the phrase "relational ontology" in theology and philosophy.

Why Do Philosophers Puzzle over Relations?

Relations are an everyday part of life that most people take for granted. We are related to other people and to the world around us, to our political leaders and our economic systems, to our children and to ourselves. There are logical, emotional, physical, mechanical, technological, cultural, moral, sexual, aesthetic, logical, and imaginary relations, to name a few. There is no particular problem with any of this for most people. Philosophers have

I am grateful to the members of the conference working group for discussions of this paper and to Robert Cummings Neville for his typically astute advice.

55

been perpetually puzzled about relations, however, and they have tried to understand them theoretically and systematically. Convincing philosophical theories of relations have proved extraordinarily difficult to construct for several reasons.

First, the sheer variety of relations seems to make the category of "relation" intractable. Philosophers have often tried to use simple cases as guides to more complex situations, but how precisely can this method work in the case of relations? Which relations are simple or basic, and which complex or derivative? If we suppose that the simplest relations are those analyzable in physics, we come across a second problem. Ordinary causes (such as collisions), ordinary fields (such as electromagnetic fields), quantum physics (especially entanglement), cognitive science (especially the mind-brain relation), and complexity theory (especially the relation between emergent properties and the constituent parts in complex systems) represent such a diversity of relations that a unified philosophical account of these supposedly simple cases in physics seems out of the question. Third, relations commonly convey or encode or express value, especially in personal contexts, but also in aesthetic and moral contexts. For example, the relation between a nation and its flag confers dignity on the flag and identity on the nation. But how can a philosophical theory of relation simultaneously embrace fundamental physics and the valuational contexts of flags and nations? Fourth, and finally, some important relations are theological in character, and these present special problems. Theistic traditions speak of the God-world relation, for example, and some Christians speak of the relation between Christ and the believer, and the relations among the Persons of the Trinity. Non-theistic religious traditions such as Buddhism speak centrally of relations, and some Buddhists claim that it is liberating to realize that we have no substantive being of our own but are only ephemeral bundles of relations. Are ordinary relations mere analogies for these theological relations, or is there a metaphysical theory that can register them all literally?

In view of these difficulties, the question of the ordinary person, "Why bother trying to construct a theory of relation?" assails any reasonable philosopher. The philosopher worries that the "problem" of a theory of relation may be a pseudo-problem, a mere artifact of a misbegotten love of philosophical abstraction. Perhaps we should cultivate a more common-sense and less metaphysically obsessive approach to life, even in philosophy, as Wittgenstein famously suggested. The metaphysically minded philosopher would answer that indulging philosophical curiosity need not be a dangerous pastime and, moreover, there are important practical consequences of philosophical understandings of relations.

This claim of important practical consequences may seem far-fetched, but there are reasons to take it seriously. One type of reason comes from religion. In the context of Christian theology, if the God-world relation is the metaphysical basis for all relations, then in some beautiful sense the divine suffuses all of reality, making everything sacred and worthy of respect. In Trinitarian thought, to believe that everything is an outward expression of the energies flowing from the loving relations among the Persons of the Trinity ought to transform our spiritual and moral attitudes to everyday life. In the context of Buddhist thought, if the doctrine of *pratītya-samutpāda* (dependent co-origination) is correct, then every kind of relation is a cause of suffering and simultaneously an opportunity for enlightenment, which dramatically changes the way we engage the world. In both the Buddhist and Christian cases, the ruling understanding of relations suggests that we are intimately connected with aspects of the world we normally think have no claim upon us, and this in turn may evoke greater compassion and responsibility among human beings, thereby helping to overcome bigotry, oppression, injustice, cruelty to animals, and ecological neglect (see, for example, Tucker and Grim 1994).

Another reason for thinking philosophically about relations bears on ontology and worldviews. For example, the well-documented human characteristic of overactive pattern recognition leads people to see supernatural causes all around them, thereby inspiring a "folk theory of relation" in which natural and supernatural worlds are intimately related to one another (see Atran 2002, Boyer 2001). If the pervasiveness of this belief is due to cognitive error, then the idea of relations with supernatural entities may be a fiction and we are best off setting the record straight. Similarly, the cognitive tendency to oversimplify leads some people to accept an ontologically reductive view of reality as separated atoms bumping and clumping, after which value, meaning, and responsibility seem to be utterly arbitrary social constructions. If this simple atomism is based on cognitive laziness (Polkinghorne's essay for this volume compiles the evidence from physics alone that shows relations are much more complex than this), then this atomistic view is an oversimplification and, once again, lovers of truth are best off setting the record straight.

Right understanding of the world, responsible engagement within it, and religious concerns all call for a philosophical interpretation of relations. These reasons to think that the metaphysics of relations might be important are mere invitations to a difficult task, however, not any advance on the task itself. Merely pronouncing the phrase "relational ontology" achieves little of significance for nurturing compassion for all beings, promoting ecological responsibility, discriminating between reality and wishful thinking, or attaining any other worthy goal — especially because proponents of substantivist ontology claim to support similar moral and spiritual outcomes. There is significant philosophical work to do, evidently, after which a relational ontology needs to be operationalized in imagination-forming traditions (such as religious worldviews with compelling ritual practices) if it is to have practical effects. I am concerned here with the philosophical phase of this transformative process rather than the social engineering phase. And I will have to bracket the controversial issue of whether a relational ontology activated in imagination-forming traditions really does have superior practical benefits. So what have philosophers been saying about relations?

Philosophical Issues Surrounding Relations

The history of philosophical and theological reflection on relations has surfaced a number of contentious issues with implications for any conception of relational ontology. I discuss four such issues in what follows.

First, if we are to speak of a relational ontology, we first need to know whether relations are ontologically real or merely attributions made by conscious entities and expressed in language. Some strict nominalist empiricist philosophers, heirs of William of Ockham, think of most relations merely as linguistic attributions of significance lacking independent ontological standing. For example, David Hume believed that relations exist in minds and if nobody attributes a relation then none exists (see Hume 2006). By contrast, non-nominalist empiricists such as William James argued that causation furnishes an ontological basis for speaking of the reality of relations (see James 1976). Meanwhile, idealist philosophers believe that the conceptual world of reason is the fundamental reality, which confers ontological status on logical, conceptual, and value relations. In fact, some idealists such as Hegel go so far as to reduce causal relations to logical relations, treating causal necessity as a species of logical necessity (see Hegel 1979). Theistic philosophers affirming an omniscient and omnipotent deity utterly reframe these arguments because, for them, God is the fundamental reality, and both entities and relations between entities have to be understood in terms of their primary relation to the ontologically fundamental entity, God (see Neville 1968).

Second, a pertinent question for a relational ontology concerns the ontological priority of substance and relation. Aristotle thought that relations are ontologically subordinate to entities. We can think of the manifold relations attributable to a set of keys on a key ring — what they can unlock, whether we know where the keys are, and so on — but those relations only exist while the key ring itself exists. Moreover, the key ring's relations can easily be changed (say, by changing locks) without affecting the substance of the key ring. This is why Aristotle included relation on his list of categories as subordinate to the primary category of substance, which he interpreted in his *Metaphysics* as the bearer of all properties, including relational properties (see Aristotle 1971). Some idealist philosophers have argued that Aristotle erred when trusting common sense as a guide in this instance. In fact, the key ring's substance, *properly understood* (i.e., understood contrary to common sense), *does change* when its relations change. Change the locks and the key ring is no longer useful in the way it once was, and this affects the substance of the key ring because substance is more than merely chemical constituents and shape. Alternatively, the category of substance is actually an empty placeholder and not something with independent ontological standing. Thus, on this non-Aristotelian view, either substance ontologically subserves relations or the two are ontologically co-primal or co-subordinate to something else.

Third, if we say relations are ontologically primary (relative to substance), then we need to specify what kinds of relations are ontologically primary. As we have seen, there are extremely diverse kinds of relation, so there is a host of decisions to make. Are the ontologically basic relations causal? conceptual? logical? axiological? What about imaginary relations? perceptual relations? the God-world relation? the intra-Trinitarian relations? At this point I shall consider just a single example that has been central in both Western and South Asian philosophical traditions. Common sense seems to demand a distinction between internal relations that constitute a thing (in the sense that Scotland would not be Scotland if it did not lie to the north of England) and external relations that are merely contingent conditions on a thing (in the sense that Scotland might have an extra tree here or there without changing its very nature). Philosophers have battled over whether relations are all ultimately internal or all ultimately external (both contrary to common sense), or whether individuals have both internal and external relations, as common sense suggests. This matters a great deal for a religiously relevant relational ontology. For example, some philosophers try to see the world from an omniscient, omnipotent God's-eye point of view, in which there are no chances or coincidences, which suggests that ultimately there is no possibility of external relations, despite the way things look to us. Again, most traditions of Buddhist philosophy in South Asia reject the idea that determinate particulars have "own-being" or independent substance, and hold that things are constituted exhaustively by their relations. This particularly strong form of the "all relations are internal" view was one of the defining intellectual distinctions between Hinduism and Buddhism, which shows how religiously potent this philosophical issue can be.

Finally, a major division in theories of relation bears on strategies for connecting scientific, philosophical, and religious understandings of the world. On the one hand, science studies causal relations, and only causal relations, though not all causal relations. The prospects of interdisciplinary conversation, and thereby of morally relevant consensus, might be enhanced if we could somehow conceive all relations as causal. We saw this benefit in connection with the non-nominalist empiricist approach to relations that treats causal relations as real in order to fit with science while insisting that other relations are mere conceptual attributions made by conscious observers. Perhaps the first part of this approach can be broadened by means of a more inclusive theory of causation that extends well beyond commonsense ideas of causation. This would furnish a basis in the theory of causation for conceptual and value relations, as well as for the physical relations we normally associate with causation. In fact, there are several theories of causation — some ancient (e.g., Aristotle's) and some devised specifically with this modern strategy of enhancing interdisciplinary conversation in mind (e.g., Whitehead's) — which are tuned to register the conceptual and valuational qualities of relations that simple scientific analyses tend to miss. Such theories involve stretching causal concepts far beyond commonsense "hitting," but fundamental physics has shown that such commonsense understandings of causation are not feasible. In this instance, therefore, physics and philosophy seem to be pointing in the same direction — toward the need for an enhanced theory of causation to register the diversity of relations that we want to say are real.

On the other hand, some philosophers pay no attention to causes at all in developing theories of relation. Science does not register the value issues that partly inspire us to develop a theory of relation in the first place, so tying a theory to causal relations for the sake of conversation with science strikes such philosophers as self-defeating. In particular, value relations, conceptual relations, and logical relations do not seem straightforwardly causal, so we may be better off trying to theorize relations by richly registering their qualities through phenomenological analysis (in the tradition of Edmund Husserl and Maurice Merleau-Ponty and others) rather than approaching them through causation. Martin Heidegger's analysis of the relation between being and time in human life is an astonishing exhibition of what this sort of approach can achieve (see Heidegger 1962).

If we are meaningfully to speak of relational ontology, then we will have to take a stand on most or all of these philosophical issues and others that philosophers have debated in connection with relations.

An Exploratory Proposal

At this point I move from surveying philosophical debates to taking a stand on the issues relevant to a relational ontology. My view on these matters is highly tentative, but there are important precedents for it so I do not travel alone. I hope that articulating one hypothesis in whatever detail space permits will help to make more concrete the rather abstract but intrinsically interesting considerations so far discussed. In fact, I will explore a hypothesis not about a single theory of relations but rather about an entire class of theories, paying attention to the theological significance of my hypothesis.

Hypothesis: All Relations Are Causal

I appreciate the strategy for dialogue among philosophy, theology, and science just mentioned in connection with a causal theory of relations. Despite the complexities involved, therefore, I propose that all real relations are causal and thus that we should develop a theory of relation by means of a wide-ranging theory of causation that can register the diverse qualities of relations. If a causal account is not possible in a given case, then the word "relation" would be used in a non-literal, honorific sense. The types of relations that could be covered in such a causal theory would be appropriately rich and diverse if the theory of causation were well structured, so there need be no concern that obvious sorts of relation are being left out of the account. The theological ramifications of a sound causal theory of relations are quite promising, also, so there should be no reservations from that point of view. I have space here to indicate what would count as a successful theory of causal relation, to mention the major examples of causal theories of relation, to indicate what a causal theory of relations portends for a relational ontology, and to provide some illustrations of how a causal theory of relation might illumine topics of interest to physicists and theologians. In fact, it will turn out that these are *causal theories of relations and entities,* and thus that they support neither relational ontology nor substantivist ontology but both relations and entities equally.

Criteria for an Adequate Causal Theory of Relation

The capacity of relations to embody and convey value means that a satisfactory theory of causation must explain how causes mediate value. The phenomenological approach to relations naturally registers the value dimensions of relations but abstracts these from their physical substratum and, in extreme versions, also from their psychological and social contexts. The theory of causation we need would span all the way from physical interactions to the mediation of value in relations of social, psychological, moral, and spiritual importance.

A useful theory of causation must take account of the varied and puzzling relations treated in physics. This means registering quantum phenomena such as entanglement, measurement, absorption, and mass-energy transfer, all of which render a commonsense "local hitting" theory of causation untenable. Yet the theory of causation must also handle particle collisions as well as the causal interactions between simple macroscopic physical systems such as billiard balls that have always exemplified commonsense causation.

A serviceable theory of causation will honor the diversity of relations in the whole of reality, within and beyond physics. This requires calling on complexity theory to explain how causation between complex entities emerges with structural complexity from the causal relations among their constituent parts. For instance, the fact that societies achieve things must relate to the way the little parts of a society cause things to happen (see Martin's contribution to this volume for a reflection on this), and this in turn has to reach all the way down to the level of physics. This also requires careful handling of the distinction between basic causes and derivative causes. For example, the basic ontological account of causation might be entered at the "lowest" level of physical reality while higher-order instances of causation such as the way human beings move objects in a game of chess might require additional concepts, such as organization or form, to explain how they work. Derivative causes (in this special sense) would have to be handled without depreciating their philosophical and practical importance, which thus avoids careless reductionism. If this is done correctly, the idea of top-down causal relations (see Polkinghorne in this volume, as well as Murphy and Ellis 1996) may take on an honorific, non-literal status, while top-down modes of analysis would remain crucial for understanding complex systems.

Finally, a comprehensive theory of causation should concern itself with classic theological problems. For example, from a theistic point of view, a theory of causation must either treat the God-world relation, including divine action, within the causal theory of relation (as in process metaphysics) or else regard it as an exception and indicate the sense in which "causal relation" can be a meaningful analogy for the God-world relation (as in Thomist metaphysics). Also, a theory of causation should make sense of spiritual experiences. From a specifically Christian point of view, for example, a comprehensive causal theory of relations should provide leverage for understanding relational concepts such as salvation, communion, sanctification, theosis, love, and judgment. From a Buddhist point of view, a comprehensive causal theory of relations should make sense of attachment and enlightenment, the experience of Samadhi and the nurturing of karuna (compassion).

Contemporary philosophical theories of causation typically ignore some of these criteria. There are counterfactual theories, probabilistic theories, psychological-descriptive theories, and a host of other approaches to causation. But these do not satisfy the criteria listed here. A more ontological approach is needed, and this requires a species of metaphysical reflection that has been somewhat out of fashion in Western philosophy for the last century or more.

Examples of Causal Theories of Relation

Five causal theories of relation that might claim to meet these criteria are participation metaphysics (classically in Plato and later in Neoplatonism), *pratītya-samutpāda* metaphysics (classically in Nâgârjuna and the Madhyamaka school of Mahâyâna Buddhist philosophy), process metaphysics (classically in Alfred North Whitehead), semiosis metaphysics (classically in Charles Sanders Peirce), and implicate-order metaphysics (classically in David Bohm). We can distinguish these views based on how they view entities, contexts, causes, and ultimacy.

Participation metaphysics takes a hylomorphic (matter-form) approach to entities. The form of a thing expresses its participation in a well-ordered realm of goodness, truth, and beauty, and is the pattern by which particular process and entities embody ideal value and intelligent purpose. This realm of transcendental value is the ultimate context for a particular entity, its ontological basis and fundamental cause. Entities participate in this ultimate context by virtue of their form. The meaning of participation through form was much debated in ancient philosophy. Aristotle's idea of a formal cause (see Aristotle 1971) was an attempt to clarify (or simplify) his teacher Plato's very complicated use of the concept of participation (say, in the dialogues *Parmenides* and *Republic;* see Plato 1963). In all of its various versions, the participation metaphysics has little specifically to say about matter, which makes connections with physics difficult, but it does support a powerful link between form and mathematical models for physical processes (Heller's contribution to this volume presupposes a similarly powerful link between mathematics and metaphysical accounts of nature). This view is also excellent for understanding the God-world relation as the presence of goodness, truth, and beauty in the form of everything that exists. John Zizioulas's view interprets all relations as participating in the divine Trinitarian relations using a participation metaphysics (see Zizioulas 1985 and various places in this volume).

Pratītya-samutpāda metaphysics propounds *anatta,* the doctrine that entities have no essence or own-being (*svabhāva*), but rather are agglomerations of relations that arise within the context of pre-existing conditions. Context exhaustively determines the character of an entity, which means that any given thing is what it is solely by virtue of its relations with other things. The religious virtues of this view are its stimulation of compassion and its provocation toward non-attachment, which leads to enlightenment, the ultimate state for Buddhists. In a narrow sense, causation does not apply when entities have no own-being; causation is an impression just as own-being is an impression, and both are misleading. Yet *pratītya-samutpāda* does require entities to arise, which requires causes. So the Madhyamaka School of Buddhist philosophy also rejects illusionistic skepticism by insisting on a middle way between the extremes — entities and causes are both real and not real (the doctrine of two truths; see Eckel

1992). This delicate framing of the idea of causation in contexts is quite promising as a framework for making sense of entanglement and other strange relations in quantum physics but is difficult as a partner for commonsense causation in the rest of physics and in ordinary experience.

Process metaphysics centralizes the ideas of prehension (sensing or feeling) and concrescence (becoming actual). The basic entities in this view are occasions that prehend other fully actualized entities and respond creatively to become actual themselves through harmonizing everything prehended (concrescence), after which they can influence other entities. The environment is not a spatio-temporal container, in this view, but rather that which can be prehended, which opens up possibilities of non-proximate influences, action at a distance, and the like. In Whitehead's version, the prehended environment always includes God, which conveys a value-optimized vision of possibilities to lure the occasion toward fulfillment (see Whitehead 1978). Relationality in this case is the causal influence made possible by prehension.

Semiosis metaphysics, deriving especially from Peirce, regards the basic entities of reality as signs, which are constituted by their interpretative relations to other signs. Each sign stands for (or interprets) another configuration of signs in some way. The resulting flux of signs expresses transformations of meaning, which at one level are mere physical changes, and at a higher level are thoughts. This defines simultaneously a primitive kind of interpretation sufficient to ground value and an ontologically basic kind of causation sufficient to ground the morally laden relations we care most about. The environment is defined as that which conditions interpretation (see Peirce 1991, Corrington 2000). As in process metaphysics, this subordinates spacetime to the construable environment, thereby helping to make sense of some of the peculiarities of fundamental physics, including the non-local phenomena of quantum mechanics. Like *pratītya-samutpāda* metaphysics and unlike process metaphysics, the flux of semiosis goes all the way down, ontologically, so that there is no fundamental ontological atomism. This offers considerable flexibility in dealing with both fundamental physics and cross-cultural variation in ontological ideas of reality. Like participation metaphysics, this view supports a concept of transforming engagement through interpretation that has valuational and religious importance.

Implicate-order metaphysics derives from physicist-philosopher Bohm's attempt to show that a deterministic interpretation of quantum mechanics was possible. Bohm developed Louis de Broglie's idea of a quantum potential or "pilot wave" that directs particles in accordance with the quantum formalism. This takes particles with definite positions seriously but also invokes the idea of a wavelike entity that links objects behind the scenes in ways that ordinary experience does not register. This implicate order is dense with relations and entities, and from it emerges the explicate order of conscious experience as a kind of interactive perspective on the whole. Implicate-order metaphysics is especially good for making a place in nature for conscious experience while also suggesting that ultimate reality is a deterministic flow of interactions of which human consciousness registers only a tiny part. Bohm's later metaphysics was profoundly influenced by the philosopher Krishnamurti and by South-Asian and East-Asian metaphysics (see Bohm 1980) but is somewhat underdeveloped in relation to philosophical concerns such as the reality of value.

The Import of a Causal Theory of Relation for Relational Ontology

Most of the causal theories just discussed subordinate *both entities and relations* to a causal flux that is ontologically more fundamental. That is, the entities and relations that are so important in human moral and spiritual experience emerge from a complex causal web that underlies every aspect of our experience. I think this is a wiser philosophical approach than the one-sided strategies of either substantivist ontology or relational ontology. If the moral downside of substantivist ontology is that we pay insufficient attention to the important relations that morally oblige us, then the equivalent problem with a relational ontology is that it does too little to interfere with our selfish tendency to pay insufficient attention to the intrinsically valuable entities all around us. The symmetry of these theoretical difficulties shows that *we are better off supporting a theory that treats as fully real both entities and relations at the morally and spiritually relevant levels.* A causal theory of relations and entities is just such a metaphysical theory.

Keeping in mind the criteria for an adequate causation-based metaphysics, and acknowledging that I cannot make a case for my view here, I am inclined to think that the semiosis metaphysics may offer the most promising general approach (Nicolaidis's contribution to this volume concurs). In fact, each of the five views has special strengths and distinctive weaknesses, so they can serve as templates in the development of a philosophically more comprehensive and satisfying causal theory of relations and entities.

Illustrating the Causal Theory of Relation

I am setting aside internal battles among causal theories of relations, which are technical debates pursued among a group of specialist philosophers, in order to illustrate how a causal theory of relations and entities works for understanding the various relations that we observe and contemplate in the world around us. I mention one example in fundamental physics, one example in the commonsense world of human experience, and a couple of examples in theology.

Explaining Relations in Fundamental Physics

Commonsense "hitting" views of causation are local, in the sense that we can ignore all events beyond a collision in figuring out how the collision itself works. But "hitting" views of causation cannot make sense of the strange relation of quantum entanglement (technically, non-factorizable, multi-particle superposition), which applies in both deterministic and indeterministic versions of quantum mechanics. Entanglement is non-local, which means that it demands analysis in terms of relations between non-contiguous events. The experimental confirmation of entanglement thus marks the demise of commonsense "hitting" theories of causation.

A causal theory of relations and entities solves this problem by deriving spacetime and the light-speed limits on commonsense causal interactions from the underlying causal nexus, rather than the other way around. On these views, causal interactions are the fundamental reality (e.g., Bohm's implicate order or Peirce's semiotic flux) and spacetime contiguity merely one of several (explicate) manifestations of the underlying flux of real causal relations. This leaves room for non-informational influences and non-local processes of the sort needed to account for entanglement.

Entanglement is popularly taken to be evidence for a mystical view of action at a distance, and has been a favorite reference point for folk versions of relational ontology that explain how I know in Sydney the very moment when my brother suffers a traumatic accident in London. But such folk theories tend to neglect the fact that entanglement prohibits non-local information transfer, which ruins the ideal of instantaneous mystical knowledge. I infer from the non-informational character of entanglement that it is useless for making sense of paranormal phenomena, if they occur at all. The philosophical force of a causal theory of relations and entities in relation to entanglement lies not in supporting paranormal knowledge, therefore, but rather in making space-time relations subordinate to causal relations. What phenomena actually occur in the world is an empirical question.

Explaining Relations in the World of Experience

Moving to the commonsense world of toasters and cricket, decisions and friendship, the main challenge for a causal theory of relations and entities is to show how both macroscopic entities and the relations that obtain between them emerge from the underlying, value-laden causal flux. For example, if Joe decides to make toast for his friend while they watch cricket together, there are a host of causal relations involved, from the mechanics of toasters to Joe's mental causation, and from the meaningful cultural phenomenon of a cricket game on television to the considerateness of an affectionate friendship. How do the causal theories of relation I defend make sense of such ordinary yet often morally and aesthetically loaded life events?

Whitehead has led the way in showing how a causal theory at a very low level can be built up into an account of the causal powers of organisms and cultures, entities and processes. This account is complex, not completely satisfactory (as he realized), and somewhat isolated from the details of physics, so much more work is needed. For example, the atomism of process metaphysics demands a tight theoretical integration of actual occasions with the fermions (matter elementals) and bosons (force elementals) of fundamental physics that has not been achieved. Causal theories of relations and entities such as the semiotic metaphysics, which are not dependent on a fundamental ontological atomism, might be better placed to account for the diversity of relations in ordinary life. Nevertheless, Whitehead did more than any other modern thinker to show that a causal metaphysics is capable in principle of furnishing the sought-after explanation of Joe's toaster adventures.

The key idea in Whitehead's framework is a society of actual occasions that inherits its determinate character and causal powers from the organization of its constituent parts. This account of macroscopic causes and properties is elegant because it requires only the mechanics of causation — prehension and concrescence, in Whitehead's case — joined with the organizational form of enduring objects to explain their complex behavior. Similar ideas also work for the semiotic theories of causal relations. Richly developed causal theories such as the process and semiotic views handle the phenomena of intentional causation and consciousness (such as Joe's decision to cook toast) as naturally as they do lower-level mechanical causes (such as the workings of the toaster). The flux of ordinary causes is constrained and organized in such a way that ordinary causes have complex top-down, bottom-up, and whole-part effects. These very real effects do not need to be ontologized in terms of top-down causes in this sort of causal theory, but there are ways of doing this.

A causal theory of relations and entities of the sort I defend can explain the wealth and diversity of ordinary causal relations far more competently than a commonsense view of causation can explain the world of the small and the emergent world of complexity. An adequate causal theory of relation is also superior to a non-causal theory of relation when it comes to handling the causal rigors of the natural sciences. This expresses the genius of the contemporary creators of causal theories of relation: Peirce, Whitehead, and Bohm developed their metaphysical theories of causation with the sorts of criteria I listed above strongly in mind. They broke away from commonsense causation in just the way required to produce stable causal interpretations of the whole range of relations and entities.

Explaining Relations in Theology

Finally, let us move to the world of theology. The claims of contemporary religion pose a fascinating challenge to a causal theory of relations and entities. Consider the idea of communion with God, which is a precious concept in theistic religions. The participation metaphysics is the causal theory of relation that has the longest history here (it is represented especially in this volume by Zizioulas). On that view, communion is present already in existence itself because the form and dynamics of existing beings express the transcendental values of goodness, truth, and beauty, which is to commune with God in the most basic sense of all. All of the theories of relation I have mentioned can accommodate the sort of causal relation underlying communion with God — basically, the expression of real value through form — but each invokes different ontological categories to convey the sense in which communion with God is causal in and through the being of determinate particulars. Process theism is a partial exception because it treats God as an entity and understands communion through prehension rather than through being itself. But this is a matter of process metaphysics narrowing the concept of God; the idea of being (or process) as communion with creativity itself — the God beyond the process God — can still be introduced into a metaphysical scheme richer than process metaphysics.

In the Christian context, the classical Patristic Trinitarian debates were centered exactly on making sense of a causal theory of relations and entities. What does it mean that the Second Person is identical to the First Person save that it is ontologically begotten by the First Person? What does it mean that the Third Person is distinguished from the first two only by proceeding from them or from the First alone (depending on which side of the Great Schism one adopts)? Causal metaphysics was the field in which the Trinitarian doctrine of God was developed. The perichoretic relations among the Persons of the Trinity are especially interesting. Once again, the participation metaphysics has the longest history here. It supports perichoresis without explaining many details, whereas some causal theories of relations and entities can be much more specific. In particular, the semiotic metaphysics is useful for constructing a rational model of the perichoretic interrelations because the semiotic metaphysics naturally handles inherently interpretative relationships of engagement and participation that also ontologically constitute individuals.

Is Anything Left Out?

Is there any type of relation or entity that a causal theory of relations and entities cannot handle? The usual candidates are logical relations such as identity, entailment, or negation; conceptual relations such as comparison of magnitude, part-whole judgments, or attribution of properties; and metaphysical relations such as non-causal miraculous divine action. A properly elaborated causal theory can handle all of these, including logical and conceptual relations (here the semiotic type of theory has special advantages). But there is one serious difficulty: causal theories of relations and entities have difficulty with the idea of a God-world relation involving non-causal miraculous divine action. While I am not sure that non-causal divine action is even a coherent notion, the causal theories of relations and entities of the sort I am defending tend to line up with theologies that rule out the possibility of a specifically non-causal God-world relation. This can be achieved by rejecting supernatural forms of theism (see Tillich 1951,

Neville 1968, Kaufman 2004). It can be achieved by treating God as a causal agent similar to other causal agents (see Cobb 1965, Suchocki 1989). It can be secured by adopting varieties of theism in which divine action is causal in character even if the causes involved are not the same as those evident in ordinary experience of the world (see Ellis 1995, Murphy 1995, Russell 1998).

Conclusion

The practical moral advantages of a relational metaphysics do not require any philosophical work to realize; inspiring rhetoric is enough. It can be life-changing to feel a profound connection to nature or to other people, and the practical effects can be significant. Religion promotes visions of such relationality and routinely achieves the corresponding effects. To think this through philosophically requires considerable effort — all the more so when we aim to take account of the wide variety of entities and relations that exist in the world, including everything from morally relevant value-laden relations to relations in fundamental physics.

When we do this philosophical work, we are led immediately to wonder whether awarding ontological priority to relations rather than entities has any significant practical advantages over ontologically prioritizing entities over relations. I have argued that both are one-sided approaches to metaphysics and that we are better off with a causal theory in which both entities and relations co-emerge with organizational complexity out of an ontologically fundamental flux of causes (with this flux understood differently in different theories).

An adequate causal theory of relations and entities establishes a philosophical defense both against careless dismissal of value in the relations we know about but do not notice or ponder very often, and against the sorts of reductionism that cannot acknowledge intrinsic value in entities. In a world where people and even the natural environment seem routinely disposed of as if they have no value, we would do well to understand that our relationships with the plants and animals, people and processes on the underside of our lifestyles or outside the immediate focus of our attention are causal, value-conveying connections — grounded in the divine life itself. To be true to oneself is to acknowledge this value-laden interconnectedness among entities, and the responsibilities we incur because of it.

BIBLIOGRAPHY OF WORKS CITED

Aristotle. *Metaphysics*. In *The Complete Works of Aristotle*, 2 volumes, ed. J. Barnes. Princeton: Princeton University Press, 1971.

Atran, Scott. *In Gods We Trust: The Evolutionary Landscape of Religion*. Evolution and Cognition Series. New York and Oxford: Oxford University Press, 2002.

Bohm, David. *Wholeness and the Implicate Order*. London and New York: Routledge, 1980.

Boyer, Pascal. *Religion Explained: The Evolutionary Origins of Religious Thought*. New York: Basic Books, 2001.

Cobb, John B., Jr. *A Christian Natural Theology: Based on the Thought of Alfred North Whitehead*. Philadelphia: Westminster Press, 1965.

Corrington, Robert S. *A Semiotic Theory of Theology and Philosophy*. New York and Cambridge: Cambridge University Press, 2000.

Eckel, Malcolm David. *To See the Buddha: A Philosopher's Quest for the Meaning of Emptiness*. San Francisco: HarperSanFrancisco, 1992.

Ellis, George. "Ordinary and Extraordinary Divine Action: The Nexus of Interaction." In *Chaos and Complexity: Scientific Perspectives on Divine Action*, ed. Robert John Russell, Nancey Murphy, and Arthur R. Peacocke. Vatican City State: Vatican Observatory; Berkeley, CA: The Center for Theology and the Natural Sciences, 1995.

Hegel, Georg Wilhelm Friedrich. *The Phenomenology of Spirit*. New edition. Translated by A. V. Miller. New York: Oxford University Press, 1979.

Heidegger, Martin. *Being and Time*. New York: Harper & Row, 1962.

Hume, David. *An Enquiry Concerning Human Understanding*. Edited by Tom L. Beauchamp. Clarendon Edition of the Works of David Hume. New York: Oxford University Press, 2006.

James, William. *Essays in Radical Empiricism*. The Works of William James. Cambridge, MA: Harvard University Press, 1976.

Kaufman, Gordon D. *In the Beginning . . . Creativity*. Minneapolis: Fortress Press, 2004.

Murphy, Nancey. "Divine Action in the Natural Order: Buridan's Ass and Schrödinger's Cat." In *Chaos and Complexity: Scientific Perspectives on Divine Action*, ed. Robert John Russell, Nancey Murphy, and Arthur R. Peacocke. Vatican City State: Vatican Observatory; Berkeley, CA: The Center for Theology and the Natural Sciences, 1995.

Murphy, Nancey, and George F. R. Ellis. *On the Moral Nature of the Universe: Theology, Cosmology, and Ethics*. Minneapolis: Fortress Press, 1996.

Neville, Robert Cummings. *God the Creator: On the Transcendence and Presence of God*. Chicago: University of Chicago Press, 1968.

Peirce, Charles S. *Peirce on Signs: Writings on Semiotics by Charles Sanders Peirce*. Chapel Hill: University of North Carolina Press, 1991.

Plato. *Plato: The Collected Dialogues*. Edited by Edith Hamilton and Huntington Cairns. Princeton: Princeton University Press, 1963.

Russell, Robert John. "Special Providence and Genetic Mutation: A New Defense of Theistic Evolution." In *Evolutionary and Molecular Biology: Scientific Perspectives on Divine Action*, ed. Robert John Russell, William R. Stoeger, and Francisco J. Ayala. Vatican City State: Vatican Observatory; Berkeley, CA: The Center for Theology and the Natural Sciences, 1998.

Suchocki, Marjorie Hewitt. *God Christ Church: A Practical Guide to Process Theology*. Revised edition. New York: Crossroad, 1989.

Tillich, Paul. *Systematic Theology*. Volume 1. Chicago: University of Chicago Press, 1951.

Tucker, Mary Evelyn, and John Grim, eds. *Worldviews and Ecology: Religion, Philosophy, and the Environment*. Ecology and Justice Series. Maryknoll, NY: Orbis Books, 1994.

Whitehead, Alfred North. *Process and Reality: An Essay in Cosmology*. Corrected Edition. Edited by David Ray Griffin and Donald W. Sherburne. New York: Free Press, 1978.

Zizioulas, John D. *Being as Communion: Studies in Personhood and the Church*. Crestwood, NY: St. Vladimir's Seminary Press, 1985.

Scientific Knowledge as a Bridge to the Mind of God

PANOS A. LIGOMENIDES

The Peculiarities of Our Relational World

Unbounded Variety of Entities

From its elementary particles to the observable limits of the galactic clusters, we perceive our physical world as an evolving, complex, and dynamic system; a system that is made up of a huge variety of different interacting material objects and physical processes, and composed of an immense number of constituents. We refer to any physical entity that we perceive as a material object or a physical process as a "physical phenomenon." As a result of direct experience and observation, a physical phenomenon can be described as arising from the collective statistical behavior of innumerable elementary constituents.

In everyday life, as well as in scientific experimentation, we can testify that nothing remains stationary in nature; everything is in perpetual change, motion, and transformation. In addition, all things are derived from other things, and cause different things to appear. This generates the sense of "before" and "after" as well as the perception of the flow of time.

Causal Relationships

It is possible to experiment with both interactions between, and transformations for, specified categories of physical phenomena, which can be repeated over a wide variety of similar conditions. As a consequence, it is possible to suggest that, besides coincidences, there exist canonical relations that are preserved, invariant, and necessary. Such necessary canonical relations within evolutionary processes that involve objects, events, conditions, and other physical entities are referred to as "causal relations." When formally stated as "causal laws," they allow predictions to be made, as well as various kinds of control to be exerted on the evolution of physical phenomena. A common characteristic in all such cases is that the predictions and controls achieved in one experiment will continue to occur in the future if similar conditions are reproduced.

Reductionism

Democritus' atomistic theory provided science with an insightful worldview for explaining the enormous variety contained within the physical world around us. This is specifically conceptualized as the movement of large aggregates of constituent and elementary "atomic building blocks" that travel and interact in a more or less mechanical manner, much like the components of a machine, within the void of space. This theory, confirmed and empowered by experiential evidence and empirical attestations, was eventually promoted to the status of universal truth. Furthermore, given the weight of the scientific evidence behind the theory, it ultimately became a source of major support for a fragmentary approach to reality.

From the earliest development of the applied scientific method, physical phenomena have been studied by reduction of the properties of their constituents as well as by subsequent inferential synthesis. At the core of this method of "studying by reduction" is the belief that the structure and function of physical phenomena (objects or processes), on all scales of space and time, as well as of the universe in its totality, can be investigated and interpreted by disassembling the physical phenomenon to its constituent parts. These constituent parts are assumed to exist independently outside of each other and to interact through forces of external contact. This contact, however, does not bring about any changes in the essential nature of the constituent parts, and this allows the parts to act in a manner analogous to the components of a machine.

By assuming that the "whole" is simply the sum of its "parts," the properties of the constituent parts are studied and the findings are subsequently assembled, again in the way one might do when analyzing the structure and function of a "machine."

A Mechanistic Worldview

The notion that the order of the universe is basically fragmentary and "mechanistic" maintained its status as a universal truth up until the end of the nineteenth century, amassing an impressive record of scientific successes, especially in the field of thermodynamics and in the manufacturing of thermal machines. Furthermore, this "mechanistic" or "classical" worldview, which is based on the unrestricted application of the deterministic laws of classical physics (e.g., the laws of classical Newtonian mechanics), is to a great extent still dominant in technological applications. In fact, it can be considered as having been the working base of technological progress in Western civilization. With an unshakable faith in the independent behavior (albeit an approximation of independent behavior) of physical phenomena based on our experience, most of today's technological industry has its roots in the mechanistic approach to handling matters of prediction and control of physical phenomena.

Despite the persisting theoretical and experimental affirmations of a "holistic physical world," which have come mainly from discoveries within the field of quantum physics, the reductionistic and analytical notion concerning the modus operandi of our physical world is still part of the worldview held by many scientists concerned with cosmological issues and matters relating to nature's evolution. A widespread commitment to the fragmentary idea about the order of the universe is based on the assumption that our world is comprised of a set of indivisible and unchangeable "elementary building blocks," not yet fully discovered and explained. The broadly propagated expectation is that this approach will make a "theory of everything" (TOE) possible, a complete and coherent explanation of everything related to the evolution of our world.

The common perception concerning the evolutionary process of our physical world is also predominated by reductionistic and deterministic ideas — specifically, that our world of material objects and physical processes is composed of elementary constituents because it was wound up at the beginning of time and was started in a self-governed perpetual deterministic evolutionary course thereafter. A significant shift to contingent evolutionary processes has, however, greatly altered our worldviews during recent decades, primarily due to the undeniable scientific discoveries made by quantum physics.

A Relational World: A Holistic Worldview

The reductionistic approach of analyzing a mechanistically related, physical world has led to confusion and serious contradictions in many important, experimentally verified cases. This can be observed within the continuous, causally determinate, and well-defined relativity theory, as well as the discontinuous, not causally determinate, not well-defined quantum theory. In a number of noteworthy experiments both theories have manifested behaviors that imply an unbroken wholeness of nature. As a direct result of this phenomenon there is a growing consensus that a new notion of order may be needed. Quantum physics reveals that the primordial phenomena, which concern the elementary constituents of matter and radiation, make no sense and offer no possibility of description if they are assumed to be isolated from their physical environment.

Expressing a kind of traditional Eastern mysticism, David Bohm and other eminent scientists have maintained that life is indissolubly connected to the whole of the physical universal system. Indeed, they proposed that all material objects of the observable phenomenological world of our experience, the trees, the stones, the clouds, and also biological beings, are nothing but "holographically encoded" (Bohm 1980, p. 11) projections on our spacetime of unbelievable complexity and variety, originating from an out-worldly holographically encoded reality. This view, however, has not gained acceptance from the majority of the scientific world.

Entanglement and Bohm's Quantum Potential

During his long-drawn-out argument with Niels Bohr, Albert Einstein used many syllogisms in an attempt to prove that quantum indeterminacy is due to the effect of certain "hidden variables" and physical processes yet to be discovered and specified by physical theory. Using reasoning and clever hypothetical experimental arguments, he strove to prove that under the illusory quantum madhouse there exists and acts the intuitive classical world of perfect and exact relations of cause and effect. If he could prove that he was right, it would then be possible to preserve the principle of determinism and to ascribe the illusory whims of indeterminate quantum behavior to the incompleteness of our knowledge as well as to the technical limitations of the experimental apparatus used for measurement.

Bohr's counterarguments to Einstein's proposals proved successful and, at the time, they were demonstrated as sound and faultless. Defeated but unyielding, the great Einstein together with two younger companions, Boris Podolsky and Nathan Rosen, challenged Bohr again in 1935 by proposing one more elegant and excellently elaborated hypothetical thought experiment, which has since become known as the "experiment of Einstein-Podolsky-Rosen," or "EPR experiment."

The basic concept of the EPR experiment was to use two quantum entities such as two elementary particles which, under specific conditions of natural coexistence and interaction, separate to an arbitrary distance in space. The experiment was designed to disprove Heisenberg's quantum principle of indeterminacy by attempting to provide the possibility of simultaneously determining the value of either conjugate property of one of the particles, without disturbing it by direct measurement. This was achieved by measuring the value of the same property on the other remote particle only, leaving the first untouched.

In 1964, John Bell provided an important theorem, stating that quantum theory is indissolubly related to the phenomenon of "entanglement." In other words, Bell's theorem enforces rigorous conditions on the character of physical reality. This conclusion is derived from a detailed examination of the statistical predictions of quantum theory, which concern measuring both interpositions under specific experimental conditions and follow-up observations of the experimental results. Bell's theorem proves beyond a doubt that it is impossible to compromise the general validity of the statistical predictions of quantum theory by the idea that the results of observation on the two faraway and separated quantum phenomena would be independent of the free selection of the experimental conditions. In other words, the validity of quantum theory's predictions demands the "non-local" entanglement, which materializes for arbitrarily great separations in space. We should note here again that the non-local entanglement, which Bell's theorem demands, materializes on two faraway physical systems after they have come into a close physical communication, i.e., after they have become entangled.

Approximately fifty years after the intellectual controversy between Einstein and Bohr, technological progress allowed the experimental verification of the quantum interpretation of the EPR experiment and of the phenomenon of the instantaneous entanglement from a distance, i.e., the phenomenon of non-locality, with the well-known experiment of Alain Aspect, Jean Dalibard, and Gérard Roger of the Institute for Optics at the University of Paris in 1982.

In 1952, in an effort to reconcile the strange "entangled" behavior of the EPR experiment with the generally accepted theory of relativity, David Bohm put forward a non-linear model of physical reality. Specifically, this is a mathematical extension of Schrödinger's equation, which proposes the existence of a preferred rest frame and the action of a "sub-quantum potential," which permeates all space, defines instantaneous "nows," and permits the introduction of undiminished and instantaneous action-at-a-distance. Bohm's quantum potential acts like a radar, affecting subatomic entities by providing an infinitely sensitive information feedback about the "active information state" of the environment.

Bohm assumed that the universal property of "non-locality" was due to the illusionary nature of the separation of material objects (contra to instructive intuition). Using allegorical demonstrations to justify this assumption, he proposed that material objects are, in effect, projections on our three-dimensional space (maybe holographic images) of a unique multidimensional reality.

In accordance with this point of view, the separation of elementary constituents of matter or radiation is only an abstraction, a projected image of a unique multidimensional reality, which exists as a seamless indivisible "whole" somewhere outside the space and time of our own world. It is apparent that our description of an illusionary "reality," which is a three-dimensional projection of an integrated entity beyond our world, will always stand in our way of ever knowing the underlying creative reality.

Bohm's logical and self-consistent propositions about complex, non-linear quantum dynamics of an imaginary reality are hard to digest and have not been widely accepted by the scientific community. This is mainly due to the strange and arbitrary assumptions they make about the notion of quantum potential, but also because of the complete lack of any experimental evidence to back them up. Despite attacks on their plausibility, Bohm's propositions have been valuable in bringing attention to the importance of the "infinitely holistic notion" of the reality of nature. The interpenetrating, possibly analyzable aspects of a holistic reality that rejects the idea that our world is the aggregate outcome of independently interacting constituent parts of a cosmic machine, have ever since become increasingly accepted.

Today, when engaged in scientific reflection, we are becoming increasingly aware of the growing need to look beyond the veil of the physical world. Quantum physics is one way in which this might be achieved.

Panos A. Ligomenides

The World of a "Divine Organizing Principle"

The revolutionary developments in science during the twentieth century have uncovered a world that is evolving in an undetermined, probabilistically driven creative manner; one that, under appropriate conditions, may manifest holistic behavior. During the last few decades of the twentieth century in particular, the idea of "wholeness," in structure and in function, has been developed and made applicable to our universe. An increasing number of scientists engaging with ontological questions want to believe in the undivided wholeness of our world, and in the suggestion that the observed separation and independence of physical entities is, in effect, an illusionary perception. Furthermore, the new idea of a "creative evolution" has begun to replace the old mechanistic ideology, and is now becoming increasingly popular.

The idea of an "unbroken, universal, flowing motion of unlimited potentiality for manifesting our evolving world" has recently gained increasing credibility. This idea expresses "a divine organizing principle," which, in a sense, reflects "the mind of God."

The ideas of a supreme Creator and Lawmaker, a machine-making Demiurge, sharply contrast with the revolutionary idea of a "divine organizing principle," a world-manifesting "agency," which has often been modeled by the scientific concept of a *field*. Specifically, the proposal suggests that the manifested universe is not "created," but that it is manifestly emergent and evolving as part of an integrated, undifferentiated, and changeless "whole." Analogous to an undifferentiated stream of consciousness that evidently comes before definable forms of thoughts and ideas, so does the undifferentiated flow of a "propensity-driven field," with unlimited potentiality to manifest a countless variety of differentiated and probabilistically evolving world-forms, come before "form." This can be conceptualized as being similar to emerging waves, splashes, vortices, and swirls; it cannot be said that they are already contained within the body of water, like pebbles in a box, but rather are potentially and latently subsumed within the turbulent stream of undifferentiated water-flow. The splashes and vortices, which emerge from the undifferentiated turbulent stream, are not created; *they are the stream.*

The world-manifesting "stream," or "the mind of God" as we might call it, is potentially coded in the dynamics of each emerging and evolving "world-form." It plays a genuine part in the "existence" of each one of these world-forms, just as the "whole" is coded in each "part" in the evolving "holomovement" of a hologram.[1] In fact, the infinite subsumed potentiality of the state of undifferentiated flow, "the mind of God," would be mere abstraction without its coexisting differentiated "bodily" expressions.

Albert Einstein, responding to the question, "Do you believe in God?" answered: "I believe in Spinoza's God, who is manifest in the harmony of all being, not in a God that is preoccupied with the fate and actions of men."

Benedict Spinoza, the seventeenth-century philosopher, rejected the Judeo-Christian idea of a transcendent God who created this universe as an act of free will, but regarded all things of this world as attributes of God, rather than God's creations. For Spinoza, God had no choice in the matter; the universe exists in its particular state because of logical necessity or inevitability. In a manner similar to how the Ancients thought, Einstein himself had flirted with the idea that "pure thought can grasp reality." This type of thinking is becoming increasingly prevalent among scientists today, with some even viewing the world as a closed and complete loop of logical explanation.

If everything in this universe follows from logical necessity, its content and form should be deducible from reason alone, with no experimentation or observation necessary for its complete description. Mathematical constructions alone would suffice for discovering the concepts and laws necessary to understand all natural phenomena. John Barrow, in his book *Theories of Everything: The Quest for Ultimate Explanation*, at-

1. A few words may be said here about "holographic coding and imaging." The "hologram" is a three-dimensional image of an object, which is created in space with the help of a laser light beam. The term "hologram" is also used for the coded record of the image on a photographic film from which, with the help of laser lighting, the holographic image of the object is created in space. A "holomovement" refers to a hologram that changes with time. When, with the help of a laser lighting beam, we project a holographically coded and recorded image of an object from a film, its three-dimensional image will appear in space behind the film. The amazing fact is that if we cut the holographically coded film in two and illuminate each piece with a laser beam, we will obtain two images of the object, identical except for a small loss of information and corresponding slight deterioration of the fidelity of each image. Notice that the act of division of the film into smaller pieces can be repeated with a corresponding progression of deterioration of the fidelity in the projected images.

In this sense, one may define as "holographic" the property of a special and peculiar kind of coding of an object, so that the total amount of information concerning the object is embedded almost wholly in the parts of the encoded form. In addition, the information of each part of the object is embedded throughout the entire coded form.

See Ligomenides, *The Peel of the Apricot,* 2nd ed. (Athens: Ellinika Grammata [in Greek], 2003).

tributes the long history of undertakings to achieve a graspable and logical explanation behind physical existence to "the passionate belief in a rational cosmos."

If this shift in fundamental worldviews were to occur, or if they were simply justified as possible, it would profoundly alter our conception of the cosmos and our place in it, and would generate a shift in contemporary theological dispositions, due to the way in which it would change our thinking about our relationship to nature and to God. The God of a mechanistic world would, therefore, be very different from the God of a creatively evolving world.[2]

The Non-Random Nature of Our World: "Why Is Our World Knowable?"

We know now that a peculiar conjunction of simplicity and complexity pervades our universe. Given the limitless variety of ways in which matter and energy can arrange themselves, almost all of which are "random," a striking feature in need of scientific explanation is the non-random nature of many functionally important complex physical systems (specifically biological organizations), and the fact that *they form coherent collections of mutually tolerant, quasi-stable entities.* Within the unbounded variety of entities and relations, the non-random nature of cosmic complexity is captured by the concept of "organization" or "depth."

We can say that our world is knowable because it is redundant, i.e., it contains "order," and therefore it is "algorithmically compressible." In the search for prediction and control of our physical world, scientists interpret the endless quantities of observational data with "compressions" that yield simple laws and theories. In other words, within the scientific framework it is possible to create remarkably concise and universally valid descriptions, usually in the form of mathematical rules and "laws," and often stated concisely "with the precision and compression of an algorithmic statement." It should be pointed out, however, that the mental representations of our brain, our memories, and our knowledge of things are, in essence, also "algorithmic compressions."

---

2. The concept of an emerging auto-germinating and self-contained universe is a viewpoint to which several prominent scientists have alluded recently with growing persistence. The "divine organizing principle" is derived from an elaboration on related viewpoints.

The possibility of algorithmic compressibility makes the world *describable,* and therefore renders it "knowable." Of course, a "shallow," non-compressible world would not contain any "form." There is, however, little point of deliberating on such issues.

"Order" is the property that not only makes observation and experimental repetition and recurrence possible but also makes the physical world *practically* describable, as well as being the property of "locality of presence in space and in time." In addition to "order," every relation and, in the language of physics, every "field of force" displays a "locality," which is due to fast attenuation from the influence of increasing distance, decay of effect as a consequence of the passage of time, or even to the existence of thresholds, as well as other causes that are yet to be discovered. This property of "locality of presence" is responsible for the approximate delimiting of objects and processes of our world, and is therefore pivotal for its evolutionary nature as it permits both the "approximate autonomy" and the "identification" of things, objects, and processes. Without this delimiting property of "relations," the interpenetrating interaction of things would make it impossible for us to know "something" without knowing "everything."

Intrinsic Evolutionary Values: Humans and Society

The Evolutionary History of Our World Through Intrinsic Values

The beginning and the evolutionary history of our world is a topic on which unintelligible relations are being discovered and theories that may never be experimentally validated are being constructed. It is commonly suggested that our world is derived from a stupendous event, the Big Bang, which to this day we do not fully understand. There are also many other suggestions that follow this pattern, such as the belief that our universe has originated from "nothing," that this miraculous physical world evolved and developed from some kind of "quantum chaos made up of ghosts," which could not have any "material" nature yet could weave all that we can sense: our expanding space, a relativistic time, and an unendingly diversified material world!

It is also believed that our world evolved with structures and functions — specifically, that it evolved through synthesis, increased complexity, differentiation, and interaction; by intercommunication, morphogenesis, and morphodestruction; and by behaviors, habits, and rules, which have developed to become the regular laws of nature.

Some believe that, from the beginning, this world had a capability of *motion* by rolling states of "propensities," rather like the Aristotelian "in potential" states (ἐν δυνάμει καταστάσεις). This world is evolving by "inherent probabilistic choices" and incomprehensible "morphogenetic jumps" among potential developmental outcomes in the evolving phenomena of our world, and by equally incomprehensible "quantum jumps" in the fantastic microcosmos of the elementary quantum phenomena. Some think that these "jumps" may constitute "the beat of Creation" in our world.

A product of this largely incomprehensible cosmogonal procedure is the development of enduring and sustaining structural and functional forms (μορφές = "morphes") in nature, which we shall name the "evolutionary inherent values" of our world. Such are the various atomic nuclei, the chemical elements, the molecules, macromolecules, and various biological organisms, the interstellar dust particles, the stars and the galaxies of our evolving physical universe.

The Greenhouse-Earth and Humanity as Intrinsic Evolutionary Value

At this point I would like to refer to the development of our planetary "greenhouse-Earth." It has been suggested that our Earth, a planetary rock, was created 4.5 billion years ago as a result of incredible, yet unintelligible, evolutionary activity. It served as a "greenhouse," with air, earth and water, and other environmental conditions necessary for the development of life, mind, and consciousness. After billions of years of evolutionary morphogenetic development of heavy chemical elements (nitrogen, oxygen, phosphorus, and carbon-12), and in the midst of the vast stellar stage of an inert universe deprived of mind and consciousness, the necessary conditions were developed in an environment with soil, water, air, and fire, for the creation and the evolution of life, intellect, and consciousness. Today it seems logical to believe that many more such greenhouses are dispersed throughout our universe.

The evolution of life on Earth is attributed to the development of *special* self-reproducible and self-sustaining "intrinsic evolutionary values." These, for example, could be biological megamolecules, living cells, biological organisms, human beings, mind, consciousness, even human societies, as well as social and moral "values." It may be argued that "living-greenhouses" and humans as a form of conscious being, together with all the other biological forms of this greenhouse, constitute undeniable intrinsic eigenforms, i.e., "intrinsic evolutionary values" that give a special character, maybe even a singular character, to its evolutionary course. It is likely that these evolutionary values endow our world with an intrinsic meaning. Supporters of the "anthropic principle" argue that clues obtained from observation endorse the hypothesis that the evolutionary course of this universe permits, maybe even foresees, the formation of evolutionary "planetary greenhouses" like our own.

If this is to be considered true, then we might suggest that the evolutionary course of our universe matured around the same time as other greenhouses (we can only know of *our own* greenhouse-Earth). This creates the possibility that, while our Earth developed, creatures with intellect and consciousness, existing on another greenhouse, were wondering about the reason of their own existence.

As a result of the evolution of humankind within the "greenhouse-earth," this universe acquired "consciousness." Because of our consciousness, we may also extrapolate that the universe "came into being" or into "aware existence." As the carrier of this miraculous property of consciousness, humans have developed the capacity to "observe and theorize." As a consequence of our ability to observe, interpret, communicate, and agree, it has been possible for the construction of scientific theories, among them various non-provable scientific myths about cosmology. According to the most predominant scientific theories, it has even been suggested *that the universe now "exists" in the minds it has generated.* Humanity and universe evolve in a wondrous "loop of self-reference," in which the most improbable things are both possible and feasible!

Through the billions of participating consciousnesses, the human community, which itself constitutes one more evolved universal "inherent value," is empowered by the human enterprises of religion, the arts, and the sciences. It builds societies, makes rules of organized cohabitation, and forms long-lasting survival contracts of "human values." We fabricate myths about the origin and the evolution of this universe, and about our own role in it, as well as erecting the four bridges of *knowledge, aesthetics, insight,* and *faith,* to the "Mind of Infinite Divinity."

One may wonder whether we, as human inhabitants of this greenhouse, or maybe every living creature with mind and consciousness, construct *solely by our own existence and our communicative activity* the reality of this unintelligible world of ours!

The evolutionary propensities of nature for morphogenesis and morphodestruction continually put our communities and our human values to the test, mainly due to the intervening acts of human beings. Today we witness the effects of our technology on the physical, social, and psychological environment, and on the possibilities of altering our genetic inheritance. This may be the end of childhood for humankind; we hear the voice of Mephistopheles. We face a Faustian choice: either to subdue our ethical values and to accept the risky technological corrosion of our environment and of our genetic nature as a necessary price to pay for power and worldwide economic development, *or* to reappraise our evolutionary trajectory, and to develop a new morality and new values.

A noble "human value" of our times is reflected in the words of Voltaire, who, more than 250 years ago, counseled us "to cultivate our garden."

The Possible Singularity of Humankind

Within a more general framework one may ask if the development of "biological organisms" from inert matter, with the subsequent emergence of intellect and consciousness, bears some specific meaning. Why is it that human beings, and the greenhouse on which we have developed, exist? Could it be a procedural accident in the blind course of a "divine organizing principle"? Could it be that the theological reference to the hidden will of God is the answer? If this world was created *for us,* as the anthropic principles suggest, then we may propose that we live in a world that is noteworthy because we distinguish it by our own existence.

Science and Spirituality

What Is "Existence"?

What kind of existence can we attribute to the various entities, both to the physical and the more abstract phenomena of our world? Based on our direct empirical observations of the physical world, we justifiably accept the independent existence of material objects that affect our senses directly on repeated inspection; we may even consider such perception uncontested.

In some metaphysical sense we extend the distinctiveness of a "shadowy existence" to the ghostly "wave-particles" of the microcosmos, which we cannot see, touch, or smell, but for which we can acquire knowledge about their activities indirectly through specially designed experimental means.

In a similar fashion, based on more direct corroborative experimental evidence of their effects, we may attribute "existence" to relational "fields of force," like the gravitational field. It is possible to do the same even when it comes to some other postulated, mysterious, often experimentally testified but mostly unexplained "relational fields," like the hypothetical relational "fields of force" that are inferred to act among specified quantum systems of the microcosmos.

The idea of a "relational field," the mechanism for which physics has only been able to explain and verify experimentally for gravity, is conveniently applied to confer the attribute of "existence" to various interpersonal forces that, in turn, may relate to people and other biological organisms. It is possible, therefore, to refer to "fields" when talking about several kinds of interpersonal relations, such as love, or other mysterious relational forces that can regulate or modify personal behavior, even *collective* behaviors of living organisms. We may add here that the "field of force" is also reflected in the perichoretic exchange of love in the Trinitarian thinking of orthodox Christian theology.

Other kinds of subjective entities that we may assign the attribute of "existence" to, could concern personal sensations, emotions, thoughts and memories, and even dream-images. Their substantiation is actualized on the material sub-base of the brain, just as the actualization of computer software depends on hardware.

A category of abstract, less-than-sensorial entities whose existence is affirmed collectively by the societal cohabitation of people includes such things as a national anthem or other cultural or artistic works, logical and mathematical theorems, and ethnical, religious, or political identities. Also belonging to this category are the all-important laws of nature.

The Laws of Nature: Do They Reflect Reality?

There are good reasons why we commonly assume that our physical world is somehow built on the independent existence of theoretically or experimentally probed "laws of nature." Ever since the rise of the scientific-experimental method, which has allowed the observation of subtle and repeatable regularities of nature, one basic question has been asked: whether the laws and theories constructed by humans are indeed the "discovered" laws of nature, or whether they simply constitute our inventions, tailored to suit our need for a believable understanding of nature. Furthermore, do the formulated physical laws enjoy a transcendent existence, thus portraying what may be referred to as the "discovered" physical reality out there (albeit in an approximate, or even warped manner), or do they simply represent the results of our best inventive effort to describe what we observe, limited by the means of observation and interpretation that are available to us? The majority of physicists want to believe in the transcendent existence of physical laws, which endow the scientific enterprise with the all-important and meaningful mission of searching for the "truth."

Some well-known researchers, notably the distinguished physicist James Hartle, as well as other distinguished scientists and philosophers, are skeptical of this viewpoint and wonder whether physical laws may prove to be no more than provisional inventions for meeting our particular scientific and cultural need to conveniently interpret what we observe about the physical world. The doubters claim that the formulated laws of nature are no more than an illusion of "reality," which may, potentially, converge towards an ultimate "truth." To support such a claim the skeptics point to notable past failures of well-known physical laws, which for a very long time were regarded as undisputable truths. Such cases include the model of universal geocentric astronomy and the theory about the universal validity of Euclidean geometry. Another factor that may be considered to justify this viewpoint is that frequently there may be several different incompatible theories attributed to a given set of experimental data, with no obvious preference for some deep transcendent truth.

Even if we accept the transcendent existence of physical laws, another fundamental question may be raised as to whether the laws of nature reveal the work of a God, of a benevolent Platonic *Demiurge* who created the universe, or whether the existence of the laws of nature is accidental, a profound mystery no more remarkable than the existence of the material world itself.

Heinz Pagels named the subtle, mathematically expressed laws of nature as the "cosmic code" which, many have suggested, constitutes a message for us from "the Encoder." For some, the natural laws are also regarded as strong evidence for the existence of an Encoder. Pagels and others, however, find no scientific evidence for the existence of this Encoder within the laws of nature.

Diversity and Wholeness

Today's growing conviction in physics is that nature cannot be fully explained by a reductionistic-mechanistic examination. Nature's "local" diversifying ways of separating things can be conceived only in an "approximately delimiting" manner. A deep understanding of the reality of our world must be able to reconcile the coexisting manifestation of diversity and wholeness.

The approximate separation between things, which is brought about by the "locality of the fields of force" that give rise to approximate autonomy and identification of things (physical phenomena, properties, etc.), must in some deep sense be reconciled with the universal relationality that underscores the wholeness of our world.

The fundamental significance of wholeness and relationality, which are so decidedly manifest in recent scientific discoveries, could be underscored by the essential character of orthodox Christian Trinitarian theology.

What Then Is God?

When discussing matters relating to the notion of "divinity," it is possible to refer to a whole variety of roughly synonymous terms derived from perceptions pertaining to scientific, theological, artistic, or mystical perspectives. We often use terms like the Unknown, Absolute Truth, Unmanifest State, Infinite Mind, or more often, "God." In truth, none of these terms, and indeed no verbal description, could possibly do justice to the ineffable and sublime notion of "divinity." Nevertheless, seeking to gain some insight into the meaning behind the abstract notion of "divinity" and to avoid misconceptions, we often use the term "God," or make reference to "the mind of God," although this is not necessarily always in terms of its formal theological connotation.

The popular notion in mainstream Christian doctrine views God as an anthropomorphic and personal Creator of the universe, who interferes with and "personally" relates to creation. Other religious or philosophical viewpoints also accept the notion of a Creator who, according to their particular viewpoints, may or may not interfere with creation.

Scientists and Religious Faith

I am always impressed to discover that many of my close scientific colleagues practice a conventional religion, managing to keep their scientific and their religious views separate. This usually entails a very liberal view of common religious doctrines, while emphasizing a sense of reverence for the "sacred" and for nature (which is akin to religious awe), as well as often unavoidably attributing unmerited and unappealing significance to physical phenomena.

It appears that most practicing scientists tend only to accept scientific truth from Monday to Friday. On weekends they too join the dogmatic spiritual covenant of religious beliefs. Many well-known scientists, when faced with the limitations of human scientific enterprise, are, in a fundamental manner, deeply religious.

Most non-scientists, when embracing a viewpoint concerning ultimate questions about nature and our place in it, are not always won over by scientific explanations. Although it might be suggested that these explanations are endowed with the authority of scientific objectivity, entrenched religious attitudes and beliefs can seem more congenial to subjective intuitive experience, especially when one is not familiar with the scientific concepts and mathematical symbolism necessary to fully understand scientific explanations. Without elements of spirituality, therefore, scientific knowledge as an approach to the "truth" feels remote to most people unfamiliar with the scientific field.

In recent years there has been an enormous resurgence of interest in what might be crudely described as the interface between science and religion, a widespread dialogue between scientists, philosophers, and theologians about the fundamental questions of existence.

A Better Way of Doing Science

Mainly for historical reasons, scientific research has traditionally distanced itself from ontological debate and the fundamental questions concerning existence. It is possible to suggest that the traditional Cartesian separation of science from spiritual matters has been the cause of crises of ecological devastation, and has promoted the debility and the desperation of the desolate individual in schizophrenic and segmented human societies.

Before beginning to both search and take a position on the fundamental questions concerning existence, we must discover what science has to tell us.

We must question the positions that philosophy brings forth and take a deep dive into our own "selves" through artistic expression and spiritual seeking. To approach "God's mind," therefore, we must cross the bridges of rational knowledge, aesthetic appreciation, mystical insight, and spiritual seeking.

The amazing accomplishments of scientific research have provided new visions and strong enticements regarding the investigation of nature and the function of our physical world, as well as our place in it. These new possibilities of scientific research offer, in my opinion, a unique opportunity for a significant contribution to the development of spirituality, and even to the development of a new kind of religiousness. The reconciliation of rational science and religious spirituality, two powerful institutions of human society, is perhaps our best hope for awaking a new sense of the meaning in our life. It may also offer us the best perspective when searching for an intrinsic meaning in the evolutionary course of nature.

Many believe that a possible attestation of the existence of God, in accordance with any notion of divinity, may come only from scientific endeavor.

*Rational and Aesthetic Scientific Cerebration
and the Insightful Experience of "Sacred"*

From a wider sociological point of view, if separated from spiritual cogitation, a dry technological civilization may deter creative social change, channeling its energy into anger and ethical deviations. In terms of our attitudes about coming to terms with various religious doctrines, it is now time that those who are thinking, searching, and deliberating should distinguish between the relics of paganism and the sublime experience of "religiousness," and the experience of the "sacred," which awakens the human spirit instead of tiring it with boredom and tastelessness.

There have been many important occasions where scientific rationality alone has found itself weak and unable to deal effectively with the ultimate mysteries of nature. Scientific research must be empowered with an appreciation of the aesthetics of nature's order and with a kind of spiritual wisdom. With regard to the essential idea of scientific research we need to conjoin spirituality, cerebration, and inspiration with austere rational scientific methodology. As Einstein proclaimed, "religion without science is blind, while science without religion is lame."

If we wish to empower our research and go further than institutional science, while at the same time overcoming the limitations of mechanistic religion, then we must strip down religions to their essence, which is spirituality. The search for scientific knowledge must be endowed with intuitiveness and inner discernment, and a dialogue must be opened between insightful science and liberated theology. Then, perhaps, a better and more interesting way of doing science would emerge.

BIBLIOGRAPHY

Baars, B. J. *A Cognitive Theory of Consciousness.* Cambridge: Cambridge University Press, 1988.

Barrow, J., and F. Tipler. *The Anthropic Principle.* Oxford: Oxford University Press, 1984.

Bohm, David. *Wholeness and the Implicate Order.* London and New York: Routledge, 1980.

Capra, Fritjov. *The Tao of Physics.* London: Wildwood House, 1975.

Davies, Paul. *The Physics of Time Asymmetry.* London: Surrey University Press, 1977.

Dawkins, Richard. *The Selfish Gene.* Oxford: Oxford University Press, 1977.

Dennett, D. *Consciousness Explained.* Boston: Little, Brown, 1991.

Dyson, Freeman. "Energy in the Universe." *Scientific American,* September 1971.

Glashow, S. L. "Quarks with Colour and Flavour." *Scientific American,* 1975.

Heisenberg, Werner. *Physics and Philosophy.* New York: Harper & Row, 1958.

Heisenberg, Werner. *The Physicist's Conception of Nature.* London: Hutchinson, 1958.

Hindmarsh, Russell W. *Science and Faith.* London: Epworth, 1968.

Hofstadter, D., and D. Dennett. *The Mind's I.* New York: Basic Books, 1981.

Hofstadter, Douglas. *Gödel, Escher, Bach.* New York: Basic Books, 1979.

Ligomenides, Panos. *Peeling the Apricot.* Forthcoming.

Ligomenides, Panos. *The Peel of the Apricot.* 2nd ed. Athens: Ellinika Grammata (in Greek), 2003.

Ligomenides, Panos. Fifty-four related lectures 1994-2006. Proceedings of the Academy of Athens.

Nicolis, G., and I. Prigogine. *Self-organization in Non-equilibrium Systems.* London: Wiley, 1977.

Polkinghorne, John. *The Quantum World.* Reading, MA: Addison Wesley Longman, 1994.

Popper, K., and J. Eccles. *The Self and Its Brain.* Berlin, Heidelberg, London: Springer, 1977.

Prigogine, Ilya. *From Being to Becoming.* San Francisco: Freeman, 1980.

Searl, J. R. *The Rediscovery of the Mind.* Cambridge, MA: MIT Press, 1992.

Taylor, J. G. *Science and the Supernatural.* London: Smith, 1980.

Whitrow, G. *The Natural Philosophy of Time.* London: Thomas Nelson & Sons, 1961.

Relational Nature

ARGYRIS NICOLAIDIS

The present chapter explores the subject of nature: the relationships we build, the images we create, and the extent that we are part of it. These are questions with deep historical roots and, in keeping with this tradition, the present paper wishes to explore these by considering the following three proposals:

PROPOSAL ONE
Nature is a *cosmos,* a place where logos and harmony reign. Nature therefore encourages us to become inspired by the order and perfection existing within it. This is an attitude shared especially by the Ionians, Greeks living in Asia Minor in 600 BCE.

PROPOSAL TWO
Nature is inert; the sole source of knowledge and authority comes from the human being. This contemporary proposal has a leading proponent in R. Descartes.

It is important to note, when drawing similarities between the first two models, that both are hierarchical in nature. The first, the paganist model, comes very close to the deification of nature, where the human being tries to reach the divine cosmos. In the second model, the human being and the human intellect are raised to become of greatest importance, with nature clearly becoming debased. For example, in the latter Cartesian approach, God appears as the end point of human argumentation. Nietzsche, however, inverted the Cartesian argument, providing the ultimate offense:

if God is the outcome of human argumentation, then God loses his onto-logical status, the death of God is decreed, and the human being is presented as a supreme being.

PROPOSAL THREE

The first two models can be conceptualized as polar opposites, with one defining the power of nature and the other of the human being. When exploring a third option, however, it may be useful to think of an "interaction" model, where the human being and nature interact, affect, and influence each other. In this type of approach, the emphasis is not on the "subject" (avoiding the "monism of the subject"), but rather on the *relation*, the interaction that brings the different entities together into community and communion. This proposed interaction is so strong that it would be inconceivable to consider the involved entities as isolated subjects; conversely, the relation and the interaction itself establish their very existence.

Moving into the realm of Relational Ontology, a seminal work with deep insight has been provided by Metropolitan John Zizioulas, in his well-known book *Being as Communion*.[1] In this work, the relationality principle is immersed in God's existence. Here relationality is the supreme ontological predicate of God and serves as the constitution of God's being. To quote,

> Nothing in existence is conceivable in itself, as an individual, such as the τόδε τι of Aristotle, since even God exists thanks to an event of communion. . . . it is communion which makes beings "be": nothing exists without it, not even God. (p. 17)

Furthermore,

> The expression "God is love" (1 John 4:16) signifies that God "subsists" as Trinity, that is, as person and not as substance. Love is not an emanation or "property" of the substance of God, but is constitutive of His substance, i.e., it is that which makes God what He is, the one God. Thus love ceases to be a qualifying — i.e., secondary — property of being and becomes the supreme ontological predicate. (p. 46)

1. John D. Zizioulas, *Being as Communion* (Crestwood, NY: St. Vladimir's Seminary Press, 1985).

The question then is unavoidable and pressing: *How is the Creator's relationality reflected and embodied in the creation?* We will try to explore this issue by studying developments in modern science, notably in special relativity, general relativity, quantum mechanics, complex systems, cosmology, Cantorian infinities, and Gödel's theorem.

Our preliminary study indicates the emergence of strong relational patterns, unifying nature and presenting it as "hypostasis," a unique and concrete entity. Furthermore, the unification process is part of a dynamic evolution, leading from the realm of necessity (at lower levels of reality) to the realm of spontaneity and freedom (at the higher levels of reality). This can be taken to suggest an intentional character or *telos* in the evolutionary process. The findings from this preliminary study vindicate, in many different ways, the ideas and methods of the great thinker Charles Sanders Peirce.[2] Peirce advanced the study of the semiotic process by proposing a triadic relation for the sign (object-sign-interpretant). The Peircean semiotic system provides the framework for the analysis of any creative human activity. Furthermore, Peirce, an ardent advocate of evolutionary philosophy, proposed three modes of evolution: anancastic, tychastic, and agapastic (see below). The relational approach of Peirce is exemplified in the introduction of a new logic, the logic of relatives. We suggest that Peircean logic may provide the ground for a logical foundation of modern theories concerning nature.

The picture of relational nature, occurring as a consequence of the scientific theories developed over the last century, merges with the old *sophia* and *gnosis,* and especially with key aspects of Eastern Christian theology. The Cappadocian fathers insisted that no nature exists "in the nude," but always has its "mode of existence" (τρόπος ὑπάρξεως). We therefore propose that relational ontology is both the framework and "mode of thinking" that brings closer together the created and uncreated.

---

2. For a brief introduction to the work of Peirce, see E. Oakes, "Discovering the American Aristotle," *First Things* 38 (1993): 24-33. The historical and intellectual context of Peirce's life can be traced in J. Brent, *Charles Sanders Peirce: A Life* (Bloomington: Indiana University Press, 1993).

Argyris Nicolaidis

The Journey of Modern Science

Special Relativity

Einstein unified space and time into a continuum: spacetime. He achieved this by raising the speed of light c (the speed of information transfer) to an absolute, a universal constant.[3] The relational considerations that guided Einstein are evident; he insisted that different experiences in spacetime are linked together and reflect a unique, concrete, and unified nature. By accepting the Einsteinian point of view one must also accept the unity of nature or, phrased differently, that nature constitutes a *hypostasis*.

Following Einstein, spacetime is structured by the events taking place. The same event is described in various ways by different observers, thus obtaining a multiplicity of "personal languages." Thanks to the Lorentz transformations, there is a "dictionary" allowing "translation" from one language to another. Events connected by causality belong to the same light cone, a cone in spacetime bordered by signals traveling at the speed of light.

Theoretical physicists considered limiting cases regarding the value c of the speed of light:

i. Everyday life, where all speeds are very small ($v \ll c$) and gravity is weak, is reproduced by the limit $c \to \infty$. In this limit the light cone expands, strict causality determines the whole of spacetime, and the Poincaré group is reduced to the Galilei group.

ii. For very high energies and strong gravity, it has been shown[4] that the appropriate physics is reproduced in the limit $c \to 0$. In this limit the light cone shrinks, causality disappears, and all events are uncorrelated and spontaneous.[5] The Poincaré group is therefore reduced to the Carroll group.[6]

---

3. A. Nicolaidis, "Space, Time and Matter in Modern Physics," a talk given at the University of Athens, published in the journal *Outopia* (May-June 2000): 77 (in Greek).

4. H. De Vega and A. Nicolaidis, "Strings in Strong Gravitational Fields," *Physical Letters* 214 (1992): 295B.

5. J.-M. Lévy-Leblond, "Une nouvelle limite non-relativiste du groupe de Poincaré," *Ann. Inst. H. Poincaré* 1 (1965): 3A.

6. Lévy-Leblond christened it the Carroll group, in honor of Lewis Carroll, author of *Alice's Adventures in Wonderland*.

It is possible to note a change as we move from the presently perceived universe (low speeds, weak gravity), to the very early universe (high speeds, strong gravity). Specifically, there is a shift from the realm of necessity and causality to the realm of spontaneity and freedom.

General Relativity

The General Theory of Relativity provides more radical changes. The spacetime continuum acquires a dynamic character and its geometry becomes determined by the distribution of matter. Within this framework the Kantian considerations of space and time, as terms of an *a priori* intuition, are disfavored. This is due to spacetime being represented by a particle-field, the graviton, much like all the other particle-fields. The whole spacetime is under a continuous evolution, and General Relativity provides the framework that allows the history of the universe to be studied. Furthermore, the "relativity" aspect is even more accentuated; the same phenomenon is described by different accounts or histories. Thus scientific language appears as an "energy" or, in other words, as a locus for the encounter of the external reality and the specific observer.

Quantum Mechanics

A strong rift within the "Cartesian program" (as defined by Husserl and Heidegger) occurred with the birth and development of quantum mechanics. The state of a quantum particle is represented by a linear superposition of two opposite eventualities A and Ā, with a third term T existing to serve as a bridge between them. As a result a binary logic is defied and triadic relationships emerge. In this interpretation the quantum particle is not localized, and the prime feature of Cartesian matter, *res extensa,* is destroyed. Heisenberg's uncertainty principle brings the observer and observed, or the subject and object, closer to one another until they appear as an interrelated couple. Bell's inequalities and Greenberger-Horne-Zeilinger equalities point to the outmost relational character of quantum theory; this has been succinctly encapsulated by Mermin,[7]

7. D. Mermin, "The Ithaca Interpretation of Quantum Mechanics," quant-ph/9609013, "What Is Quantum Mechanics Trying to Tell Us?" quant-ph/9801057.

"Correlations have physical reality; that which they correlate does not. . . . Quantum mechanics is a theory of correlation without correlata."

Complex Systems

Complex systems are highly non-linear, and each individual trajectory is chaotic and undetermined. However, in this framework, if rather than considering the evolution of a single particle, the evolution of a density distribution of points is considered, smooth and universal behavior can be observed.[8] Thus, while the individual event is not predictable, the overall probabilistic features of the system are well determined and universal. It is important to emphasize that in a non-linear system, large and small scales are mixed, resulting in fractal structures. In other words, the statement "the dynamics of a grain of sand may be linked to the dynamics of the entire universe" is rendered credible by complex systems.

Cosmology

The most remarkable discovery of the twentieth century is the evolution of the universe. Contrary to established conceptions regarding the permanence and stability of the universe, dating back to the ancient Greeks, the universe now appears to be an ever-changing entity, with distinct stages in its evolution. The universe, therefore, is an ideal laboratory in which matter and its behavior may be explored in diverse conditions, the "unified models" may be tested, and the ultimate "laws" of nature probed.

The current understanding of the evolution of the universe is impressive.[9] All major "cosmic events," dating from a few minutes after the "birth" of the universe, are now rather well understood, and the inflationary expansion, seeded by the energy of the inflaton field, has been confirmed by the recent cosmic microwave background (CMB) data. Furthermore, the rich structure of the universe (galaxies, clusters of galaxies) can be considered as a manifestation of the quantum fluctuations of the inflaton field. Considering the random character of the quantum fluctua-

8. A. Lasota and M. Mackey, *Probabilistic Properties of Deterministic Systems* (Cambridge: Cambridge University Press, 1985).

9. A. Linde, "Particle Physics and Inflationary Cosmology," hep-th/0503203.

tions (verified by studying the gaussianity of the CMB data), it is beginning to be understood that the current structure of the universe is the end result of *random* dynamics. It is important to note, however, that the present universe also appears strangely unique, with a multitude of parameters having very specific values. This issue is usually analyzed within the "Anthropic Principle" framework.[10] The question then arises whether the possibility of a "guided randomness" should be considered.

A theoretical arsenal has been deployed in the attempt to trace back the history of the universe to its very first instant. This has been enriched with theories such as string theory, M-models, extra dimensions, branes, and noncommutative geometry — to name some strategies. Without entering into any theoretical detail, I would like to stress what may be rather evident: that the first moments of the universe are defined elements of randomness, spontaneity, and freedom, released from the strict causality characteristic of the established scientific frameworks.

Recently, an exciting theoretical development has been the discovery of "dualities."[11] Adopting long-established terminology, theorists suggest the existence of analogies between different and disparate theories. For example, under certain conditions, gravity (the theory determining the large scale of the universe) looks like QCD (the theory determining the inner structure of the microscopic hadrons — proton, neutron, pions). The whole of nature, therefore, appears *strongly interrelated,* forming a unique and coherent entity, to which we belong and remain in constant interaction.

Cantorian Infinities

An infinite quantity breaks the usual axiom that "the whole is greater than one of its parts," for in the infinite case the two can be in one-one correspondence. Cantor analyzed and quantified the notion of infinity, and established that there exists a hierarchy of infinities: $\aleph_0$, $\aleph_1$, $\aleph_2$, $\aleph_3$. . . .[12]

10. J. Barrow and F. Tipler, *The Anthropic Cosmological Principle* (Oxford: Oxford University Press, 1986).

11. J. Maldacena, "TASI Lectures on AdS/CFT," hep-th/0309246. G. Veneziano, "A New Approach to Semiclassical Gravitational Scattering," in Second Paris Cosmology Colloquium, World Scientific, 1995. A. Nicolaidis and N. Sanchez, "Signatures of TeV Scale Gravity in High Energy Collisions," *Modern Physical Letters* 20 (2005): 1203.

12. The "simplest" infinity, $\aleph_0$, corresponds to the infinity of integers (set N). The next level of infinity, $\aleph_1$, is represented by the real numbers (set R).

The question, therefore, is how the two levels of infinity are connected. We may move from one level of infinity to the next by invoking the *requirement of totality*.[13] For example, starting from the set of integers N, the set of *all* subsets of N belongs to R (the set of real numbers). Every time we use the requirement of totality we move to a higher level of representation, where different laws apply (for example, the rules of arithmetic with $\aleph_0$ are not the same as the rules of arithmetic with $\aleph_1$). Since a subset is an effective way of determining a relationship among its members, we may rephrase Cantor's theorem by stating that a "community-communion" of individuals (the ensemble of all the relationships among the individuals) is a more multitudinous and powerful entity than the collection of distinct individuals.

Gödel's Theorem

In 1931, in a brilliant mathematical demonstration, Gödel established that mathematical systems cannot be shown to be free of any internal contradiction, i.e., that we cannot separate mathematics from metamathematics. Gödel, using the diagonal lemma of Cantor, formulated the proposition G: "There is a theorem, which is self-referenced as a non-theorem." Gödel showed that a dichotomy into true and false statements cannot be established. These are undecidable statements that we cannot classify as true or false. It is suspected therefore that analysis, and language in general, lags behind reality.

In summary, it can be gathered from the previous exposition that, rather than having uniform laws that are valid on any determined scale, there are different levels of organization and different levels of knowledge. At each definite level of knowledge, we create a number of predicates, each one appearing as a pair of opposites, A and Ā. To establish identity, unity, and the totality of the cosmos once more, we have to reconcile the opposites by introducing the previously mentioned third term T at a higher level of knowledge, to act as a bridge between the two ends. At each new level of reality there are fewer predicates; the corresponding "language" is further evolved, more complicated, and abstract, as well as less connected

13. A. Nicolaidis, "The Metaphysics of Reason," in *Science and Religion: Antagonism or Complementarity?* ed. B. Nicolescu and M. Stavinschi (Bucharest: Eonul Dogmatic, 2003), p. 231.

to immediate experiences. Lower levels of reality are dominated by strict causality, while at the higher levels we encounter the dominance of spontaneity and freedom. Each level of knowledge is characterized by a *relative apophaticity*[14] with regard to the previous one. It is not possible, therefore, to use the predicates of a lower level to determine an entity living at a higher level (for example, the quantum beable is *not* a particle and is *not* a wave).

Although a complete overall picture is not available, it is quite clear that we should avoid the old dualisms, the dissociation of matter from energy, and placing subject and object in opposition. Modern science indicates that matter, rather than a compound state of Democritan atoms, appears as a concrete manifestation of energy.[15] Quantum realities also imply strong interrelations between the subject and object, rendering the sharp distinction of ontology from epistemology as a counterproductive scheme.[16]

The Peircean Paradigm

Our findings strongly resonate with the ideas and notions developed by the great American thinker Charles Sanders Peirce, who was noted by Bertrand Russell as one of the most original minds of the late nineteenth century. Peirce made important contributions to science, philosophy (notably philosophy of religion), semiotics (theory of signs), and logic.[17] He rejected Cartesian strategies in philosophy, as well as the notion that ideas are "locked up" in the dungeons of the human soul. He proposed that, instead of the isolated Cartesian subject, an intersubjective relational community existed. Peirce treated philosophy as an interactive and experimental discipline ("laboratory philosophy"), and his pragmatism should be understood as a method to link the meaning of concepts to their operational or practical consequences.

Peirce, an ardent advocate of evolution, identified three modes of evolutionary development:

14. A. Nicolaidis, "The Science of the 20th Century as a Sign," talk given in the workshop "The Apophatic Tradition in Theology and Modern Science," University of Thessaloniki, May 2003, to appear in the proceedings "Cosmos in Science and Religion."

15. J. Polkinghorne, in this volume.

16. A. Zeilinger, in this volume.

17. H. Putnam, "Peirce the Logician," *Historia Mathematica* 9 (1982): 290-301.

i. *anancastic* evolution, where mechanical necessity reigns — the best example being Newtonian mechanics;
ii. *tychastic* evolution, where chance predominates; here Darwin's theory serves as an example; and
iii. *agapastic* evolution, where agape (ἀγάπη) is the source of creative growth and intelligible novelty.

In a brilliant proposal, formulated in 1888, Peirce presented a cosmological model, foreshadowing the developments in modern cosmology.

> Our conceptions of the first stages of the development, before time yet existed, must be as vague and figurative as the expressions of the first chapter of Genesis. Out of the womb of indeterminacy we must say that there would have come something by the principle of firstness, which we may call a flash.[18]

The universe is born out of *nothingness,* a "completely undetermined and dimensionless potentiality," characterized by freedom, chance, and spontaneity. The initial flash was followed by other flashes, until the events formed a quasi-continuous flow. Different streams of flashes might coalesce while others remain separated, leading to many different worlds that would know nothing of one another. Secondness is reached when a flash is genuinely second to another flash. It is thus that time has been suggested to have been developed, as well as the first germ of spatial extension. Trends are formed when certain states are connected to others, and these will constitute a spatial continuum that differs from our space by the irregularity in its connection. The spatial continuum might have a certain number of dimensions in one location, and a different number in another. This may also differ for one moving state vis-à-vis another. A collection of these trends will constitute a definite substance. For Peirce, a substance exists as a precise web of relations. The permanence of some trends or tendencies will lead, via thirdness, to the laws of nature.

Peirce held that all knowledge relies on the ability to manipulate signs, and he developed a semiotics (theory of signs) in an attempt to model human thinking. Peirce's definition of "sign" reads as follows:

> A sign is something which, for a given person (the interpretant), stands for something (the object) in some respect or capacity.

---

18. "A Guess at the Riddle," in *The Essential Peirce,* vol. 1, ed. N. Houser and C. Kloesel (Bloomington: Indiana University Press, 1992).

The sign itself may be an icon, an index, or a symbol.[19] An icon is a sign that represents an object by resembling it (e.g., a picture of a dog); an index one that represents an object by actually being connected to it (e.g., the bark of a dog); and a symbol one that represents an object essentially because of its given interpretation (e.g., the word d-o-g).

One of Peirce's most important insights was the realization that signification (meaning) is not based on a relationship between two phenomena (the sign and its object), characteristic of the traditional approach; it is the result of a *triadic* relation, which always involves an interpretant. Thus, the recognition that a sign is indeed a sign lies with the interpretant, underlying his or her *freedom* and *creative intelligence.* The multiplicity of interpretants does not lead to chaotic signification. For Peirce, semiosis is a social activity undertaken by the community of inquirer-interpretant participants in the web of semiosis, whose collective opinion would, given sufficient time, converge.

Thanks to Peirce we have a unified scheme from which to analyze and study all human creativity in science, philosophy, art, and religion, and the necessary means to navigate in the "ocean of signs."

Peirce, a mathematician and logician of highest standing, contributed enormously to a logic of relations, based on triadic relations. Consider two individuals ("terms") S_1, S_2. The relationship of S_1 to S_2 is denoted by R_{12} ("relative"). If we have a class of individuals-subjects S_1, S_2, S_3, ... S_n, Peirce, considering the relationship as the defining operation of the subject, suggested that the subject is represented by the ensemble of all its relationships:[20]

$$S_1 = R_{11} + R_{12} + R_{13} + \ldots + R_{1n}$$
$$S_2 = R_{21} + R_{22} + R_{23} + \ldots + R_{2n}$$
$$\cdots \cdots \cdots \cdots \cdots \cdots \cdots \cdots$$
$$S_n = R_{n1} + R_{n2} + R_{n3} + \ldots + R_{nn}$$

The relationship R_{ij} defines an algebra that has been found[21] to be isomorphic to the algebra of string theory. Since string theory is the theory unifying all interactions, we suspect that nature itself embodies the mathematical structures implied by relational logic.

19. *The Essential Peirce,* vol. 1.

20. Peirce runs against the traditional approach in both science and philosophy, where first the "subject" is defined, and afterwards its actions on "objects" are considered.

21. A. Nicolaidis, *Logic and String Theory* (in press).

The Eastern Sophia

In a search for the vestiges of God's relationality within creation, the present paper has embarked on a journey through the scientific achievements of the twentieth century. It is apparent, in retrospect, that nature has been portrayed by science as a vast and very dense web of relations. It is important to note that, not only are these relations linked together, but they also form a continuum and follow the patterns suggested by relational logic. As a consequence there is no room for dualisms within this framework; they appear as inadequate approximations, poor descriptions, or degenerate forms of an underlying genuine triadic relationship.

Another important factor that deserves consideration is that of evolution; specifically, that all things are subject to the process of change. The human being has a very rich biological history within nature. Nature, however, is also in a continual state of transformation, and as a consequence human beings also have an unpredictable future.

Our own forms of knowledge and experience can, therefore, increase in a dramatic way, leading to the appearance of new forms of intelligibility. Evolution can be conceptualized as both resulting from a very complex set of dynamics and acting as the driving force behind them.

On appraisal, it is also clear that as the course of history has taken place we have turned our backs on traditional Greek preoccupations. The Greek mind searched behind the appearance, the multiplicity, the change, behind the γίγνεσθαι (becoming). It was looking for the invariant element — the first principle and the foundational εἶναι (being). In our case we are faced with the omnipresence of time as "the all-begetting one," and becoming-ness as the essential condition for the fulfillment of the existing.[22] These notions, the pre-eminence of temporality and becoming, may be traced back to their biblical roots. Another important shift is the transfer of ontological interest from "τι ἐστί" (what is it) to "πώς εστίν" (how is it). Specifically, the category of relation, or functionality, takes precedence over that of essence (οὐσία). The question remains, however, whether it is possible to formulate a coherent framework incorporating

22. An "ontology in the temporal" has been developed by Heidegger. M. Heidegger, *Being and Time* (New York: Harper & Row, 1962). Expanding on Heidegger, Levinas insisted that "intelligibility does not arise from the identity of the same which remains in himself, but from the face of the Other who calls upon the same." E. Levinas, *Discovering Existence with Husserl and Heidegger* (Evanston, IL: Northwestern University Press, 1998). E. Levinas, *Totality and Infinity: An Essay on Exteriority* (Pittsburgh: Duquesne University Press, 1969).

these aspects. It appears that within the Eastern Christian tradition we may find the key elements for restructuring our thought and intuition in the necessary direction.[23]

According to Dionysius the Areopagite, the human being may perceive God's creative energies by considering the "πάντων των ὄντων διάταξις" (ordering of all beings). Specifically, the truth does not reside in the beings themselves, but in their positioning and the way in which they exist and correlate. This διάταξις can, therefore, be considered as analogous to the "icon" of the "divine paradigms." St. Maximus, by putting the emphasis on the "τρόπος ὑπάρξεως" (mode of existence), also underscored the prime importance of relationships, for both gnoseological and ontological purposes. Furthermore, it can be suggested that the immanent-transcendent nature of creation is best presented by St. Maximus. Sidestepping Plato and Aristotle,[24] St. Maximus suggested that the human being, on entering the universe of the intelligible, explores the logoi of all beings, and then unifies all different logoi to the unique Logos. Nature, therefore, appears as the "inanimate incarnation" of Logos. A fundamental aspect of Orthodox theology, as advanced by St. Gregory Palamas, is the distinction between divine essence and divine energies. This distinction allows the creation to be viewed as a manifestation of the divine energy and will, but at the same time preserves the ontological gulf between creation and God. For St. Gregory Palamas the divine energies are ἀνείδεοι (unspecified) and ἀσχημάτιστοι (unformed). Following this interpretation, it is possible to view the indeterminate and vague character of the newly born universe (as discussed previously) as a sign of God's energy and will.

It is important to note that there is an ongoing dialogue between the human logos and the divine Logos. Next to creation, the human being creates an entire universe composed of signs and therefore becomes a "created creator." With humans created in the image of God, nature becomes "the image of the image" (St. Gregory of Nyssa). The profound interconnection and affinity between cosmos and anthropos, therefore, forms the basis for what can be suggested to be a hidden "duality": anthropos is a microcosmos and the cosmos is a macroanthropos (St. Maximus). At the

23. Our undertaking is motivated by the need to provide a foundation to the semiotic process occurring in nature. We acknowledge that in this process there is a non-negligible risk of misapprehending deep theological issues.

24. For Plato, the meaning of a thing is separated from the individual object and exists *a priori (ante res)*, while for Aristotle the meaning is located in things *(in rebus)*.

end of evolution, man, in a Eucharist, presents the whole unified universe as an offering to God.[25]

Agape as the Existential Condition

The work of Peirce has greatly informed the current analysis. Drawing on his work once more it is possible to pose two questions: *What is the ontological basis of the archetypal Peircean triadic relationship?* and *Within a universe, what is the ultimate meaning of discourse on nature?*

Following the "iconic" ontology of Christian theology, we are tempted to consider the triadic relationship shaping creation as an "icon" of the divine Trinitarian relationship. If this path is accepted, then the Maximian understanding is invoked: that we may reach God by adopting a "τρόπος ὑπάρξεως" (mode of existence) identical to the divine.

These questions are beyond both the scope of the present paper and the capabilities of the author. To cite a comment by Peirce himself, however:

> Here, therefore, we have a divine trinity of the object, interpretant, and ground [sign]. . . . In many respects, this trinity agrees with the Christian trinity; indeed, I am not aware that there are any points of disagreement. . . .

In conclusion, a mode of thinking has been reached where the primacy focuses on an "interacting being," a being constantly in relation to the other and a being in continuous *ek-stasis* to reach the other. This relational mode of existence, which has been associated with creative growth, novelty, and free development, is qualified as agape. Agape then is something more than an emotional state or sentimental experience, it is the very principle of existence: relating in a creative manner. Ο Θεός αγάπη εστί signifies that God is relationality and the whole exists as an endless and continuous manifestation of agape. Against the tides of modernity we may affirm the statement "SOCIATUS SUM, ERGO SUM" *(I relate, therefore I exist).*

---

25. Metropolitan John of Pergamon (J. Zizioulas), "Creation as Eucharist," talks given at King's College London, published by Editions Akritas, 1992 (in Greek).

26. Brent, *Charles Sanders Peirce.*

The Holy Trinity:
Model for Personhood-in-Relation

METROPOLITAN KALLISTOS WARE

Personal relations are the important thing for ever and ever, and not this outer life of telegrams and anger.

E. M. Forster, *Howards End*

God as Communion

"When I say God, I mean Father, Son, and Holy Spirit," states St. Gregory of Nazianzus (c. 329-90), or Gregory the Theologian, as he is known in the Orthodox Church.[1] For him, the doctrine of the Trinity is not just one possible way of thinking about God. It is the only way. The one God of the Christian church cannot be conceived except as Trinity. Apart from the unity-in-diversity of Father, Son, and Holy Spirit, God cannot be known in the full truth and reality of his being. There is no authentically Christian experience that is not, either explicitly or implicitly, a Trinitarian experience. In this way Gregory's approach is not abstract but personal. In his understanding God is not a theoretical concept, not a philosophical axiom or postulate, but a living communion of three per-

---

1. *Oration* 45.4. In this present chapter I develop ideas found in my articles, "The Human Person as an Icon of the Trinity," *Sobornost incorporating Eastern Churches Review* 8, no. 2 (1986): 6-23, and "The Trinity: Heart of Our Life," in *Reclaiming the Great Tradition: Evangelicals, Catholics and Orthodox in Dialogue*, ed. James S. Cutsinger (Downers Grove, IL: InterVarsity Press, 1997), pp. 125-46, 204-7. These two articles, extensively revised, will appear in my book, *In the Image of the Trinity* (Crestwood, NY: St. Vladimir's Seminary Press, forthcoming). I am grateful to Professor Sarah Coakley for her helpful suggestions.

sons or hypostases, joined inseparably to one another in a union of mutual love.

Such is equally the approach of the Nicene-Constantinopolitan Creed (325/381). After the opening words, "We believe in one God," the Creed does not go on to say, "We believe in an Ultimate Ground of Being, in Primordial Reality, in an Unmoved Mover, an Uncaused Cause." Doubtless these ways of referring to God have their value, but such is not the starting-point of the statement whereby Christians in both East and West confess their faith. On the contrary, the approach of the Creed is personalist, not abstract: "We believe in one God, the Father . . . and in one Lord Jesus Christ the only-begotten Son . . . and in the Holy Spirit." For the authors of the Creed, as for St. Gregory the Theologian, God signifies Father, Son, and Spirit.

This means that the idea of relationship is central to the Christian doctrine of God. In the words of Metropolitan John (Zizioulas) of Pergamon, "The being of God is a relational being: without the concept of communion it would not be possible to speak of the being of God."[2] As Trinity, the Christian God is not just a unit but a union, not just personal but interpersonal. God is not merely self-love but shared love. The Christian God is, in the words of Karl Barth, "not a lonely God."[3] God is not a single person, loving himself alone, isolated, turned inwards. God is a triunity of persons loving each other, and in that reciprocal love the three persons are totally one without losing their specific individuality. It has been rightly said that relationship implies both connection and distinction, and that where there is total fusion there is no relationship. This applies precisely to the intersubjectivity of the Trinitarian God. In the phrase of St. John of Damascus (c. 660–c. 750), the Three are "united yet not confused, distinct yet not divided."[4] We are to see God's oneness, not as a bare mathematical unity, but as an organic, structured unity, an internally constitutive unity. The divine simplicity is a complex simplicity.

Let us explore the relational character of divine being in two ways. Let us first consider briefly how the three members of the Trinity are to be seen

2. John D. Zizioulas, *Being as Communion: Studies in Personhood and the Church* (Crestwood, NY: St. Vladimir's Seminary Press, 1985), p. 17. Metropolitan John's latest book, *Communion and Otherness: Further Studies in Personhood and the Church* (London and New York: T. & T. Clark, 2006), appeared too recently for me to make use of it in the present chapter.

3. Karl Barth, *Dogmatics in Outline* (New York: Harper & Row, 1959), p. 42.

4. *Exposition of the Orthodox Faith* 1.8 (ed. B. Kotter, §8, line 25).

working together in the main events of salvation history, as recorded in the Bible, and how they are likewise active in the two chief sacraments of the Church, Baptism and Eucharist, and in the experience of Christian prayer, as understood by St. Paul. Second, let us note how the doctrine of the Trinity is interpreted by three leading authors from the Patristic and medieval period, the one Greek and the other two Latin: St. Basil the Great, Archbishop of Caesarea (c. 330-79), St. Augustine, Bishop of Hippo (354-430), and the Scotsman Richard of St. Victor (d. 1173). With this as our basis, we can then appreciate how the relational understanding of God sheds light upon the Christian doctrine of creation and of human personhood.

Salvation History, the Sacraments, and Prayer

Any exploration of Trinitarian theology needs to start, not from some abstract notion such as "relationship," nor from the concept of mutual love considered in general terms, but rather from the specific events of salvation history, as revealed in Scripture and interpreted in the tradition of the church. These are found to possess a clear Trinitarian structure:

Creation

God creates through his Word and his Spirit: "God said, 'Let there be light'; and there was light . . . the Spirit of God swept over the face of the waters" (Gen. 1:3, 2). "By the Word of the Lord the heavens were made, and all their host by the Breath [or Spirit] of his mouth" (Ps. 33:6).

Incarnation

At the Annunciation the Father sends the Spirit upon the Blessed Virgin Mary, so that she conceives the Eternal Son of God (Luke 1:35; Matt. 1:18).

Baptism

Here the Trinitarian structure of God's action is particularly plain. At Christ's Baptism by John in the Jordan, the Father speaks from heaven, bearing witness to the Son, while the Spirit descends in the form of a dove (Mark 1:9-11 and parallels).

Transfiguration

There is a similar Trinitarian pattern. On Mount Tabor the Father speaks from heaven, testifying to the Son, while the Spirit descends in the form, not on this occasion of a dove, but of a cloud of light (Mark 9:2-8 and parallels).

Resurrection

After Christ's death on the Cross, the Father raises the Son in and through the power of the Spirit (Rom. 8:11; cf. 1:4).

Pentecost

At the Annunciation it is the Spirit who sends Christ into the world. At Pentecost the relationship is reversed; the risen Christ sends down upon the disciples the Spirit that proceeds from the Father (John 15:26; Acts 2:1-4, 33).

Thus, although the actual word "Trinity" is not to be found in the Bible, the triune character of the Godhead is implicit in the creation story, and is clearly apparent in the Gospel narratives and the Book of Acts.

The basic sacramental actions of the church have likewise a definitely Trinitarian ethos:

Baptism

While Baptism may initially have been conferred simply in the name of Jesus Christ (cf. Acts 2:38; 8:16; 10:48; Rom. 6:3), from an early period it came to be administered in the name of Father, Son, and Holy Spirit, as is evident from the conclusion of Matthew (28:19) and from the *Teaching of the Twelve Apostles* (late first–early second century).[5] Thus the Christian's en-

5. *Didache* 7.1.

try into the church is unmistakably Trinitarian in its orientation. The same Trinitarian emphasis is evident at many other points in the baptismal service, as performed in the Orthodox Church. For example, during the preliminary rite the catechumen, after reciting the Creed, makes a profession of faith in the Trinity: "I worship Father, Son and Holy Spirit, the consubstantial and undivided Trinity." Shortly afterwards the actual baptismal office begins with a Trinitarian blessing: "Blessed is the Kingdom of the Father, the Son and the Holy Spirit."

Eucharist

Here there are similar references to the Trinity. The Divine Liturgy of St. John Chrysostom begins with the same Trinitarian blessing as was used at the start of the baptismal office. Before the recitation of the Creed the deacon says to the people, "Let us love one another, that with one mind we may confess . . . ," and the people complete his statement by responding in words that recall the profession of faith by the catechumen, ". . . Father, Son and Holy Spirit, the consubstantial and undivided Trinity." We shall return later to the parallel affirmed here between the interpersonal character of the Trinitarian God and the mutual love of Christian believers. Most significantly of all, at the culminating moment in the consecratory anaphora, there is an epiclesis or invocation of the Spirit that is directly Trinitarian. The celebrant prays to God the Father to send down the Holy Spirit upon the gifts of bread and wine,[6] so that they may become the Body and Blood of Christ. Here the relationship between the three divine persons is similar to that which is evident at the Annunciation: the Father sends the Spirit, whose ministry it is to make Christ present in our midst.

There is also a Trinitarian pattern in the personal prayer of the Christian believer, as St. Paul indicates in Romans 8:9-27 and 1 Corinthians 2:9-16. He envisages the Holy Spirit as praying for and within us: "The Spirit also helps our weakness . . . the Spirit himself intercedes for us" (Rom. 8:26). Now the function of the Paraclete Spirit, when he prays in this way for and within us, is precisely to enable us to share the "mind of Christ" (1 Cor. 2:16). Through the Spirit, then, we participate in the Son's response to the Father, crying out with Christ, "Abba, Father!" (Rom. 8:15), thus be-

6. There is in fact a double invocation of the Spirit, upon the assembled congregation as well as the bread and wine.

coming "sons in the Son": "The Spirit himself bears witness with our spirit that we are the children of God" (Rom. 8:16). So, in and through the Spirit, we participate in the eternal dialogue that passes between the Father and the Son. Prayer, then, is not to be seen simply as a conversation between two subjects, me and God. At a more profound level I do not just speak to God, but rather I am taken up into the exchange of mutual love that passes unceasingly between the three divine hypostases of the Trinity. Prayer, then, in its fullest and most authentic expression, is nothing less than to enter into the life of the Trinity. It is to become part of the interpersonal relationship of the threefold God.

From all this it is abundantly clear that the reality and truth of God as Trinity is directly disclosed to us alike in the events of salvation history, in the church's sacramental acts, and in our personal prayer. The doctrine of the Trinity is, in this way, not primarily a philosophical hypothesis that we seek to "prove" through rational arguments or speculative analogies. It is, on the contrary, something that is *revealed* to us in Scripture and in the experience of the church, whether corporately or through our prayer "in secret" (Matt. 6:6).

All this serves to indicate that our Christian God is a God of Trinitarian relationships. But it does not explain *why* God should be Trinity. Doubtless a full and exhaustive explanation is impossible: we should never lose sight of the apophatic dimension of our Trinitarian faith. The doctrine of the Trinity is indeed a mystery. But a mystery, in the proper theological sense, is not simply a conundrum or an inexplicable enigma, but it is something revealed to our understanding, although never completely revealed, for it extends beyond our comprehension into the unfathomable depths (or heights) of divine being. How then can we attain at least a partial understanding of why God should be Trinity? More specifically, what discernible effect does our Trinitarian faith have upon our daily life? As Christians we are not polytheists, believing in many gods as did the pagan Greeks, nor yet are we in a restrictive and unqualified sense monotheists, as are the Jews and the Muslims, but we believe in a God who is not simply one but one-in-three and three-in-one, that is to say, a God who combines within his perfect being both absolute unity and genuine personal diversity. Yet what practical difference does this make?

God as Mutual Love

In attempting to answer these questions — why? and what difference? — let us adopt as our way of entry the notion of God as love. This is not merely a hypothetical analogy proposed by philosophical theologians, but a way of speaking about God that possesses clear scriptural authority, especially in the Johannine writings. "God is love," it is said, "and those who abide in love abide in God, and God abides in them" (1 John 4:16; cf. 4:7-8). More particularly the Fourth Gospel speaks of the love of the Father for the Son: "The Father loves the Son" (John 3:35; cf. 10:17). This love is an eternal relationship prevailing "before the foundation of the world" (17:24). This timeless love of the Father for the Son is then extended within time so as to embrace equally the community of believers. Thus Christ says to the disciples, "As the Father has loved me, so I have loved you; abide in my love" (15:9); and to the Father he says likewise, "You have loved them even as you have loved me . . . may the love with which you have loved me be also in them, and I in them" (17:23, 26). Drawn into the mutual love of Father and Son, the believers are not only to love God but to show the same love towards each other: "Since God loved us so much, we also ought to love one another" (1 John 4:11).

The divine relationship of interpersonal love that exists between the Father and the Son is thus a model and paradigm for all human relationships: "As you, Father, are in me and I am in you, may they also be one in us . . . may they be one, *even as* we are one: I in them and you in me, may they become completely one" (John 17:21-23). Full weight should be given to this Trinitarian "even as." Our highest vocation as human persons is to reproduce on earth, so far as this is possible for us, the movement of mutual love that passes eternally between Father, Son, and Holy Spirit. Although the Johannine texts quoted above allude only to the love of Father and Son, it is clear that the circle of mutual love can be easily extended so as to include the Spirit, whose relationship with Christ and the Father is in any case explicitly mentioned at other points in the Fourth Gospel (John 14:16-17, 26; 15:26; 16:13-14, etc.).

The qualification made here, "so far as this is possible for us," needs to be constantly kept in view. There is a decisive difference between the infinite and uncreated love that unites the three divine persons, and the finite love that we human beings show towards God and each other; and this difference is rendered all the greater by the fact that we human beings are not only finite but fallen. Yet, while there needs to be a definite distinction of levels, the Johannine writings underline that there is also a true parallel, a life-giving similarity, between the divine level and the human. There is not only discontinuity but continuity.

Needless to say, when the First Epistle of John states that "God is love" (1 John 4:8), or when St. Paul affirms that "the greatest of these is love" (1 Cor. 13:13), they do not mean by love simply an emotional feeling. On the contrary, love signifies in this context a fundamental stance or attitude that allows the other, in the words of Metropolitan John of Pergamon, *to be* and *to be other.*[7] To love, that is to say, is to exist not for the self but for the other. And this fundamental stance or attitude involves the totality of our human personhood: not only the feelings and emotions (although these do indeed play an important part), but also the will, the imagination, the rational faculty *(dianoia),* and the visionary intellect *(nous).* It is only when love is understood in this inclusive and all-embracing sense that it can serve as an analogy for the interpersonal mystery of God.

It is time to turn to our three chosen witnesses from the Christian tradition, and to see how they interpret this understanding of God as a mutual relationship or *koinonia* of interpersonal love.

St. Basil

In his masterwork *On the Holy Spirit,* one of the key terms that St. Basil the Great employed was the word *koinonia,* "communion" or "fellowship." St. Athanasius of Alexandria (c. 296-373) spoke of God predominantly in terms of essence or substance, assigning cardinal significance to the term *homoousios,* "consubstantial." But Basil and the other two Cappadocians, Gregory of Nazianzus and Gregory of Nyssa (c. 330–c. 395) — while retaining (with some modifications) the Athanasian notion of consubstantiality — chose also to expound God's unity in terms of the communion that subsists between the three hypostases or persons. In the characteristic words of Basil, "The unity of God lies in the communion *(koinonia)* of the Godhead."[8] Developing the point, Basil's younger brother, Gregory of Nyssa, spelled out the doctrine of God in terms of the two words "communion" *(koinonia)* and "distinction" *(diakrisis):*

7. See the article by John Zizioulas in this volume, "Relational Ontology: Insights from Patristic Thought," p. 150.

8. *On the Holy Spirit* 18 [45].

In the life-creating nature of Father, Son and Holy Spirit, there is no division but only a continuous and inseparable communion between them. . . . It is not possible to envisage any severance or division, such that one might think of the Son without the Father, or separate the Spirit from the Son; but there is between them an ineffable and inconceivable communion and distinction.[9]

Divine unity, that is to say, is not to be interpreted exclusively or predominantly in essentialist terms, as a unity of nature or substance; but it is to be understood equally in personalist terms, as a unity established through the interrelationship or *koinonia* of the three divine subjects. We cannot speak of the triune God without using the language of interpersonal communion. In this connection Gregory of Nazianzus observed that the names "Father" and "Son" do not denote either the divine essence or the divine energy; they are terms that indicate a *schesis* or personal relationship. Whoever speaks of "Father" implies also the existence of the Son; and whoever invokes God as "Son" points also towards the Father. Thus the three "modes of subsistence" within the Godhead are to be envisaged as *scheseis* or relationships.[10]

The point that Gregory is making here applies much better to the interrelationship of the first and second persons than it does to that of the first and the third. The terms "Father" and "Son" imply a specific relationship, although this needs of course to be understood in an apophatic sense: as Athanasius insisted in his polemic against the Arians, God is not "Father" in exactly the same way as a human being is such. On the other hand, the terms "God" and "Spirit" do not in themselves signify any particular and distinctive kind of relationship. The term "generation" has a reasonably precise sense, whereas the term "procession" does not. This raises the question of how far the Cappadocians, or at any rate Basil and Gregory of Nazianzus, succeeded in defining adequately the distinguishing characteristic of the Holy Spirit. As Fr. Pavel Florensky among others has pointed out, they fail to indicate in a convincing manner the difference between "generation" and "procession."[11]

The Cappadocians considered that the *scheseis* or relationships within the Trinity are causal in character. Gregory of Nyssa, for example, de-

9. *On the Difference between Essence and Hypostasis* [= Basil, *Letter* 38] (*PG* 32: 332A, D).

10. *Oration* 29.16.

11. Pavel Florensky, *The Pillar and the Ground of Truth* (Princeton: Princeton University Press, 1997), letter 5: "The Comforter," especially pp. 85-89.

scribed the Father as the unique causative principle *(aition)* within the Trinity, while the Son and the Spirit are "caused" *(aitiata)* by him.[12] At the same time, Gregory insisted that this causation does not signify any subordination of the second and third hypostases in their relationship with the first; all three are in every respect co-equal and co-eternal. Western theology, by contrast, has been more reluctant to apply the notion of causation to the doctrine of the Trinity. Much depends, of course, on the way in which the term "cause" is understood. If the notion of causality is to be applied to intra-Trinitarian relationships, then it is important to differentiate between three levels: (1) the way in which one created thing acts as the cause of another created thing; (2) the way in which God is the cause of the world; (3) the way in which, within the Trinity, the Father is the cause of the Son and the Spirit. In the case of (2), "to cause" means "to produce out of nothing" *(creatio ex nihilo)*, but this is manifestly not the sense that "to cause" possesses on levels (1) and (3). On level (3), the noun "cause" is being used in a special sense, to signify that the Father is the *arche* and *principium*, the fountainhead, source, and origin of the hypostatic existence of the other two persons. As Gregory of Nazianzus put it, "The three have one nature: God. And the basis of unity is the Father, from whom and to whom the order of the persons runs its course."[13]

On a number of occasions the Cappadocians interpreted the doctrine of the Trinity in what appear to be "social" terms, using the analogy of three human subjects engaged in dialogue and mutual relationship. But at the same time they were keenly aware of the need to restrict and qualify this analogy. To suggest that the divine unity is no stronger than the unity existing between three human persons, so they recognized, would lead directly to tritheism, that is to say, to a belief in three Gods, not one. They therefore sought to underline that the unity existing between the three divine persons is altogether unique and *sui generis*. In the words of Gregory of Nyssa:

> The persons *(prosopa)* of the Godhead are not separated from one another either by time or by place, either by will or by practice, either by energy *(energeia)* or by passion *(pathos)*, nor by anything of this sort, such as is observed in regard to human beings.[14]

---

12. See, for example, Gregory of Nyssa, *To the Greeks: From the Common Notions*, ed. W. Jaeger and F. Mueller, *Gregorii Nysseni Opera* III.i, p. 25; and compare Gregory of Nazianzus, *Oration* 29.3.

13. *Oration* 42.15.

14. *To the Greeks*, III.i, p. 25.

To indicate the unique character of the divine unity, in contrast to the unity prevailing between human beings, the Cappadocians used in particular three main lines of argument. First, there is their teaching, already mentioned, about the Father as the sole source and fountainhead within the Divinity (the "monarchy" of the Father). Second, they stressed what was later to be termed the *perichoresis* of the three persons, their mutual indwelling and "coinherence."[15] Third, and most importantly, they insisted that the three, Father, Son, and Holy Spirit, share a single energy and a single will. Human beings cooperate on joint projects, but in such cases each retains his or her specific inner energy and conative impulse. With the three divine persons of the Godhead, on the other hand, this is not so. This teaching concerning the single energy and the single will of the three members of the Trinity is fundamental in particular to Gregory of Nyssa's theology of the divine unity, as is manifest from his treatise *To Ablabius: that there are not three Gods.*[16]

For the Cappadocians, then, the concept of relationship is applicable not to the divine essence or substance *(ousia)* but to the divine hypostases or persons. It is the hypostatic relationships within the Trinity that make the divine essence particular and personal; for the person, as Metropolitan John says, is that which achieves particularity through relation.[17] This is not to say, however, that within the Godhead — or, for that matter, on the human level — the person *is* the relation. Thomas Aquinas (c. 1225-74) went so far as to assert baldly, *Personae sunt ipsae relationes subsistentes,*[18] but this is not the standpoint of Eastern theology. As St. Gregory Palamas (1296-1359) affirmed, "Personal characteristics do not constitute the person, but they characterize the person."[19] The relations within the Trinity, that is to say, while designating the persons, in no way exhaust the mystery of each. For the Cappadocians, as for Gregory Palamas, Father, Son, and Holy Spirit are not merely relations but entities. At the same time, from an epistemological standpoint we human beings have no access to the cate-

---

15. See Nonna Verna Harrison, "Perichoresis in the Greek Fathers," *St. Vladimir's Seminary Quarterly* 35 (1991): 53-65.

16. *Gregorii Nysseni Opera* III.i, pp. 37-57. See Lewis Ayres, "On Not Three People: The Fundamental Themes of Gregory of Nyssa's Trinitarian Theology as Seen in *To Ablabius: On Not Three Gods,*" in *Re-thinking Gregory of Nyssa,* ed. Sarah Coakley (Oxford: Basil Blackwell, 2002), pp. 15-44.

17. See Zizioulas, "Relational Ontology: Insights from Patristic Thought," p. 153.

18. *Summa Theologiae* I q. 40 a. 2.

19. *Letter to Daniel of Ainos* 4 (ed. P. Christou, II, 377).

gory of divine personhood in the abstract; we can only begin to apprehend the divine persons through their relationships of origin, insofar as these are revealed to us.

It should not be overlooked that even though the Cappadocians thought sometimes of the Trinity on the analogy (carefully qualified) of three human persons in relationship, at other times they also employed uni-personal analogies, likening the three divine hypostases to the interaction of faculties within a single human person. Gregory of Nazianzus, for example, compared the three divine persons, Father, Son, and Spirit, to the three faculties of *nous* (intellect), *logos* (reason or word), and *pneuma* (breath or spirit) within a particular human being.[20] It is usually assumed that such uni-personal or "psychological" analogies are more characteristic of St. Augustine and the Latin West than they are of the Greek East. While this is basically true, the "uni-personal" approach is by no means absent from Greek Patristic authors. It is found, for example, in Gregory of Nyssa, Theodoret of Cyrrhus, John of Damascus, Nicetas Stethatos, Gregory of Sinai, Theoleptos of Philadelphia, and Gregory Palamas, all of whom saw the interaction of faculties within the human soul as a reflection of the Trinity.[21]

St. Augustine

By insisting that the persons within the Trinity are to be understood as "subsistent relations," Augustine placed the concept of relationship at the very heart of his doctrine of God. In his work *On the Trinity* he worked out the relational character of God's being in terms of two different kinds of analogy. First, adopting an interpersonal model, he proposed a "trinity of love." Love, he said, involves three elements: the lover *(amans)*, that which is loved *(quod amatur)*, and the love *(amor)* that passes reciprocally between the lover and the beloved.[22] Applying this to the Trinity, the Father is to be seen as the lover, the Son as the beloved, and the Spirit as the

20. *Oration* 23.11.

21. See Robert E. Sinkewicz, in the introduction to his edition of St. Gregory Palamas, *The One Hundred and Fifty Chapters,* Studies and Texts 83 (Toronto: Pontifical Institute of Mediaeval Studies, 1988), pp. 16-34; Kallistos Ware, "The Human Person as an Image of the Holy Trinity: From Augustine to Palamas," *Archiv für Mittelalterliche Philosophie und Kultur* 9 (Sofia: Lik, 2003): 7-19, especially 14-18.

22. Augustine, *On the Trinity* 8.14 (10).

vinculum amoris, the bond of love uniting Father and Son, the "commu-nion" that subsists between them. Adopting next a uni-personal model, Augustine went on to develop two "trinities of the mind." He devoted far more space to these than he did to the initial "trinity of love." He likened Father, Son, and Spirit first to mind, knowledge, and love within the hu-man psyche, and then to memory, understanding, and will.[23] It is com-monly assumed by modern writers on Augustine that his interpersonal "trinity of love" was no more than a brief preliminary reflection, and that what really interested him were the uni-personal analogies based on the faculties of the human soul. At the end of his work *On the Trinity,* however, Augustine returned to the interpersonal paradigm of mutual love, and he suggested that among all the different analogies this is perhaps the least in-adequate.[24] If full value is given in this way to the "trinity of love," Augus-tine's interpretation of the relational being of God turns out to be less "essentialist" and more "personalist" than is usually assumed.

Recent research has rightly called in question the tendency, found among many twentieth-century historians of early Christian doctrine, to posit a sharp contrast between the "Eastern" or "Greek" approach to the Trinity, typified by the Cappadocians, and the "Western" or "Latin" ap-proach typified by Augustine. The East, so it used to be claimed, starts with the three hypostases or persons of the Godhead, and works from that to the one *ousia* or essence; the West moves in the opposite direction, starting with the one essence, and working from that to the three persons. This in-terpretation of early Christian doctrine, often termed "the de Régnon par-adigm," has been popularized in Orthodox circles by Vladimir Lossky (1903-58), who quoted in particular the statement of the Jesuit scholar Théodore de Régnon (d. 1893):

> Latin philosophy first considers the nature in itself and proceeds to the agent; Greek philosophy first considers the agent and afterwards passes through it to find the nature. The Latins think of personality as a mode of nature, the Greeks think of nature as the content of the person.[25]

23. *On the Trinity* 9.4 (4); 10.17 (11).
24. *On the Trinity* 15.10 (6); cf. 15.27 (17).
25. Vladimir Lossky, *The Mystical Theology of the Eastern Church* (London: James Clarke, 1957), pp. 57-58; citing Théodore de Régnon, *Études de théologie positive sur la Sainte Trinité* (Paris: Victor Retaux, 1892), vol. 1, p. 433. See Michel René Barnes, "De Régnon Re-considered," *Augustinian Studies* 26, no. 2 (1995): 51-79.

De Régnon's views were in fact considerably more subtle and complex than this brief quotation suggests. Be that as it may, the assertion that the Cappadocians started with the three persons and worked from this to the one essence is certainly misleading. It would be more correct to say that a thinker such as Gregory of Nazianzus considered that the divine threefoldness and the divine unity were both equally ultimate, so that neither can be derived from the other. Thus he writes, "When I speak of God, you must be encircled by one flash of lightning and by three";[26] the single and the threefold envelopment are simultaneous. By the same token, David Bentley Hart rightly claims that Augustine "evinces no less keen a sense of the distinct integrity of the divine persons than does Gregory [of Nyssa]."[27]

Nevertheless, there are certainly significant differences in perspective between the Cappadocians and Augustine. Even though, as we have seen, Gregory of Nazianzus was prepared on occasion to posit a uni-personal "trinity of the mind," yet he placed far less emphasis upon it than did Augustine, and he worked it out far less systematically. He did not "psychologize" the Trinity in the way that Augustine did. Moreover, whereas the Cappadocians treated the notion of "communion" as applicable jointly to all three persons of the Trinity, for Augustine this was more specifically the distinctive characteristic of the Holy Spirit.

From the standpoint of the Christian East, Augustine's "trinity of love" seems to suffer from two defects. First, in making the Spirit the mutual love that passes between the Father and the Son, it seems to lead directly to the standpoint of the *Filioque,* that is to say, to the doctrine of the double procession, according to which the Spirit proceeds from both the Father and the Son. In reality, however, Augustine was never a "Filioquist" in any stark and unqualified sense. He was careful to insist that the Spirit proceeds from the Father *principaliter,* "principally" or "principially," and from the Son only in a secondary and derivative sense, *per donum Patris,* "by the Father's gift." In other words, all that the Son has he receives from the Father, and so it is from the Father that he receives also the power to cause the Spirit to proceed.[28] This means that, in common with the Cappadocians, Augustine regarded the Father as the *principium* and *arche*

26. *Oration* 39.11.
27. "The Mirror of the Infinite: Gregory of Nyssa on the *Vestigia Trinitatis*," in Coakley, ed., *Re-thinking Gregory of Nyssa*, p. 112, citing Augustine, *On the Trinity* 15.5 (7-8).
28. *On the Trinity* 15.17 (29).

within the Godhead, the ultimate source and sole origin of hypostatic being within the Trinity.

A second and more serious difficulty in Augustine's "trinity of love" is that it likens God to two persons, not three. For, while the lover and the beloved are both persons, the mutual love that passes between them is not a third person additional to the other two. In this way Augustine's interpersonal model is in danger of depersonalizing the Holy Spirit, although this was certainly not his intention.

Richard of St. Victor

This defect in Augustine's "trinity of love," that it is bi-personal rather than tri-personal, is fortunately avoided in the last of our three witnesses, Richard of St. Victor. In the third book of his work *On the Trinity,* Richard succeeded in developing an analogy of love that was fully triadic. "God is love" (1 John 4:8): such was his starting-point. Love is the perfection of human nature, the highest reality within our personal experience; and so it is the quality of love that brings us closest to God, expressing — better than anything else that we know — the perfection of the divine nature.

Richard then took a second step in his argument. Self-love, the love of one turned inwards, is not true love.[29] Love signifies self-giving and exchange, and so it cannot be genuinely present unless it is mutual; it presupposes a "thou" as well as an "I." True love can only exist, in that case, where there is a plurality of persons: "The perfection of one person requires fellowship with another," wrote Richard. This is the case not only with human beings but likewise with divine being: divine love, as well as human, is fundamentally relational, and is characterized by sharing and communion. The fullness of glory, he affirmed, "requires that a sharer of glory be not lacking." In God's case, as in that of human persons, "nothing is more glorious . . . than to wish to have nothing that you do not wish to share." If, then, God is love, it is inconceivable that he should be merely one person loving himself. He has to be at least two persons, Father and Son, loving each other.[30]

Next, Richard took a crucial third step in his analysis of God's rela-

29. There is, of course, a self-love that is not negative but creative; this, however, is not the point with which Richard is immediately concerned.

30. Richard of St. Victor, *On the Trinity* 3.4, 6.

tional being. To exist in its plenitude, love needs to be not only "mutual" but "shared." The closed circle of mutual love between two persons still falls short of the perfection of love; in order that such perfection may exist, the two have to share their reciprocal love with a third. "Perfect love casts out fear" (1 John 4:18); love in its perfection is without selfishness or jealousy, without fear of a rival. Where love is perfect, then, the lover not only loves the beloved as a second self, but wishes the beloved to have the further joy of loving a third, jointly with the lover, and of being jointly loved by that third. "The sharing of love cannot exist among any less than three persons. . . . Shared love is properly said to exist when a third person is loved by two persons harmoniously and in community, and the affection of the two persons is fused into one affection by the flame of love for a third." In the case of God the Trinity, this "third" with whom the first two, the Father and the Son, share their mutual love is precisely the Holy Spirit, whom Richard termed *condilectus,* the "co-beloved."[31]

In this way Richard of St. Victor, in common with the Cappadocians, saw God in terms of interpersonal *koinonia* or communion. Following Augustine, he started with the relationship between lover *(amans)* and beloved *(quod amatur).* But then, instead of making the third member of the Trinity simply the love *(amor)* that passes between the first two, he treated the Holy Spirit as a fully personal subject, not just "love" but "co-beloved." Instead of being dyadic, as in Augustine, the relationship affirmed by Richard is genuinely triangular. In Richard's Triadology, then, there is a movement from self-love to mutual love, and so to shared love: from the love of one (the Father alone) to the love of two (Father and Son), and from this to the love of three (Father, Son, and Holy Spirit). There is, according to Richard, no need to go beyond the number three; for, when the circle of the mutual love between lover and beloved is enlarged to include the co-beloved, the pattern of love is complete. In the words of Gregory of Nazianzus (not actually quoted by Richard), "The monad, moving forth into the dyad, came to rest in the triad."[32]

I do not imagine that either Augustine or Richard regarded their "trinities of love" as constituting in the strict sense a *proof* of the doctrine of the Trinity, as if the threefoldness of God were a logical necessity. Both of them would surely have insisted that the Trinity is a mystery beyond our understanding, incapable of rational demonstration, and known to

---

31. *On the Trinity* 3.14-15.
32. *Oration* 29.3.

us only through revelation; and they would have readily acknowledged that all analogies fall far short of the transcendent plenitude of the divine unity-in-diversity. It has sometimes been urged, as an objection to Richard's analogy of shared love, that, while it is true of human beings that they can only enjoy good in fellowship, the same cannot be asserted of God. Since God is all-good, he needs no fellow, no *consociatus,* for his self-fulfillment and perfection. Love, according to this objection, is a striving to gain that which one does not as yet possess; it implies a lack or deficiency, and it is inconceivable that God should be lacking in anything. Thus the analogy of love, as shared among humans, is not applicable to God. But this is to misconstrue Richard's intent. Surely he was right to regard love, at its highest and best, not as an effort to acquire what one lacks but as an attitude of self-giving. To love is to offer oneself as gift to the other. According to Richard, then, the doctrine of the Trinity is a way of saying that God's eternal being is a threefold shared self-giving in reciprocal love.

The Augustinian and Victorine notion of the "trinity of love" has played a notable part in Russian religious thought during the nineteenth and twentieth centuries, being used by such writers as Vladimir Solovyov, Pavel Florensky, Nikolai Berdyaev, and Sergei Bulgakov.[33] They were particularly interested in the implications of this Trinitarian love paradigm for a Christian understanding of the human person; and to these implications we shall shortly turn. But, before doing so, let us first consider how the notion of God as Trinitarian interrelationship sheds light on the doctrine of creation.

Trinitarian Creativity

God, it is commonly affirmed in both Eastern and Western theology, created the world *ex nihilo,* "out of nothing." This signifies, not simply that God did not fashion the world from pre-existent matter, but also, much more profoundly, that he created the world in total freedom; he was not in any way under constraint or compulsion when he brought the universe into existence. There is no necessity whatsoever for the existence of the

---

33. See Michael Meerson-Aksenov, *The Trinity of Love in Modern Russian Theology: The Love Paradigm and the Retrieval of Western Love Mysticism in Modern Russian Trinitarian Thought (from Solovyov to Bulgakov)* (Quincy, IL: Franciscan Press, 1998).

world. The world could have not existed. God is necessary to the world, but the world is not necessary to God. The sole foundation of the world consists in God's freedom.

This last statement, however, requires to be expanded. The sole foundation of the world consists in God's freedom — *in the freedom of love.* Precisely here, in the freedom of divine love, we find an answer — insofar as any answer is possible — to the question: Why did God create the world? God, we reply, is creator because he is a God of Trinitarian love. Nothing compelled him to create. But at the same time, since he is a God of interpersonal relationship, of Trinitarian love, it is altogether appropriate and in conformity with his nature that he should have chosen to create the world, so that others besides himself might share in the movement of his love. It is altogether appropriate, that is to say, that the circle of intra-Trinitarian love, the love of the three divine persons, should be enlarged, so that it engenders and embraces created persons outside God. In the words of St. Dionysius the Areopagite (c. 500), "Divine *eros* is ecstatic."[34] The Areopagite had here in view the literal sense of *ekstasis,* meaning "standing outside oneself." God created the world because his love, as an interpersonal Trinitarian love, is outgoing and self-diffusive; and without this overflowing love the world would not exist. Rather than speak of creation *ex nihilo,* "out of nothing," would it not be better to speak of creation *ex amore,* "out of love"?

Love is closely connected with joy, and so what has just been stated about creation as an expression of mutual love can be spelled out equally in terms of mutual joy. Joy, like love, is outgoing and self-diffusive. In the words of St. Maximus the Confessor (c. 580-662), "God, full beyond all fullness, brought creatures into being, not because he had need of anything, but so that they might participate in him in proportion to their capacity, and that he himself might rejoice in his works through seeing them joyful."[35] Whether, then, we choose to speak in terms of mutual love or of mutual joy, the notion of God as a Trinity of interrelated persons provides us with a foundation for the doctrine of creation in a way that a strictly unitarian doctrine of God cannot do.

34. *On the Divine Names* 3.14.
35. *Centuries on Love* 3.46.

The Human Person as Icon of the Trinity

Coming now to the understanding of the human person, let us see how this too can find a sure foundation in the doctrine of the Trinity. Having sought to interpret God in relational terms as shared love, let us now attempt to do the same for humankind. As human persons we are created in the divine image. In the Christian tradition this has usually been understood to mean that we are formed in the image of Christ the divine Logos; but it can also be interpreted to signify that we are formed in the image of God the Trinity. It is therefore our vocation as human persons to reproduce on earth the eternal *perichoresis* that joins in unity the three persons of the Trinity. Let us recall in this context the many statements already cited from the Johannine writings that develop this idea, and in particular Christ's prayer, "May they be one, *even as* we are one" (John 17:22). A similar parallel between the unity of Father and Son and the unity of Christian believers is made by St. Ignatius of Antioch (c. 110).[36] Obviously all human forms of communion fall infinitely short of the divine *koinonia,* yet there is nonetheless a real similarity between the human and the divine. It is our vocation as persons in the divine image to become nothing less than living icons of the Trinity; and the term "icon" is to be understood here in its precise signification, as denoting not identity but participation.

On the basis, then, of the Johannine writings and of the *koinonia*/love paradigm developed by the Cappadocians, Augustine, and Richard of St. Victor, let us suggest the possible outlines of a Trinitarian anthropology. In so doing, we may legitimately draw also on the insights concerning human personhood found in such works as *I and Thou* by the Jewish thinker Martin Buber (1878-1965), and in the somewhat neglected Gifford Lectures by the Scottish philosopher John Macmurray (1891-1976), although neither of these alludes explicitly to the doctrine of the Trinity. But, in using modern authors such as Buber and Macmurray, we should bear in mind that our present-day understanding of what constitutes a "person" does not exactly correspond to the Patristic interpretation of the terms *hypostasis* and *prosopon.*[37] It is entirely acceptable as we develop a relational ontology in

---

36. *To the Magnesians* 7.1.

37. On this complex and fundamental issue, see the articles of M. R. Barnes, Lucian Turcescu, and D. B. Hart, in Coakley, ed., *Re-thinking Gregory of Nyssa;* also S. Coakley, "'Persons' in the 'Social' Doctrine of the Trinity: A Critique of Current Analytical Discussion," in *The Trinity: An Interdisciplinary Symposium on the Trinity,* ed. Stephen T. Davis, Da-

the twenty-first century, to make use of this present-day understanding, so long as we do not read it back unconditionally into Patristic or medieval texts.

"Let us love one another that with one mind we may confess . . . the Trinity": without mutual love there can be on our part no true confession of faith in God the Trinity, for the Trinity is mutual love. "As in heaven, so on earth": the Trinity, in the words of the Anglican poet and theologian Charles Williams (1886-1943), is the "primary act of love,"[38] while we human beings are the created expression of that primary act. If, then, the doctrine of the Trinity is "a revelation not only of God but at the same time of man," as C. G. Jung claims,[39] then everything that we have been saying about the triune God applies also, with appropriate qualifications, to ourselves as human persons. The being of God is relational: so also is our being as human persons. Without the concept of communion it is not possible to speak about the being of God: so also without the concept of communion it is not possible to speak about human being. God is self-giving, sharing, response: such also is the human person. God is coinherence, *perichoresis:* so also are we humans. God expresses himself from all eternity in a relationship of I-and-thou: so also within time does the human person. The divine image in which as humans we are created is not possessed by any one of us in isolation, but comes to its fulfillment only in the "between" of love, in the "and" that joins the "I" to the "thou." To be a person after the image of God the Trinity is therefore to be a person-in-relationship. Selfhood is social, or it is nothing. The authentic human being is not egocentric but exocentric. I am only truly human, truly personal, insofar as I greet others as persons. It is relationship that changes me from an individual, a unit — what the Greeks call *atomon* — into a person, what the Greeks call *prosopon,* a countenance or face. As an icon of the Trinity, I become truly myself only if I face others, looking into their eyes and allowing them to look into mine.

All this is powerfully expressed by John Macmurray. As persons, he rightly maintains, we are what we are solely in relation to other persons.

---

vid Kendall, and Gerald O'Collins (Oxford: Oxford University Press, 1999), pp. 123-44. Cf. Ware, "The Human Person as an Icon of the Trinity," pp. 12-15.

38. Charles Williams, *The Image of the City and Other Essays,* ed. Anne Ridler (London: Oxford University Press, 1958), p. xiv. Williams also used to say, in an aphoristic misquotation from Genesis, "It is not good for God to be alone" (*The Image of the City,* p. xlv).

39. C. G. Jung, "A Psychological Approach to the Dogma of the Trinity," *Psychology and Religion: West and East,* The Collected Works, vol. 11, 2nd ed. (London: Routledge & Kegan Paul, 1981), p. 161.

"The Self exists only in dynamic relation to the Other," he writes. "The Self is constituted by its relation to the Other. . . . It has its being in its relationship." There is no true person except when there are at least two persons communicating with each other; to be human is to be dialogic. "Since mutuality is constructive for the personal," he concludes, "it follows that 'I' need 'You' in order to be myself."[40] As a Christian, Macmurray could well have strengthened his argument by appealing in this context to the doctrine of the Trinity. In fact he fails to do so; yet his words exactly sum up the anthropological consequences of Trinitarian belief. *Precisely because God is Trinity, I need you in order to be myself.*

"L'enfer, c'est les autres," said Sartre, but was he right? Surely T. S. Eliot came closer to the truth, when he wrote in *The Cocktail Party:*

What is hell? Hell is oneself,
Hell is alone, the other figures
Merely projections.

Yes, indeed: hell is not other people; it is myself, cut off from the others, willfully refusing to relate, and so denying the Trinity. Either we love one another, after the image of God the Trinity, or else we condemn ourselves to the void. That is why Fr. Pavel Florensky asserted, "Between the Trinity and hell there lies no other choice."[41] Without Trinitarian love, there is in the end a loss of all joy and all meaning. Without Trinitarian love, we cease to be truly human, and we each become an un-person, an "un-man," to use the word coined by C. S. Lewis in his novel *Perelandra.*

In this way faith in God as Trinity, so far from being recondite and theoretical, can and should have an immediate and transfiguring effect upon the manner in which we live out our daily life. In the words of that eccentric but shrewd Russian thinker Nikolai Fyodorov (1828-1903), the friend of Dostoevsky and Tolstoy, "Our social programme is the dogma of the Trinity."[42] Belief in the Trinitarian God, whose being is relational, whose characteristics are sharing and solidarity, has far-reaching practical implications for our Christian attitude towards politics, economics, and social action. Every form of community — the family, the school, the workplace, the local Eucharistic center, the monastery, the city, the nation — has as its

40. John Macmurray, *Persons in Relation* (London: Faber & Faber, 1961), pp. 17, 69.
41. Quoted by Lossky, *The Mystical Theology of the Eastern Church,* p. 66.
42. Quoted by Olivier Clément, *L'Eglise orthodoxe* (Paris: Presses Universitaires de France, 1961), p. 63.

vocation to become, each according to its own modality, a living icon of the Holy Trinity. When as Christians we fight for justice and for human rights, for a compassionate and caring society, we are acting specifically in the name of the Trinity. Faith in the Trinitarian God, in the God of personal interrelationship and shared love, commits us to struggle with all our strength against poverty, exploitation, oppression, and disease. Our combat for human rights — and indeed, for the rights of animals — is undertaken not merely on generalized philanthropic and humanitarian grounds, but precisely because we believe in God as Trinity. Because God is a triune mystery of shared love, we cannot as humans created in the image of the Trinity remain indifferent to any suffering, by any member of the human race, in any part of the world.

"Only connect!" says E. M. Forster in his novel *Howards End;* and my history master at school used to exclaim, as his constant refrain, "It all ties up, you see, it all ties up." Both these remarks aptly apply to the theme of the present paper. There is an integral connection between the Christian doctrines of God the Trinity, of creation, and of the human person; it all ties up. The human experience of mutual love provides us with the least inadequate analogy for the mystery of the Trinitarian God; and the doctrine of the Trinity, in its turn, enables us to understand in some small measure why the world exists and what is the meaning of our own personhood. If we ask, "Why is there a world?" and "Who am I?" for an answer let us look to the relational being of the Trinity.

SELECT BIBLIOGRAPHY

Barnes, Michel René. "De Régnon Reconsidered." *Augustinian Studies* 26, no. 2 (1995): 51-79.

Coakley, Sarah, ed. *Re-thinking Gregory of Nyssa.* Oxford: Basil Blackwell, 2002.

Davis, Stephen T., David Kendall, and Gerald O'Collins, eds. *The Trinity: An Interdisciplinary Symposium on the Trinity.* Oxford: Oxford University Press, 1999.

Harrison, Nonna Verna. "Human Community as an Image of the Holy Trinity." *St. Vladimir's Seminary Quarterly* 46, no. 4 (2002): 347-64.

Harrison, Nonna Verna. "Perichoresis in the Greek Fathers." *St. Vladimir's Seminary Quarterly* 35, no. 1 (1991): 53-65.

Meerson-Aksenov, Michael. *The Trinity of Love in Modern Russian Theology: The Love Paradigm and the Retrieval of Western Love Mysticism in Modern Russian Trinitarian Thought (from Solovyov to Bulgakov).* Quincy, IL: Franciscan Press, 1998.

Ware, Kallistos. "The Human Person as an Icon of the Trinity." *Sobornost incorporating Eastern Churches Review* 8, no. 2 (1986): 6-23.

Ware, Kallistos. "The Trinity: Heart of Our Life." In *Reclaiming the Great Tradition: Evangelicals, Catholics and Orthodox in Dialogue,* ed. James S. Cutsinger, pp. 125-46, 204-7. Downers Grove, IL: InterVarsity Press, 1997.

Zizioulas, John D. *Being as Communion: Studies in Personhood and the Church.* Crestwood, NY: St. Vladimir's Seminary Press, 1985.

Zizioulas, John D. *Communion and Otherness: Further Studies in Personhood and the Church.* London and New York: T. & T. Clark, 2006.

(Mis)Adventures in Trinitarian Ontology

LEWIS AYRES

Problems with "Relational" Ontologies

Over the past few decades a considerable number of theologians — Orthodox, Catholic, and Protestant — have sketched "Trinitarian" or "relational" ontologies. For many of these theologians these ontologies are
more fully reflective of what they take to be the relational nature of the
Trinity than the accounts that have been standard in Western theological
tradition. Some of these theologians focus on overcoming perceived
disjunctions between the implications of Trinitarian theology and previous Christian accounts of what is; others employ developments in various
sub-fields of philosophy and science in order to re-envision the relationship between Creator and creation. In many of these figures (Elizabeth
Johnson and Miroslav Volf being good but very distinct examples)
relationality is exemplified by the mutual interrelationship of the three divine persons. This relational life is, in turn, understood as analogous to the
relations obtaining between three human persons, and is also (in some
sense) predicated of the created order at a fundamental level. For others,
most notably, John Zizioulas, the category of "the personal" becomes cen-

---

I am grateful to all of the participants in our seminar and to Ian McFarland and Tommy
Humphries for comments on earlier drafts. Throughout I take the term "ontology" to refer
to the investigation of "being." "Being" is of course highly freighted: more prosaically I assume that ontology considers a range of questions from the attempt to sketch what sorts of
beings there actually are to questions considering what it is to exist, and why and how there
is what there is.

tral. Zizioulas uses the *monarchia* of the Father to ground an ontology in which "person" defines "being" and in which redemption is partly understood as the basic category.[1]

In the first section of this paper I will suggest a series of interrelated flaws in some arguments common to this diverse theological movement; in the second I will suggest the outlines of an alternative construal of the relationship between classical Trinitarian theology and ontology. It is important to note that throughout this paper my concern is with theologians interested in "relational ontologies," and with the question of how far current proposals can be understood as sufficiently theological in relationship to classical Christian traditions. Those exploring relational ontologies without theological and Trinitarian commitments will have little reason to find many of my arguments persuasive — although I hope they may see the possibility of demonstrating that many of their concerns have actually been part of the Western Christian tradition at least from the late fourth century! In what follows I will begin by discussing the use of analogy in some recent "relational" theologies. I will suggest that key inadequacies in this usage are best addressed by reconsidering the reflections on analogy in the very traditions that these relational theologies tend to reject. It will, however, become clear that I also think notions of analogy are inseparable from the theologies in which they are embedded. Accordingly, I will have to discuss the deeper theological background that sustains the notions of analogy for which I will argue. At the same time, an appeal to reconsider classical Christian resources that have been rejected on the basis of misapprehensions cannot but also involve inviting a reconsideration of the histories of theology implicit in all of these recent proposals. Thus what begins as an attempt to suggest inadequacies in the use of analogy in some recent "relational" theologies cannot but end as an attempt to sketch an alternative theological approach to how we conceive of the relations between God and world. In this sketch there is little that is new: a return to our sources will serve us better than any rejection of them in favor of a new beginning.

I turn first, then, to analogy. In many of those who advocate for a rela-

---

1. One fundamental difference between these groups is that for the first, Trinitarian relationality is fundamental to the Christian conception of God in a way that the traditional *taxis* of Father-Son-Spirit is not. Clearly enough, Bishop Zizioulas's account depends on assuming the fundamental importance of that *taxis*. Despite my critique of his position it is perhaps here that it becomes clear that I share far more with his position than with the first group I name here!

tional Trinitarian ontology, I would suggest that key terminology is used in an imprecise manner that ultimately reveals the lack of an appropriate account of analogy. Perhaps most importantly, it is unclear in what way "relationship" can function as a useful general descriptor of being — divine, human, and non-human. When it is said that relationship is fundamental to being, does this identify basic spatio-temporal features of things (e.g., discrete sensible realities in physical or temporal relationship), or does it identify the complex emotional and psychological content of human relationships as basic to the cosmos?

If the former, then the features that supposedly identify the cosmos as *imago Trinitatis* are those that all classical theologians agree are not to be predicated of the Trinity. If the latter, then it is not clear how the material structures of our universe exhibit the qualities intrinsic to relationship. But, in turn, if the term "relation" is actually used primarily of divine being, then created being surely exhibits the qualities of relationship by analogy. If the term is being used broadly or analogically to encompass both (or all) kinds of relationship described here, then clear and precise indication will need to be given about the common thread that links them together, and about how each sort of relationship may be read as revealing the creation's mirroring of the triune God. Thus, "relationality" as a general category may well define both the relations between Father and Son and between two bricks, but only in the most minimal sense and only usefully so within the context of a robust account of how one thinks analogically.

Wesley Wildman's paper in this volume illustrates the problems with many of these accounts particularly clearly. Recognizing that a great plurality of varieties of "relation" needs to be marshaled into some sort of unity in order to give philosophical coherence, Wildman suggests that all relations may be described as "causal." I am unconvinced that much is achieved by placing an extremely wide variety of "relations" under a general rubric that itself covers a wide variety of notions of causality. If we say that "the-capacity-of-causing-effects" is the fundamental marker of all forms of existence, all we have done is to push to the forefront the need for careful definition of the various varieties of causality and for careful definition of the analogical practice within which we can use these terms to describe causal relations in Creator and creation.[2]

---

2. This statement also leaves out of consideration the question of whether one can conceive of the relations of Son and Spirit to Father as "causal."

John Zizioulas's version of a Trinitarian ontology faces a number of similar and distinct problems. In the first place one may ask similar questions about his use of person and relation: Zizioulas makes little effort to distinguish clearly the relationship between divine and human personhood, predicating of divine personhood attributes that seem to owe most to modern personalism and little to the Patristic sources on which he draws.[3] In the second place, he is mistaken to assume that describing divine being as fundamentally revolving around the concept of person rather than essence carries any necessary ramifications for the structure of the creation as such. This is particularly clear in those on whom he most extensively draws. For example, Basil of Caesarea and his brother Gregory of Nyssa (figures on whom Zizioulas draws extensively) agree that the cosmos is ordered at its most basic level into a series of immutable natures (the unity and permanence of each mirroring the unity and permanence of the one divine power found in the three divine persons). They agree that divine being finds its source in the person of the Father (as do all pro-Nicenes, Eastern and Western), but their account of created being does not treat person as *the* basic category. Indeed, even in the case of divine being it is not the case that person is the fundamental category. Surely for Christians the simple divine being — one in nature, power, and will — is constituted by the unity of three persons, each of whom is the whole and yet all of whom are one? The Father as divine person eternally gives rise to the unique divine being that *cannot* be reduced to "person" as a category more basic than the union of the three.[4] That which is fundamental is the union of the three irreducible persons constituted by the Father's eternal begetting of the Son and breathing of the Spirit.

Throughout these criticisms one constant theme has been heard: the failure of these theologians to offer an adequate account of analogy. In fact, the failure of these theologians to offer an adequate account of analogy should lead, I suggest, to our recognizing a fundamental distinction between types of "relational" theology. For those relational theologians who are deeply indebted to process thought my charge may simply not hold water: if one assumes that "God" is governed by the same fundamental dy-

---

3. For a strongly worded critique see Lucian Turcescu, "'Person' versus 'Individual,' and Other Modern Misreadings of Gregory of Nyssa," *Modern Theology* 18 (2002): 527-39. On the question of the nature of divine persons I find the approach of Vladimir Lossky closer to that found in Patristic thought.

4. For a closely related point see the very helpful essay of Nicholas Lash, "Considering the Trinity," *Modern Theology* 2 (1986): 183-96.

namics that govern all reality then the need for any complex use of analogy in such predication has gone. Such thinkers are, however, radically different from theologians committed to traditional Christian belief who wish to make use of relational ontologies. For this group the distinction between God and the world is a cross-cutting theme in Christian thought. (I offer a sketch of how I understand this distinction later in the paper.) My argument will thus make different appeals to these two groups. To the first my appeal is to reconsider the rejection of traditional Christian presuppositions on which process thought is predicated; to the second my appeal is for a closer integration of the engagement with relational ontologies with the demands of those presuppositions.

Before turning in more detail to the question of analogy and classical Christian theology I want to note another set of common commitments found in the theologians with whom I am here concerned. All assume some version of the charge that the Western theological tradition has fallen prey to a metaphysics based on the primacy of "Being" or "substance," or to an account that exemplifies "onto-theology." At the same time it is frequently assumed that traditional doctrines of divine simplicity and immutability work against the need to understand the relationship between God and world in a dynamic manner. There is no space here to offer a refutation of such broad claims.[5] I can, however, suggest that it is increasingly incumbent on the proponents of such accounts that they take account of the substantial body of recent work that shows the difficulty of maintaining that the major theologians of the West subscribed to any such doctrines.[6] Thus, to take one example, an increasing body of work has demonstrated

---

5. For a particularly clear summary account of the character of a Trinitarian theology that assumes the divine immutability and simplicity, see Thomas G. Weinandy, *Does God Suffer?* (Notre Dame: University of Notre Dame Press, 2000), pp. 113-46. Weinandy's account is consciously Thomist in inspiration, and thus presents only one example of classical Trinitarianism, but the purpose of his summary focuses around the argument that "the divine attributes of immutability and impassibility are . . . essential . . . for they insure both that the trinity of persons as subsistent relations, are fully in act and cannot become any more in 'act' through change and mutation, and that God, considered as *ipsum esse*, is pure act and cannot become any more in act through change and mutation. Far from designating the Trinity or God as static and inert, these attributes affirm, protect, and sustain the absolute dynamism and pure passion of God's divine nature as a trinity of persons" (p. 146).

6. Thus, for example, in the light of a retraction such as that represented by Jean-Luc Marion, "Saint Thomas d'Aquin et l'onto-théologie," *Revue Thomiste* 95 (1995): 31-66, good practice seems to enjoin a good deal of fresh exposition on those who wish to maintain an ontotheological critique of Thomas.

that figures such as Augustine and Thomas (frequently cited as the exemplars *par excellence* of the problem) use the doctrine of divine simplicity as a way of articulating the difference between God and world and thus as a way of articulating the mystery and paradoxes of the three who are one.[7] It has also become much clearer that the assumptions of a basic distinction between Eastern and Western Trinitarian theology — at least in its Patristic versions — are equally problematic.[8]

This historical reconstruction is of significance in two ways. For those theologians who make explicit appeal to Patristic — usually Greek Patristic — theologians in constructing their "relational" accounts, it is important for their arguments to maintain the independence of those sources from the theologies found in Western tradition. If it should turn out not only that the onto-theological critique holds little water in general but that Greek and Latin theologians share similar attitudes towards the role of ontology in theology and the language of persons and essence, then far more historical scholarly effort will need to be expended by those who want to use these Greek Patristic sources as a particular resource for a distinct account of the Trinity (or of reality itself). For those relational theologians indebted to process thought and with little interest in Patristic sources, the failure of the onto-theological critique simply undercuts the necessity of some of their most basic assumptions. Given the weight of recent historical scholarship, both groups of theologians face considerable challenges, and without some extended historical work on their part one would have to judge their case at the very least "not proven."

7. I make reference later to the work of David Burrell. His work offers an excellent example of this scholarship; see especially his *Knowing the Unknowable God: Ibn-Sina, Maimonides, Aquinas* (Notre Dame: University of Notre Dame Press, 1986). On Augustine see my "The Grammar of Augustine's Trinitarian Theology," in *Augustine and His Critics,* ed. Robert Dodaro and George Lawless (London and New York: Routledge, 1999), pp. 56-71; *Nicaea and Its Legacy: An Approach to Fourth Century Trinitarian Theology* (Oxford and New York: Oxford University Press, 2004), chap. 10.

8. I will not add further notes here to my own work on this question or to the work of Michel René Barnes (*Nicaea and Its Legacy* offers relevant bibliography). One introductory recent piece that I have found particularly useful in seminar discussions of this theme is Bruce Marshall's "The Trinity," in *The Blackwell Companion to Theology,* ed. Gareth Jones (Cambridge, MA: Blackwell, 2004), pp. 183-203.

Contemplation of What Is

In the following sections of the paper I will turn to a more constructive task, suggesting some answers to the question, "How might a theologian, committed to the basic dynamics of Patristic trinitarianism, reflect on the relationships between the character of the divine communion and the structure of the created order?" But before making any progress towards answering this question I think it important to outline my answer to a question necessarily preliminary: What is the purpose of theological reflection on the created order and its relationship to God? The core of any answer must, I suggest, be that such reflection plays a key role in the development and purification of one's contemplation or *theoria* (θεωρία). In Greek Christian authors of this period the term *theoria* identifies both the contemplation of the Trinity and the correct interpretation of Scripture's figural/allegorical sense.[9] Here, by slight extension, I use the term to designate also the contemplation of all in relation to the divine being, a contemplation of all in relation to God that assumes the text of Scripture to present the "firmament" that now enables our gaze on the world and onto God's presence within it.[10] It is a fairly consistent theme in the key Patristic

9. In this latter use it is not a preserve of "Antiochene" exegetes, but may also be found in Origen. See Frances Young, *Biblical Exegesis and the Making of Christian Culture* (Cambridge: Cambridge University Press, 1997).

10. My use of "firmament" is an echo of Augustine's *Confessions* 13.15.16-17 (*Saint Augustine: Confessions,* trans. Henry Chadwick [Oxford: Oxford University Press, 1992], pp. 282-83): "Who but you, O God, has made for us a solid firmament of authority over us in your divine Scripture? . . . So you have stretched out the firmament of your book 'like a skin,' that is your words which are not mutually discordant. . . . Lord, let us look 'at the heavens, the work of your fingers.' Dispel from our eyes the cloud with which you have covered them. . . . We have not found any other books so destructive of pride, so destructive of 'the enemy and the defender.' . . . I have not known, Lord, I have not met with other utterances so pure, which so persuasively move me to confession. . . ." This image is of importance here because Augustine emphasizes both the function of Scripture in enabling knowledge and contemplation of all that is, and he does so simultaneously with an emphasis on the link between good contemplation and praise of and humility before the One who has arranged this "firmament" above us. The text reveals and guides, but it does so only as it also reveals the divine as mystery: the text is ultimately and always trustworthy, but it is not understood simply as the provider of factual information enabling the fundamentalist to resist the modernist in late nineteenth-century terms. This becomes fully apparent when one sees how this passage sits between discussion of Scripture's multi-valence and the importance of learning a multiplicity of reading strategies; see *Conf.* 13.24.35ff.; *Conf.* 12.30.41: "In this diversity of true views, may truth itself engender concord. . . ." On this topic see now Isabelle Bochet, *"Le Firmament de L'Écriture." L'Herméneutique Augustinienne* (Paris: Études Augustiniennes, 2004).

theologians of the fourth century, and following that the restoration of the soul's vision centers upon a restoration of our ability to see all things in relation to their Creator, and all things as reflecting the sustaining presence and glory of the Creator.[11] This is first and foremost a vision of God — even if understood as a vision whose form is faith in this life — but it is a vision in which all of this is seen in its anagogic reality.

Such a conception of *theoria* has a number of significant implications, of which I will highlight one. The shaping of this vision will be governed by all of the factors that govern any attempt to think theologically: the coordination of that which seems inherently persuasive at different stages in human reflection with the character of biblical evidence; the importance of taking into account the stage within the history of salvation at which one reflects. Thus, in the case of the first of these governing factors, the sort of contemplation of the created order discussed in the last paragraph involves both learning to judge which accounts of what is are most persuasive, and learning to see how the text of Scripture may guide and shape the appropriation of that which seems persuasive. This, however, involves not only being able to see where the text of Scripture insists on perspectives that must govern such appropriation, but also how the same text may stimulate creative engagement with that which seems persuasive.[12]

In the case of the second governing factor, our claims to knowledge of the created order and its relationship to the divine must always be made in the light of our faith that a necessary mysteriousness and provisionality obtains this side of the eschaton. Augustine's account, in Books XII and XIII of the *Confessions* — however clearly we want to reject aspects of the "science" he there finds persuasive — remains a model for the character of our investigations of what is. In the light of these rather broad characterizations I will now suggest some basic principles of appropriate reflection on the relationship between the divine communion and ontology.

---

11. I discuss the continuing relevance of the notion of "soul" in my "The Soul and the Reading of Scripture: A Note on Henri de Lubac," *Scottish Journal of Theology,* forthcoming.

12. One of the clearest examples of just such a perspective at work is to be found in Bruce Marshall, "Absorbing the World: Christianity and the Universe of Truths," in *Theology and Dialogue: Essays in Conversation with George Lindbeck,* ed. Bruce Marshall (Notre Dame: Notre Dame University Press, 1990), pp. 69-102. For an outline of how I understand the interrelationship of "grammatical" and "figural" modes of exegesis in key fourth-century authors, see my *Nicaea and Its Legacy,* pp. 34-40.

Lewis Ayres

Ontological Commitments

Theologians should of course engage and seek to appropriate those aspects of ontological speculation that they find persuasive in an attempt to articulate their faith in the Creator and to articulate how the created order reveals the divine. And, of course, what results will be "an ontology" in the sense that it is likely that some propositions will be accepted and others rejected from any particular set of ideas found persuasive. Nevertheless, theologians do well to recognize that while they seek for convergence with accounts of the character of existence, convergence itself remains necessarily elusive this side of the eschaton. I argue this for two theological reasons.

First, it has been a persistent theological claim that the structure of things remains partially mysterious *because* the "poem of the universe" (to use Augustine's phrase) is intended to lead the contemplating soul to the vision of the God who is truly distinct from the world. Before that vision our knowledge of how existence reveals and reflects God must remain partial. Second, but closely related, faith within the Christian tradition is a virtue precisely because it accepts the necessity of sight's absence and trust's presence. There will then be many possible ontologies consonant with Trinitarian faith. The task of the Trinitarian "ontologist" is then perhaps best delineated by looking at the fundamental concerns that should shape engagement with ideas found persuasive, and at the patterns of analogical judgment that should accompany such engagement. We should accordingly think of theologians as sustaining and developing ontological commitments, but not as shaping an ontology. Just as modern theologians should, I suggest, sustain some of the ontological commitments found in such Patristic figures as Augustine and Maximus, while rejecting others as no longer persuasive, so we should be aware of the possibility that our own ontological commitments may seem equally a mix of the persuasive and unpersuasive in future generations. What we should hope is that future generations of theologians recognize that we struggled hard to bring those commitments into accord with the demands of Christian belief.

Analogy and Participation

While my first thesis suggests a certain necessary provisionality in Christians' "ontological commitments," I want now to suggest that there are some ontological commitments deeply embedded in traditional Christian

138

accounts of this provisionality that we should continue to sustain. Our attempts to suggest ways in which the ordering of the cosmos reveals the divine existence must be governed by our acceptance that we speak analogically when we argue that any concept describes both God and world. At the same time, we must recognize that an appropriate doctrine of analogy is sustained by the combination of an account of the distinction between Creator and creation and an account of the presence of the Creator to the creation. Here we see one of the most important ontological commitments intrinsic to classical Trinitarian theology.

Robert Sokolowski made the distinction between Creator and creation central to his renowned introduction to theology. Sokolowski in particular emphasizes that God's transcendence of all in the creation is a result of God's creative and loving will. He writes:

> [God] does not appear in the world or in human experience. He is not the kind of being that can be present as a thing in the world. . . . In the distinctions that normally occur in the setting of the world, each term distinguished is what it is precisely by not being that which it is distinguishable from. Its being is established partially by its otherness, and therefore its being depends on its distinction from others. But in the Christian distinction God is understood as "being" God entirely apart from any relation of otherness to the world or to the whole. God could and would be God even if there were no world. . . . The most fundamental thing we come to in Christianity, the distinction between the world and God, is appreciated as not being the most fundamental thing after all, because one of the terms of the distinction, God, is more fundamental than the distinction itself.
>
> In Christian faith God is understood not only to have created the world, but to have permitted the distinction between himself and the world to occur . . . [and if God] was not motivated by any need of completion in the one who let it be, and not even motivated by the need for "there" to be more perfection and greatness, then the world is there through an incomparable generosity.[13]

While Sokolowski offers one of the clearest introductory statements of this distinction in recent writing, the work of David Burrell offers one of the best resources for exploring its significance for our speech about

---

13. Robert Sokolowski, *The God of Faith and Reason: Foundations of Christian Theology* (Washington, DC: Catholic University of America Press, 1982), pp. 1, 32-34.

God.[14] Taking Thomas as his example, Burrell argues, first, that traditional Christian accounts of God's distinction from the world ground accounts of the unmediated participation of all things in God.[15] The mode
of that participation may be described only in scriptural terms or in
philosophical terms that are extremely formal in nature because of the divine mystery. Although Platonic accounts of participation — especially
those found in Neoplatonic thinkers — are frequently discussed in terms
that assume a fundamental distinction between models of "emanation"
and accounts of *creatio ex nihilo,* it is important to recognize that Neoplatonic accounts of the relationship between different "levels" of existence
were complex particularly in their attention to the difficulty of understanding the mode of such participation.[16] These models provided a key
resource for Christian thinkers seeking to imagine the participation of all
things in God. They were also revised in their theological adaptation: frequently the assertion that participation was the result of the divine power
served only to emphasize with more clarity the incomprehensibility of
such participation. In such a context, for Burrell, when we speak of drawing analogies between God and world we use "analogy" analogically; we
are drawn to assert in faith that there is, for example, justice in God, but
there is no *proportionate* relationship between the justice that we know
and God's own justice.[17] Our understanding of analogy will hence be seen
in the ways that we shape patterns of analogical judgment and predication that constantly reveal this distinction and the necessity of faith.
Good use of analogy in theology promotes awareness that and how God
reveals, and it promotes awareness of how Christians wait upon the mystery of God in faith. We may thus say that analogy used in theological
context has moral and spiritual dimensions that depend on recognition
of the distinction between God and world.

14. See especially David Burrell, "From Analogy of 'Being' to the Analogy of Being," in
*Recovering Nature: Essays in Natural Philosophy, Ethics and Metaphysics in Honor of Ralph
McInerny,* ed. Thomas Hibbs and John O'Callaghan (Notre Dame: University of Notre
Dame Press, 1999), pp. 253-66.

15. One of the clearest introductions to the importance of the distinction between God
and world is to be found in Sokolowski's *The God of Faith and Reason,* chaps. 3-5.

16. A. C. Lloyd, *The Anatomy of Neoplatonism* (Oxford: Clarendon Press, 1990), offers a
particularly helpful account.

17. One of the very best introductions to the history of analogy, focusing on medieval
discussion, is E. Jennifer Ashworth's "Medieval Theories of Analogy," in the *Stanford Encyclopedia of Philosophy,* to be found at http://plato.stanford.edu/entries/analogy-medieval.

Contemplating Divine Activity

From the previous section it is already clear that outlining an account of analogy appropriate for theological thinking involves also sketching some ontological commitments that are intrinsic to classical theology. In this section I want to explore some of the theological context within which that ontological commitment has traditionally been articulated. Accounts of how the creation participates in God have been consistently shaped in Christian tradition by Trinitarian accounts of divine action. These accounts not only describe the relationship of creation to the Trinity, but also offer an account of the action of God through created temporality. Once we have seen in outline how these discourses also shape analogical reflection, we will then be in a position to suggest ways in which our imagining of parallels between divine and human communion might proceed within this context.

As I hinted in the previous section, the reframing of originally Platonist conceptions of participation in theological terms — a reframing that was central to the development of Christianity in both East and West — had the effect of emphasizing the incomprehensibility of the mode of our participation in God, or of God's presence to what is.[18] Nevertheless, one of the ways in which this assertion of incomprehensibility has been given further specificity in both Eastern and Western Christianity is through theological accounts of what it means for all to exist in the divine Wisdom or Word and how we may conceive of the Spirit as sustaining the created order. These richly textured discussions advocate a variety of ontological possibilities, but share a sense that understanding the creation's existence is dependent on grasping the distinction *and yet immediate presence* of God to the creation. Some liberal and revisionist theologies have in recent decades argued for accounts of divine action in which God is not conceived as constantly active in creation (particularly not in such a way that would allow us to speak of any "supernatural" interactions of God with creation):[19] one of the ways in which such accounts are distinct from classical Christian traditions (and I use the plural here to emphasize the variety of Eastern and Western theological traditions on which such a perspective impinges) is in their undercutting of the complex use of Trinitar-

18. This is also to say, of course, that these developments involved not simple statements of incomprehensibility, but a definition of what and where incomprehensibility lay.

19. Perhaps most clearly, Maurice Wiles, *God's Action in the World* (London: SCM, 1986).

ian theology as a framework for describing God's presence to and work in the created order.

As I suggested in the previous paragraph, one way in which Trinitarian theology gives further density to our understanding of analogy and participation is through narrating God's constant presence to the creation that God simultaneously transcends. This narration, however, is not simply a matter of formal statements asserting that just as all exists in the Word, so the Spirit sustains all in existence. It is also a narration of the progress of divine interaction with the creation. The Christian tradition's narration of God's faithfulness to Israel, the sending of the Son (in time), and the movement from crucifixion to Ascension and the awaiting of the *eschaton,* both shapes our account of the divine love (and thus gives further density to our contemplation of what it means for God to sustain all in existence) and locates our thinking at a particular stage of the divine-human drama. Earlier, in my discussion of theologians' need for "ontological commitments" rather than for "ontologies," I suggested that this was in part so because of the nature of faith. Here that statement finds its fuller context.

Narrating the divine drama is an integral part of setting out a theological epistemology. The character of our knowing and searching for knowledge, the character of the θεωρία that we most appropriately seek, depends upon how we envision the characteristics of this stage of our temporal relationship with God. To what extent and in what ways does sin affect the possibility of human speech about God? To what extent does the work of the Spirit in the body of Christ enable us to overcome those limits? To what extent does the provision of the scriptural text enable the shaping of a faith that will stand in for the vision now hidden? To what extent does our participation in the body of Christ involve a "deifying" impartation of the divine life and effect a real union with the Word's *hypostasis?* Dense answers to these questions seem to me the essential framework within which we should consider the relationship between divine and human communion. Of course, as may be clear from even these brief sentences, the shape of one's theological epistemology will be related to one's conception of salvation and (most likely therefore) to one's theological tradition.

Relationality, Human and Divine

The bulk of my argument has been occupied with critique and with suggesting the appropriate framework within which one might think about the analogical relationship between divine and created communion. I have devoted so much space to these questions precisely because it is there that I see recent work in "relational" and "Trinitarian" ontology to be most lacking. However, against the framework I have now sketched it is important for me to suggest, even if very briefly, that there are ways in which we may and should envisage theologians exploring relationships between communion in the created order and the inner divine communion. I will suggest two.

In the first place, the characteristics of the divine relationships certainly should provide material that should be of immense help in shaping our vision of the world. Envisioning the shape of the divine unity and relationality should, however, be an analogical and anagogic exercise of the kind suggested at the end of the first section of the paper. In such a context, however, our imagining of the divine community may still serve as a guide for our engagement of ontological thought. For example, our imagining of the divine peace may serve us an index against which we may judge, engage, and adapt any ontologies that envision an ultimately chaotic or violent structure to what is. Nevertheless, the shaping of our accounts of divine relationships is thus, I would suggest, an exercise not to be constructed solely by means of philosophical investigation, but also by the exegetical engagement of these resources, exploring how the relationships of God, Word, and Spirit are narrated by the text of Scripture. To undertake — and indeed to recover — such an enterprise, would also require considerable attention to the figural/allegorical readings of Scripture that traditionally have played a significant role in imagining the divine existence.[20]

I suggest we will also need to explore ways in which the fundamental principles of Trinitarian theology itself will help in our exploration of the created structures that we believe in faith to mirror the divine.[21] I suspect that detailed examination of Patristic and medieval texts within which such modes of quasi-analogical investigation are modeled would also reveal not only that such a practice is inseparable from an understanding of the divine transcendence and distinction from the world, but also recogni-

20. Sarah Coakley's "Re-thinking Gregory of Nyssa: Introduction — Gender, Trinitarian Analogies and the Pedagogy of the *Song*," *Modern Theology* 18 (2002): 431-43, offers some excellent examples of this procedure.

21. I have suggested that Augustine himself is engaged in such an exercise in his *De trinitate*. See my *Augustine's Trinitarian Theology* (Cambridge: Cambridge University Press, forthcoming), chaps. 7-8.

tion of the need for grace in the task of theology itself. It might well be possible, in other words, to sketch a phenomenology of such quasi-analogical investigation in which the intellectual practice of identifying similarity and distinction between created and divine structures is inseparable from the move towards prayer for grace. Within this context it would become much more difficult to sustain what seems to me the weak analogical procedure of projecting onto God a notion of relationality and then assuming that this description of divine being licenses prescriptions for Christian life. Our envisioning of the relationship between divine and human community must take its place within the practice of anagogical meditation and intellectual endeavor (these two terms are not antithetical, but rather overlap in meaning) that is the context for all theology.

In the second place, there are certainly contexts within which the character of the interdependence of the created order and our mode of intended participation within it are best explored by reflection on the unity, diversity, and love modeled by Father, Son, and Spirit — contexts within which the divine-human relationship established by God enables progress in understanding of the intra-divine relationships. John 17:11's ". . . that they may be one, *even as* we are one" indicates the importance of such arguments for Christians. Indeed, we should note — especially for those for whom it might come as a surprise — that in a number of places Augustine parallels the unity of the Trinity with the unity of the apostles described in Acts 4:32.[22] This should not surprise given the way in which Augustine interrelates an account of the Spirit as the eternally subsistent love between Father and Son with an account of the church as that location in which the Spirit as gift and dove unites the wills and loves of Christians.[23] However, the modes of unity and plurality that Christians seek are shaped not only by reference to that which we attempt to see in the Trinity itself, but always also by reflection on the stage of the divine-human drama within which we currently find ourselves.

In other words, the modes of unity and plurality Christians should seek to practice now are not governed solely by an attempt to imitate what we assume is to be found in God, but also by an attempt to discern what unity and pluralities are appropriate for this stage in the progress of the

---

22. E.g., *C. Max.* 2.20.1. See Roland Teske, trans., *Arianism and Other Heresies,* The Works of Saint Augustine I/18 (Hyde Park, NY: New City Press, 1995), p. 300.

23. E.g., *Ep. Io. trans.* 7. See John W. Rettig, trans., *St. Augustine. Tractates on the Gospel of John 112-24. Tractates on the First Epistle of John,* Fathers of the Church 92 (Washington, DC: Catholic University of America Press, 1995), pp. 217-27.

body of Christ towards its head. Created and *temporal* being is most certainly intended to reflect the divine existence and draw all into a communion that reflects that existence. As we have seen, the reflection of divine existence in the created order is grasped when the anagogic nature of that reflection is grasped: the reflection is understood when the grasping is part of our move towards the Creator. And certainly, the temporality of the created order enables the endless advance into the mystery of God, mirroring eternity as a sacrament of the divine limitlessness. And yet, our advance into that vision is one shaped and honed by our participation in the (sacramental) life of the church, that is, by our life in the body of Christ. There can, then, be a relational and a Trinitarian ontology: but it is one whose shape and investigation must be governed by a theologically dense and Christologically formed conception of our existence and ongoing sanctification. Trinitarian ontology, if it is to be truly theological, must be also both Christology and ecclesiology.

Relational Ontology: Insights from Patristic Thought

Metropolitan John Zizioulas

From Substance to Personhood

The term "relational ontology" results from a combination or synthesis of the idea of being with that of relation. The bringing together of these two ideas in the form of a single concept is by no means a simple matter. In the logic that our Western minds have inherited from classical Greek thought, "to be" is always prior to "relating"; the two ideas can never be thought of simultaneously. You first *are* and then you *relate*. Whereas being is a necessary condition of ontology, i.e., of any reference to being, relation is not. A stone, or for that matter an individual human being, can be conceived as existing, as being there, without necessarily being in relation to something else. In fact, the more it is isolated and individualized the more its being emerges clearly in our minds.

This kind of ontology received its fullest expression in classical Greece through the philosophy of Aristotle. The starting point of ontology for this philosopher was the *individual thing*, the ζόδε τι. Speculation about being presupposes the observation of the concrete being as it presents itself to us *in itself*. This is the "first substance," the beginning of ontology. It is from that basis that we can move to the "second substance," that is, to the category of being that can be applied to more than one being. What unites, therefore, the individual beings is substance — not relation. Relation is one of the several categories that are not necessary in order to indicate that something *is;* it is substance that performs this role.[1] There is no room in this case for a relational ontology.

1. Aristotle, *Metaphysics*, 1007 a 26 and 1028 b 3: "what is being *(to on)*, i.e., what is the

146

This priority of substance in ontology entered Christian theology and became a matter of crucial importance in the discussions concerning the Trinity. From the time that Tertullian (late second century, early third) described the Trinity as *una substantia, tres personae*,[2] Patristic theology in the West as well as in the East embarked on a theological debate that involved, in one way or another, the concept of substance in connection with that of relation. *Persona*, or *prosopon* in Greek, carried with it a connotation of relationality, and it inevitably gave rise to the question whether "person" is primary ontologically in relation to substance. Thus, Trinitarian theology offered the first historical occasion for the possibility of a relational ontology.

It is beyond the scope of the present paper to discuss the historical details of the circumstances that marked the theological debate concerning Trinitarian theology in the Patristic period.[3] It would suffice to mention two approaches to relational ontology that bear directly on our subject. The first one is exemplified by St. Augustine's Trinitarian theology, the other one by that of the Cappadocian fathers (Basil, Gregory Nazianzen, Gregory of Nyssa, and Amphilochius of Iconium). In both cases Aristotelian ontology played a fundamental role in connection with the concept of relation.

Augustine is known for his extensive use of the concept of relation in Trinitarian theology. In his attempt to escape the dilemma posed by his Arian opponents whether, in terms of Aristotelian logic, the three persons of the Trinity are substances or accidents, neither of which being proper to describe the Orthodox doctrine of the Trinity, Augustine proposed the idea of *relation:* the Three of the Trinity are neither substances nor accidents but *relations* which have real subsistence[4] — an idea already taught by Plotinus and Porphyry.[5] It would appear, therefore, that Augustine, un-

---

substance *(ousia)*." Cf. W. D. Ross, *Aristotle* (1959), pp. 155f.: "Being is not an attribute that belongs in precisely the same sense to everything that is. There is one kind of being which *is* in the strictest and fullest sense — viz. substance; and all other things *are* simply by virtue of standing in some definite relation to substance — as qualities of substance, as relations between substances, or the like."

2. Tertullian, *Against Praxeas* 11-12 (PL 2:1670D).

3. I deal with this in some detail in my *Being as Communion* (Crestwood, NY: St. Vladimir's Seminary Press, 1993), pp. 36ff., and more recently and extensively in my *Communion and Otherness: Further Studies in Personhood and the Church* (London: T. & T. Clark, 2006), esp. pp. 155ff. and 178ff.

4. Augustine, *De trinitate* 5-7. Cf. *Tractatus in Iohannes euangelium* 39; *Ep.* 170; *De civitate dei* 11, 10.

5. E.g., Plotinus, *Ennead* 6, 1, 6-8.

like Aristotle, elevated the concept of relation to an ontological level, thus contributing to the emergence of a relational ontology.

This would have been indeed the case had it not been for the fact that Augustine understood these relations, and therefore the persons of the Trinity, as subsisting within the divine substance, which acquired in this way ontological priority.[6] Substance retained in Augustine the ontological primacy attached to it by Aristotle. As Karl Rahner critically observes, Augustine is responsible for the priority of the treatise *De Deo uno* before the doctrine of the Trinity in the dogmatic manuals of the West.[7]

The Cappadocians also used extensively the concept of relation *(schesis)* in their Trinitarian theology.[8] They differed, however, from Augustine on two basic points. First, they did not identify person with relation. Relation for them is constitutive of personhood but the person is not the relation itself; it is a concrete *hypostasis,* an entity that is relational but at the same time ontologically integral. Thus whereas for Augustine the persons of the Trinity can be illustrated by the example of three psychological faculties of *one* (human) being, for the Cappadocians we would need *three* (human) beings in order to illustrate the three divine persons.[9] This elevates the person to the highest ontological status.

The second point of difference follows from the first. Since the person is ontologically integral, it does not derive ontological status from substance. Substance is not the primary ontological category. Threeness is just as primary as oneness; diversity is constitutive of unity. The many are neither *caused* by the One nor subsist as relations *within* the One. The *De Deo uno* cannot be treated before the *De Deo trino*. The one God is the Father,

---

6. *De trinitate* 5, 3 and 7f.: in dealing with the doctrine of God we begin not with the Father but with divine "substance" or, as Augustine prefers, "essence," which is the primary ontological category in our reference to God. Substance, therefore, *underlies* the relations. According to H. A. Wolfson, *The Philosophy of the Church Fathers* (Cambridge, MA: Harvard University Press, 1956), pp. 326f., this is a return to Aristotelianism: "Unlike Tertullian and like Aristotle" Augustine "identifies the substratum [of the Trinity] not with the Father but with something underlying both the Father and the Son."

7. K. Rahner, *The Trinity* (Tunbridge Wells: Burns & Oates, 1970), *passim* and pp. 58f.

8. E.g., Amphilochius, *Fragment* 15 (PG 39:112): the names Father, Son, and Spirit do not stand for essence but for "a mode of existence or relation." Cf. Gregory Nazianzus *Orationes* 29 (PG 36:96): "the name Father is not one of essence or of energy but of relation."

9. On Augustine's rejection of the illustration of three human beings belonging to one genus, see his *Tractatus in Iohannes euangelium* 39, 2-4. On the Cappadocians' repeated use of this illustration, see Basil (= Gregory of Nyssa), *Epistola* 38; Gregory of Nyssa, *Ad Graecos ex communibus notionibus* (PG 45:177f.), etc.

i.e., one of the Three, and he is the highest point of reference in divine ontology. Divine substance cannot be said to exist apart from the Father who "causes" its "hypostatization," i.e., its being the way it is.[10]

Thus, in their dealing with the doctrine of the Trinity the Cappadocian fathers developed an ontology that is of paramount importance for our subject. Ontology consists in a twofold question: in asking not only *what* something is but also *how* it exists. The *what* question refers to the substance *(ousia* or *physis),* while the *how* question applies to the way something *relates.*[11] This leads to the following equations:

"What" *(ti)* = substance *(ousia, physis)*
"How" *(pos* or *hopos)* = hypostasis/person = mode of being *(tropos hyparxeos)* = relation *(schesis).*

These equations cannot be separated from one another, yet it is only at the level of "how" that we can have access to and communion with being. The Cappadocians, and for that matter the entire Greek Patristic tradition, were quite clear: God's substance remains unknowable and incommunicable. It is at the level of the "how" that communion with God can take place. We can know God as Father (cf. John 17:13) — and as the other persons of the Trinity — i.e., as *person, as he relates to,* and not in his essence. And although their main preoccupation was with divine being, these fathers did not limit this principle to God but extended it to everything that exists: we cannot know the substance of anything, only the way it exists is accessible to us.[12] A relational ontology, therefore, takes place at the level of the way things relate with each other, and this is the only way that being is accessible to us, not only for *knowledge* — this must be stressed — but also for *participation* and *communion.*

We shall have to return to this point later, for, I think, it is of crucial significance for a dialogue between theology and the sciences. Meanwhile let me underline another implication of this kind of Trinitarian theology for the subject of relational ontology. The Cappadocian fathers are known

---

10. Cf. Gregory Nazianzus, *Theological Orations* 6; Gregory of Nyssa, *Ad Ablabium* (PG 45:133). Also, my *Being as Communion,* pp. 40f., and more extensively my *Communion and Otherness,* esp. pp. 113-54.

11. See Basil, *Contra Eunomium* 1, 14-15; Gregory Nazianzus, *Theol. Or.* 3, 16, etc.

12. See Gregory Nazianzus, *Theol. Or.* 2, 17-30: even the nature of created beings is beyond comprehension. Also, Gregory of Nyssa, *C. Eun.* 2 (Jaeger 260, 10-13); *C. Eun.* 3 (Jaeger 238, 19-22); *C. Eun.* 2 (Jaeger 257).

— and by several Western theologians strongly criticized — for having introduced the idea of "cause" into the being of God. At the level of "how" or personhood/hypostasis, and only at that, relations are *causal:* the Father causes the Son and the Spirit to exist as hypostases, i.e., as specific identities emerging through relations.[13] The significance of this is twofold. On the one hand, it introduces dynamism and movement in ontology. Being is not static, and beings are not self-explicable but *emerge* from a constant movement of relationality. On the other hand, it gives to being a quality of *love* and to love an *ontological* character: to be *is to exist for the other,* not for the self, and to love is not to "feel" something about the other, but to *let the other be and be other.*[14] Relation causes otherness, it does not amount to uniformity. Causation is as primary ontologically as the "how" of being. There is no such thing as the "unmoving mover" of Aristotle. For the Greek fathers God is unmovable in his substance but constantly and eternally moving in himself as person: in relation to himself as Trinity, and outside himself towards creation in his relation to the world. This leads the Greek fathers to use the term *eros* to describe divine being both in itself and in its relation with creation.[15] Relational ontology is erotic ontology.

From Logos to Tropos

These ideas were taken up by Maximus the Confessor in the seventh century and applied to the being of creation. Just as in the case of divine being, so in the universe, too, we must distinguish between the "what" and the "how" things are. Maximus uses two terms to describe this ontology: *logos* and *tropos*.[16] It is with the help of these two terms, which he borrows from the Trinitarian theology of the Cappadocians, that Maximus proceeds to develop his cosmological ontology. According to him, everything that is said to exist possesses a *logos physeos* or *ousias* and a *tropos hyparxeos,* a

13. Cf. n. 10 above.

14. More on this in my *Communion and Otherness, passim,* and esp. pp. 13-98.

15. Thus Dionysius the Areopagite, *De divinis nominibus* 4, 13, and Maximus, *Ambiguum* 23: God as *eros* and *agape* (there is no difference between the two terms) moves toward creation, causing at the same time a reciprocal movement toward himself from the side of creation.

16. This distinction is typical of Maximus' ontology and occurs repeatedly in his writings. E.g., *Amb.* 31; 36; and above all 42 (PG 91:1341). Cf. P. Sherwood, *The Earlier Ambigua of St. Maximus the Confessor and His Refutation of Origenism* (Rome: Herder, 1955), pp. 155-56.

hypostasis. There is no substance "in the nude," as it was already observed by the Cappadocian fathers,[17] and this means for Maximus that there is no substance in the world that does not possess its *tropos,* its mode of being.

Now, the significance of all this lies, for Maximus, in the capacity of beings to *modify* and change themselves thanks to their *tropos,* while remaining identical to themselves because of their *logos.*[18] This mysterious coincidence of identity or continuity and change or "innovation" is the core of relational ontology. It was worked out by Maximus as a way of explaining Chalcedonian Christology, according to which the two natures, divine and human, united in Christ "without division" and yet "without confusion." Relational ontology consists in conceiving all that is said to exist as a constant movement of change and modification that preserves (or rather brings about?) unity and otherness at the same time.

This movement of constant change and modification takes place in creation in or *as time.* Following the theological trend initiated by Irenaeus in the second century, Maximus conceives the universe as moving towards a *telos,* a goal or a purpose. Time is part of the dynamics of the relationality that characterizes the being of creation. Time and space are interwoven in a sort of "cosmic liturgy" — as von Balthasar successfully described Maximus' thought — in which creation moves to its blessed *peras,* its final goal which is unity in Christ without confusion. Unlike Dionysius the Areopagite, Maximus views the liturgy as a movement in time and not simply as a static revelation of hierarchical relations between divine and worldly being.[19]

I leave it to the scientists to decide whether this kind of ontology, worked out by the Greek Fathers, bears any significance for their approach to the world. In my elementary acquaintance with modern science I cannot but be reminded of what Michael Faraday wrote already in the nineteenth century about the "mutual penetrability of atoms," each of which "extends, so to say, throughout the whole of the solar system, yet always retaining its own centre of force."[20] Physics has, of course, developed consid-

17. Basil (= Gregory of Nyssa), *Ep.* 38, 2; Gregory of Nyssa, *C. Eun.* 1.

18. Maximus presents this as a universal scientific law: "Every innovation, to speak generically, has naturally to do with the mode *(tropos)* of the innovated thing but not with the logos of nature . . . the mode innovated, the logos, being preserved in its nature, manifests miraculous power." *Amb.* 42 (PG 91:134).

19. This is evident in Maximus' interpretation of the Eucharistic liturgy in his *Mystagogia.*

20. M. Faraday, "A Speculation Touching Electric Conduction and the Nature of Matter," *On the Primary Forces of Electricity,* ed. R. Laming (London: 1838), pp. 7f.

erably since the time of Faraday, and yet I seem to find an echo of Patristic ontology in it as recently as the writings of Ilya Prigogine and Isabelle Stengers, who write that physics "now recognizes that, for an interaction to be real, the 'nature' of the related things must derive from these relations, while at the same time the relations must derive from the 'nature' of the things."[21] A similar appreciation of the implications of the Patristic doctrine of the Trinity for physics is to be found in John Polkinghorne, *Science and the Trinity* (2004), and more recently in his *Exploring Reality* (2005), especially pages 105ff. And although the eschatology of the dynamic of the world as presented by Maximus (and earlier by Irenaeus) is not identical with the way modern physics speaks of the dynamism of the universe, the world is viewed by both of them as a relational reality constituted by the arrow of time. Thus, there seems to be a striking affinity between Patristic theology and modern science in what we call "relational ontology."

Creation and Personhood

The world is, for both Patristic theology and modern science, relational and dynamic. But there may be a fundamental difference between science and theology concerning the nature of this relational ontology of the world, a difference that should be considered. For the Patristic theologians whose ontology we have just discussed, the relational and dynamic character of the universe, its "how it is," is due to a *personal* presence in creation, that of the *Logos* of God.[22] Their relational ontology is personalistic in that, for them, *only in personhood can we find the possibility of a modification and "innovation" of nature,* the dynamic relationality that transforms without destroying and brings about unity in otherness. A relational ontology of this kind implies, therefore, or requires a dimension of *freedom,* a denial of determinism.

Now, physics today speaks also of indeterminacy and contingency as characteristic of the being of the world. We live in a non-determined world, and this is what allows us also, human beings, to escape from determinism, for there would have been no possibility of freedom for us had

---

21. I. Prigogine and I. Stengers, *Order Out of Chaos: Man's New Dialogue with Nature* (London: Flamingo, 1985), p. 95. Cf. C. E. Gunton, *The Promise of Trinitarian Theology* (Edinburgh: T. & T. Clark, 1991), pp. 144f.

22. This is a central idea in Athanasius, *De incarnatione verbi dei.* Maximus uses this idea also in his works.

there been determinism in the universe of which we are parts. (Only if somehow we detach the human being from its organic relation with the rest of creation, thus distancing fundamentally human sciences from physical sciences — something habitually done — can we ignore the connection between human and cosmic determinism.) But is physics ready to connect this indeterminacy, this "freedom" of the way the universe is, with a *personal presence* in it, or would physicists rather conceive it in terms of personhood simply *analogically?* Patristic theology did *not* relate personhood and creation analogically but preferred to speak of the world as *containing in itself a personal presence* (the *Logos* of God and the human being as the *imago Dei*). It is this presence that accounts, in Patristic thought, for the indeterminacy and "freedom" of the world's being. But is physical science prepared to speak in such terms?

The crucial question, therefore, in a dialogue between theology and the sciences on the basis of relational ontology is the following: If the way the universe exists resembles the way God exists (relational ontology on both sides), is there any connection between divine being and the being of the world *ontologically,* i.e., in reality, and not simply *analogically,* i.e., in the way we speak about this resemblance (identity of concepts)? If we are satisfied with the analogical connection, the dialogue can be construed with the recognition that there is a common conceptual framework in the conversation between theologians and scientists: the two sides are talking the same language — a considerable advance, of course, if not a revolution, compared with the relation, or non-relation, of theology and science in the past. If, however, we wish to pursue the dialogue further and address the *ontological* rather than the analogical aspect of the connection between divine and worldly relational ontology, we must discuss some fundamental themes of a philosophical or metaphysical kind. For, it would seem to me, when scientists speak of the world in terms of relational ontology, indeterminacy, contingency, etc., they consciously or unconsciously abolish or blur the borderline between physics and metaphysics.

Unless it is conceived only analogically, the use of the concept of relational ontology by scientists in a way similar to that applied by theologians to divine being inevitably suggests some form of personhood in relation to creation. The universe behaves *like a person,* not in the prevailing Augustinian and modern Western sense of "center of consciousness," but as "persons" were described above in connection with the Trinity, namely as *particularities emerging from relations.* There is an interpenetration between nature and relation, causality and indeterminacy, chaos and stability or structure, making predictability difficult, or even impossible, not because our knowledge of natural laws is imperfect but because there is in reality no such thing as nature "in the nude," i.e., as substance or *logos* without a *tropos*, a modifying relationality. And this is exactly what we find in personhood. It would appear, therefore, that the link between the relational ontology of divine being and that of the being of the world is to be found in the reality of personal existence, of otherness in communion and communion in otherness.

In Greek Patristic thought we can depict several ways of linking divine being with the being of the world. In a trend influenced by ancient Greek philosophy and represented by Origen, Evagrius, and others, the link between God and the world is found in the *Logos* as mind *(nous)* and intelligence. This, however, would bear no significance for a dialogue between theology and modern science, since it would have to rule out any consideration of the material world with which the physical sciences deal. In fact, the material creation is for this kind of theology ultimately unnecessary in ontology. The other major trend, to which a great deal of attention is paid in our time, is that represented mainly by St. Gregory Palamas, which links God and the world through the idea of *energy*. This seems to bear more directly on the dialogue between theology and the sciences because of the central role that energy plays in physics and cosmology. And yet this way of linking God and the world does not seem to tell us anything about relationality as relational modification of nature, which brings about particularities in and through relations, as otherness in unity and unity in otherness — i.e., precisely about what characterizes the being of the universe as well as that of God.

The only trend of Patristic thought that seems to meet the requirements of a dialogue between theology and the sciences on the basis of relational ontology seems to me to be that represented by St. Maximus, to whose ideas we have already referred. According to him, God and the world are related ontologically — not analogically — through the *Logos* of God understood not as *nous* and intelligence, but as a *person who transfers his way of being*, his *tropos hyparxeos* from the divine realm to that of creation. There is a well-known passage in Maximus' work in which he writes: "The Logos of God and God wills always and in everything the realization of the mystery of his embodiment" (*Amb.* 7). This means that the way God is and the way the world exists as relational beings coincide and relate to each other through the fact that in both God and the world nature acquires stability and duration only in and through a constant modification of its *tropos,* i.e., through a movement of com-munion similar to that which characterizes personhood, namely specific identity emerging through relationships.

Now, if we connect divine relationality with the world's relational be-ing through personhood understood as explained above, two options seem to be offered to us: either a form of personalization of the world, in which case relational ontology is equally applied to all dimensions of being (cf. Hartshorne and process philosophy); or the Patristic view of the world as owing its relational being to a personal presence which, although *in* the world, exists in a *dialectical relation with it.* The first of these options would make it difficult to disentangle ontologically God, or even the hu-man personhood, from creation, thus making it equally difficult to explain not only divine but also human freedom *vis-à-vis* the world. The second of these options would necessitate the understanding of the world as a reality that in its *very relational being calls for a way of being which the world can-not by itself fulfill.* In other words, the relational way of being that the phys-icist and the cosmologist recognize in the universe, and which resembles the reality of divine personhood, would remain not only inexplicable but unfulfilled if left to the observed reality itself. Relational ontology contains in its very nature a dimension of *transcendence,* an *openness* of being, pointing to a *beyond the self,* to *seeking communion with the Other,* an es-chatological orientation — at all levels of otherness, from the most ele-mentary to the absolute one. A relational ontology that presupposes a self-contained universe contradicts its own fundamental claims. The moment a scientist agrees to speak of the universe in terms of relational ontology he or she ceases to be a mere or "pure" scientist. The philosophical *and theo-logical* questions emerge as unavoidable.

If the being of the universe is relational it cannot but be open-ended and transcendent in all respects — with regard to all its components as well as its own integral identity. And if it is open-ended and dynamic, its nature is *eschatological,* i.e., a relationality seeking fulfillment through rela-tion with a reality other than itself. If the *Anthropic Cosmological Principle* according to which "It is not only that man is adapted to the universe. The universe is adapted to man,"[23] has any place in a relational ontology, it is not so much in the sense that the world needs or moves towards a higher level of intelligence and consciousness, humanity and the universe being

---

23. John A. Wheeler, Foreword to J. D. Barrow and F. I. Tipler, *The Anthropic Cosmologi-cal Principle* (Oxford: Oxford University Press, 1986), p. vii.

conceived in terms of computer power,[24] as in the sense that it drives at the fulfillment of its relationality, seeking its "embodiment" in a truly personal way of being in which particularities emerge as "others" in communion. And if Christ has any place in such an ontology, it is only in the sense that he is the *Anthropos* the world needs to fulfill its relational being in making the relational ontology of God and the relational ontology of the world coincide in one and the same reality, what the Greek fathers would call *theosis* of creation, in and through truly personal communion.

Conclusion

When scientists and theologians agree that being is at all levels relational, they do not tell us only something about God and the world. They throw light also on our ordinary everyday life as human beings. If we live in a relational universe, not as external visitors to it but as parts of it, any individualistic approach to existence is bound to contradict not only the will of God but also the truth of our own being. A relational ontology, if it is *ontology* in the true sense of the word, cannot but cover all aspects, all areas, and all levels of existence: the divine, the cosmic, the social. Such an ontology acquires its full significance as it helps us understand that a relational existence, a transcendence of the boundaries of the self for the purpose of communion with the other, an existence of communion in otherness, is not a matter of our *bene esse* but of the very *esse* of ourselves and of the world in which we live. In engaging with relational ontology we encounter all that ultimately matters in existence.

24. F. J. Tipler, *The Physics of Immortality: Modern Cosmology, God and the Resurrection of the Dead* (New York: Doubleday, 1994).

Relation: Human and Divine

MICHAEL WELKER

Over the past decades the terms "relation" and "relationality" have become buzzwords in many popular and academic discourses. All sorts of dynamics and structures have been associated with these terms. In most cases these terms were opposed to other forms of perceiving and thinking constellations of life (e.g., substance-oriented theories) and other attempts to organize forms of life (e.g., abstract individualism). Beyond the discoveries of deficiencies in other modes of orientation, however, they rarely provided sufficient conceptual clarity. Most dominant were conceptions of two different "points of reference" in the so-called "subject-object relation," in which the subjective side was seen as active and privileged by a basic "self-relation," whereas the objective side was regarded as passive or even as constituted by the subject. Over against this subject-object relation the intersubjective "I-Thou relation" was praised and analyzed on different levels of sophistication. Only a few theories moved beyond reflections about the "relatedness" of two self-referential "points of reference." There were, of course, many protests against these simplistic philosophical and religious modes of thinking in one-to-one constellations. But the theoretically more complex and empirically more realistic approaches toward "the subject" and "the object" and toward "intersubjective" processes of communication lost, as a rule, the clarity intended by the term "relation." The admission that the two "reference points" were in themselves of a complex "relationality," or that they were at least embedded in a complex relational setting, was most often paid for with a loss of control of thought in "relational thinking."

My contribution to this volume will challenge the talking and thinking about such "reference points." It proposes to move beyond the popular philosophical and religious thinking connected with these assumptions — even in elementary education. In the *first* part I will start with the simple question: What is the minimum structure required to call a constellation between or in so-called "subjects" or "subjects and objects" "a relation"? Is the collision of two billiard balls already a relation? Is a vague feeling of external presence a relation? Is a fleeting inner intuition already a self-relation? In order to answer my basic question I will center on a qualified contact between a human mental system and an external physical entity or a cluster of entities. What is the minimum required to call the classical so-called "subject-object encounter" a relation? In the *second* part I will reflect on the dynamics of reciprocal, interactive personal relations. The *third* part offers some preliminary reflections on divine-human relations.

The Inner Complexity of a "Relation"

One could assume that "relations" are the simplest "building blocks" or the most elementary "bridges" in natural and social forms of life. Starting from some observations and reflections by Alfred North Whitehead about the organization of thought and the emergence of science and some recent findings about mental development in early childhood, I would like to contest this view. I would like to argue that even the most basic constellations worthy to be called a "relation" (and not just a contact, an encounter without any continuity and any result) are of a breathtaking inner complexity.

"The Organisation of Thought" is the title of the Presidential Address that Whitehead gave to the British Association, Newcastle 1916. A book of his collected essays published a year later bears the same title (*The Organisation of Thought*, 1917; the following numbers in the text refer to Whitehead's article, pp. 105-33). Whitehead starts with reflections on our authentic "experience of life," which is formed by a "flux of perceptions, sensations and emotions" (p. 109). "The most obvious aspect of this field of actual experience is its disorderly character. It is for each person a *continuum*, fragmentary and with elements not clearly differentiated." Whitehead comments: "I insist on the radically untidy, ill-adjusted character of the fields of actual experience from which science starts. To grasp this truth is the first step in wisdom . . ." (p. 110). It is only through complex operations and abstractions that we create "the neat, trim, tidy, exact world which is the goal of scientific thought." We do, however, "imagine that we have immediate experience of a world of perfectly defined objects implicated in perfectly defined events which, as known to us by the direct deliverance of our senses, happen at exact instants of time, in a space formed by exact points . . ." (p. 110). But this imagination is a self-deception. It is not immediate experience, but an imagined continuum organized by thought that gives us these impressions.

Interesting experiments by the Harvard neuroscientist Charles Nelson with six- and nine-month-old babies can lead us into the first stages of the process of constructing the commonsense and later the scientific worlds that we confuse with real immediate experience. Nelson "showed a group of 6-month old babies a photo of a chimpanzee, and gave them time to stare at it until they lost interest. They were then shown another chimp. The babies perked up and stared at the new photo. The infants easily recognized each chimp as an individual — they were fascinated by each new face. . . . By 9 months, those kids had lost the ability to tell chimps apart; but at the same time they had increased their powers of observation when it came to human faces" (Wingert/Brant, *Studying the Baby's Brain*, p. 49). Quite obviously the babies had reduced one type of complexity of perception and had increased another one. In a superficial view and talk, they "related" at six months to each new chimp and lost this ability by nine months. My argument is, that staring at a photo or a real face, even with some energy and intensity, is not yet "relating" to it. By nine months, the babies had reached a higher perceptive level towards the ability to develop "relations."

Extremely complex grids and patterns of observation have to be built in order to "relate" a human mind to its environment or even small parts of it. A multitude of experienced rhythms, the experiences of interruption and discontinuity and recontinuation seem to be basic for the emergence of these patterns. Hunger, thirst, and their satisfaction by nourishment; the experience of wetness, coldness, and then of being clean and warm again; tiredness, sleep, and then awakening — a multitude of experiences generate a complex bodily self-reference. In the early stages of life and experience, however, this complex self-reference is of the untidiness that Whitehead describes; only gradually will it be transformed into a set of self-relations. From the earliest, the intake of nourishment is accompanied by a multi-sensual perception: tactile perceptions, tasting, smelling, the first forms of seeing and hearing, have to be endured, discerned, and correlated. A very complex multi-sensual bodily self-perception and complex patterns of discerning contacts with the environment have to be coordinated. An overwhelming multitude of internal and external stimuli, reactions and activities have to be attuned, hierarchized, and sequenced. Routines and rhythms are experienced and practiced, particularly with the primary contact-persons, who provide nourishment, care, and attention.

Despite the intensity of such connections and the necessity of their sustenance and renewal, it is not necessarily adequate to speak of a "relation" from the side of the infant. The constellation can still lack the *intrinsic continuity, clarity, and definiteness that we connect with the term "relation."* In principle, the cry of the infant could always be answered by new and different feeding persons, although this would probably be bad for the child's emotional development. Gradually the baby will have to sort out different worlds of sounds and noises, bodily and tactile feelings, smells, intensities of lights and colors. In a counterintuitive way the tensions between this multiple complexity and the continued central needs of the child and their satisfaction will drive towards a reduction of the overpowering complexity of perception and experience. Typical correlations of multi-sensual experience create events and areas of familiarity and comfort. Gradually a "relational" experience of familiarity with oneself sets in. On the basis of research done by Martin Hoffmann, a professor of psychology at New York University who studied the experience of empathy in earliest childhood, "researchers played for infants tapes of other babies crying. As predicted, that was enough to start the tears flowing. But when researchers played babies recordings of their own cries, they rarely began crying themselves" (*Studying the Baby's Brain,* p. 47). Obviously, a familiarity with oneself emerges that allows one to discern external and internal challenges to perception and emotion and will eventually evolve into a complex self-relation.

The development of a multitude of complex patterns of perception, their coordination, and finally the abstraction from the uniqueness of each perception and the abstraction from elementary references and self-references open the possibility to establish external relations. A most simple deictic reidentification can have the potential for a relation and can help to illuminate it. A baby points to an object in her environment: she re-cognizes it: "This! There!" What has to happen so that this event can come about?

In the midst of a flux of perceptions, sensations, and emotions, a constellation of colors and shapes somehow had to be identified visually. This external constellation had to be copied into latent memory and imagination (by processes that have to be further analyzed by scientists, if possible). A visual awareness of this constellation repeated several times caused the — potentially repeatable — activation of its memory. The "againness" of the perception became striking. The seemingly simple deictic operation — "This! There!" — expresses the excitement at the successful attunement of the inner and outer worlds, the world of memories and imagination and the world of material for externally conditioned experience.

However, even the complexity of such an operation, which requires complex self-referential and perceptual operations and their attunement, does not yet constitute a "relation." The imagined operation "This! There!" could be a unique event. Only once did the infant point to the yellow fish on the wallpaper — then lost interest in this fish forever. It became part of the wallpaper, the complex environment. The infant did *not* develop a relation to this object. But what is required in order to reach this level?

In order to speak of a "relation" in a meaningful way, a constellation of two or more actual entities in the midst of complex patterns of perception, imagination, and memory has to be actualized in such a way that the perception is accompanied by *a certainty of identity and continuity.* This certainty of identity and continuity can be internally conditioned so that the relation is more or less dominated by the self-relation, the cultivation of memory, imagination, and experience. But a relation can also primarily derive its continuity- and identity-conditioning power from the object and its self-presentation in spacetime, thus conditioning a more reactive constellation on the mental side. In the first case the vividness of the self-referential experience of a reactivation of patterns of memory and imagination sustains the relation to external constellations; in the second case an impressive continuous or repeated constellation in spacetime elicits the relation by again and again activating patterns of memory and imagination. To be sure, both sides are necessary in any "simple relation" in terms of a conscious subject-object encounter.

On this basis we can refine Immanuel Kant's famous statement about the transcendental apperception in §16 of his *Critique of Pure Reason:* "Das: Ich denke muß alle meine Vorstellungen begleiten können" (pp. 140b, "The I think has to potentially accompany all my perceptions"). Kant makes it clear that the "I think" is not an entity that can be calmly imagined and perceived, but a potential dynamic self-awareness that can be activated in all perceptual activity. This is a deeply relational awareness of a relational activity connected with a continuum that we associate with the "inner self." This continuum is neither a mere "reference-point" nor a tabula rasa, an empty intellectual space. It is rather the host of a multitude of sensually conditioned grids and patterns that allow us to copy and to re-construct the world in memories and imaginings. This emotionally loaded, highly active continuum, however, does much more than copy the world of experience into our memory and imagination. There is no such thing as a "neat, trim, tidy, exact world which is the goal of scientific thought," that rests out there, just waiting to be copied. An enormous imaginative creativity, reduced and tamed again and again by mental activity and imposing impressions, has to deal with "radically untidy, ill-adjusted fields of actual experience." Its creative potential allows it to rise far beyond the natural environment into realms of memory and imagination, either long gone by, or only in the making, or never to be incarnated in natural spacetime at all. Expressing ourselves poorly, we usually speak of the "realms of possibilities" that invite the establishment of relations far beyond perceptual relations in the realm of nature.

Reciprocal, Interactive, Personal Relations

The "simple" deictic and not even the perceptual operation that we have imagined and considered on the way to understanding the inner texture of a "relation" is not what most people have in mind when they use this term. With "relation" they usually associate a reciprocal, interactive, person-to-person constellation, a more or less stable I-Thou encounter. In addition, the term "relationality" is also used to represent not only one-on-one interpersonal constellations, but also (though most often vaguely) one-to-many and many-to-many configurations.

As soon as one is aware of the inner complexity of a "simple" perceptual relation, the extremely potentiated complexity of a person-to-person encounter can easily discourage any effort to analyze it. An at least triadic complexity has to be handled even before any explicitly verbal communication sets in. We have to differentiate and attune two realms of memory and imagination with the attempt to relate to a natural environment that we can regard as "common" in order to establish such a relation. Much higher complexities have to be considered when we include language and verbal communication.

It would be a worthwhile task to work on a typology of typical interpersonal relations with different levels of complexity. Since this task is far beyond the scope of this presentation, I will rather — in a kind of top-down approach — consider the question why the relation of "love" can be regarded as the prime example, if not the essence of, perfect interpersonal reciprocal relations.

In order to do this it will not suffice to differentiate between *eros* and *agape* (Anders Nygren), to differentiate a type of love that primarily seeks individual personal fulfillment from a type of love that primarily seeks to serve the needs of the "other." Even triadic differentiations between *eros, agape,* and a more reciprocally balanced *philia* (or *cupiditas, caritas, amicitia*) will not be sufficient to disclose the inner structure of this relation (cf. Welker, in Polkinghorne, *Work of Love;* Welker, "Liebe"). It is the Gospel of John in its description of the love between God the Father and the Son which can also open our eyes to the depth-dimension of human love. John 17:26 says, *I made known to them thy name, and I will make it known, that the love with which thou hast loved me may be in them, and I in them.* An equal manifestation of the Son and a "making home of Father and Son" among the believers is connected with the divine love in which the believers participate (John 14:21ff.).

Here love is depicted as a relation of (mutual) honoring that seeks the honor of the beloved beyond one's own relation of honor to him or her. The loving thus opens the relation for others by praising and revealing the beloved to fellow-creatures. Parental love, which seeks the inclusion of children in the love relation of the parents, is a model for a fully developed love, which also reveals the deficiencies of a romantic or erotic relation or a relation of mercy. Whitehead grasps this mature form of love in non-religious contexts when he speaks of the "love of self-devotion where the potentialities of the loved object are felt passionately as a claim that it find itself in a friendly universe. Such love is really an intense feeling as to how the harmony of the world should be realized in particular objects" (*Adventures of Ideas,* p. 289). Love seeks the unfolding of the beloved beyond one's own fixed conceptions of what would be best for him or her or for both. In the beloved one, the harmony of creation should realize itself beyond one's own preconception. In Whitehead's words, the beloved should concretize his or her relative, real world with all its potentials as well as he or she possibly can. And the loving relation will do everything so that the world concretizes itself favorably in the beloved. All things and everybody should work together for the good of the beloved.

In the relation of love a person's own memories and imaginings try to serve the memories and expectations of the loved one in a way that he or she can best unfold his or her creative potential. The loving person also tries to create and support circumstances in the shared environment that serve him or her best. And he or she does not do this in the attempt to "treat" the beloved well, but to let him or her freely find "a friendly universe." Honoring, encouragement to unfold, and the creative attempt to support this self-unfolding are characteristic of this "relation," which becomes the perfect interpersonal relation in reciprocal co-enhancement.

Core elements of what is essential in a constellation termed "relation" here come to the fore. A "relation" is at least in search of its — not infinite but indefinite — continuity. In a complex and continually changing world it thus requires the paradox of development and unfolding in order to grant relative stability. An ideal "relation" seeks the (revelatory, physical, emotional, cognitive . . .) unfolding of both (or all) sides of a simple or complex correlation, therefore making "truth-seeking communities" a perfect example of flourishing "relational" configurations (cf. Polkinghorne/Welker, *Faith,* esp. chapter 9). Here we argue that the process of co-enhancement of perceptual certainty and cognitive insight that continuously poses and challenges truth-claims in order to reach higher levels of conviction and insight is characteristic for those communities.

Although a relation is directional and clearly oriented, it seeks — at least on one side — in the case of true love, on both sides — dynamic freedom. In doing so it seeks creative continuity, permanence, or even eternity.

The Relation of God to Human Creatures

How could God and human creatures ever "relate" in the sense of the term developed here when mutual access to the other's memory and imagination — and to a common environment — are essential for this constellation? Different religions will give different answers, and some may even waive the claim that we can "relate" to God unless we accept much more one-sided or much more vague connections between God and creatures.

In the Christian perspective it is the incarnational and kenotic presence (cf. Polkinghorne, *The Work of Love,* pp. 90-106) of God — fully revealed in Jesus Christ and witnessed to by his post-Easterly body — that gives us the potential of truly relating to God. Through the Word of God — witnessed to in Scripture and clearly concretized in the person and proclamation of pre- and post-Easter Jesus Christ — we have access to God's memory and imagination.[1] In the body of Christ, in the celebration

---

1. For a discussion of the potentials and difficulties in accessing the mind of God through the exploration of nature, cf. John Polkinghorne and Michael Welker, *Faith in the Living God: A Dialogue* (London: SPCK, 2001), chaps. 1 and 2.

of the sacraments, in proclamation and discipleship, we can share an environment with the resurrected. Compared with many human person-to-person relations, however, this relation is not symmetrical. Despite his incarnational and kenotic presence, God encounters us with his eternal and salvific creativity in the Holy Spirit. God's potentials of sustenance, rescue, and ennoblement in his loving relation to us are far beyond any idea of reciprocity. This does not question the anthropological "realism" of this relation, quite the contrary (cf. Welker, in Jeeves, *From Cells to Souls,* pp. 223-32; Welker, in Soulen/Woodhead, *God,* pp. 317-42). Our doxology and praise, intensive, powerful, and beautiful as they might be, are all too poor and frail to rise to a level of reciprocity with God's creative relation to us. It is, however, in community with Christ and in the power of the Spirit that we become dignified to participate fully in the dynamics of the divine love and life. The proclamatory, sacramental, and diaconal mission of the church witnesses to this relating to, and participating in, God's merciful and ennobling love (cf. Zizioulas, 123ff.; Welker, *Communion,* pp. 167ff.; Schwöbel, pp. 379ff.).

It is the figure of the "pouring of the Spirit" and the notion of "Spirit baptism" that can open our eyes to the complexity of the *divine-human I-Thou encounter,* which is not adequately grasped with an analogy to human person-to-person encounters (cf. Martin's reflections on mobilizations and encounters, this volume; Dunn and Macchia, in Welker, *The Work of the Spirit,* pp. 3ff. and 109ff.). On the one hand, the context-sensitivity and encounter-sensitivity of the Holy Spirit (Polkinghorne/Welker, chapter 5) guarantees the individuality and uniqueness of each creature "encountered" by God. On the other hand, the "relation" of God to the individual creature is never a constellation of just "two points of reference" (cf. the critique of reductionist Trinitarian thinking by Lewis Ayres and Kallistos Ware, in this volume). God, as the triune God, with rich divine creativity, the presence of the post-Easter and elevated Christ, and the power of the Holy Spirit, encounters each creature in its embeddedness in a rich creaturely context, beginning with its differentiated body (cf. Luther's splendid realism in his explication of the first article in his Small and Large Catechisms) and the rich creaturely community — past, present, and future — without which the individual creature would not be what it is (cf. Polkinghorne on the analogy between complex spiritual and scientific "relational" constellations, and Michael Heller on "noncommutative spaces," in this volume).

Michael Welker

Summary

I have argued that "relations" are not connections between two "points of reference." They are more or less successful attempts to connect two or more continua or segments of environments in a way that allows for clarity of impact (or, in higher forms, of insight) and continuity. On this basis we can differentiate immediate and cognitively modeled experience (only on the basis of the latter concepts of "relations" in terms of two reference points). On the basis of the insights so far developed, the creative functions and tasks of "relations" can be made visible. It can be shown why the "relation of love" — in many religious and philosophical traditions — was seen to be the ideal connection between creatures. Finally, we can start contemplating on what is needed from the divine and human side in order to establish a "relation" between the realities formerly depicted as "the reference points God and man."

BIBLIOGRAPHY

Ayres, Lewis. "(Mis)Adventures in Trinitarian Ontology." In this volume.

Dunn, James. "Towards the Spirit of Christ: The Emergence of the Distinctive Features of Christian Pneumatology." In *The Work of the Spirit: Academic Pneumatology and Pentecostalism,* ed. Michael Welker, pp. 3-16. Grand Rapids: Eerdmans, 2006.

Heller, Michael. "A Self-Contained Universe?" In this volume.

Kant, Immanuel. *Kritik der reinen Vernunft.* Hamburg: Meiner, 1956. 2nd ed., 1987.

Macchia, Frank. "The Kingdom and the Power: Spirit Baptism in Pentecostal and Ecumenical Perspective." In *The Work of the Spirit: Academic Pneumatology and Pentecostalism,* ed. Michael Welker, pp. 109-25. Grand Rapids: Eerdmans, 2006.

Martin, David. "A Relational Ontology Reviewed in Sociological Perspective." In this volume.

Nygren, Anders. *Eros und Agape: Gestaltwandlungen der christlichen Liebe.* 2 vols. Gütersloh: Bertelsmann, 1930 and 1937.

Polkinghorne, John. "The Demise of Democritus." In this volume.

Polkinghorne, John. "Kenotic Creation and Divine Action." In *The Work of Love: Creation as Kenosis,* ed. John Polkinghorne. Grand Rapids: Eerdmans; London: SPCK, 2001.

Polkinghorne, John, ed. *The Work of Love: Creation as Kenosis.* Grand Rapids: Eerdmans; London: SPCK, 2001.

Polkinghorne, John, and Michael Welker. *Faith in the Living God: A Dialogue.* London: SPCK; Philadelphia: Fortress, 2001.

Schwöbel, Christof. *Gott in Beziehung. Studien zur Dogmatik.* Tübingen: Mohr Siebeck, 2002.

Ware, Kallistos. "The Holy Trinity: Model for Personhood-in-Relation." In this volume.

Welker, Michael. "The Addressee of Divine Sustenance, Rescue, Salvation and Elevation: Toward a Non-Reductive Understanding of Human Personhood," in *From Cells to Souls — and Beyond: Changing Portraits of Human Nature,* ed. M. Jeeves, pp. 223-32. Grand Rapids: Eerdmans, 2004.

Welker, Michael. "Liebe, Evangelisches Soziallexikon." In *Neuausgabe,* ed. Martin Honecker et al., pp. 959-63. Stuttgart, Berlin, and Köln: Kohlhammer, 2001.

Welker, Michael. "Romantic Love, Covenantal Love, Kenotic Love." In *The Work of Love: Creation as Kenosis,* ed. John Polkinghorne, pp. 127-36. Grand Rapids: Eerdmans, 2001.

Welker, Michael. "Theological Anthropology Versus Anthropological Reductionism." In *God and Human Dignity,* ed. E. K. Soulen and L. Woodhead, pp. 317-42. Grand Rapids: Eerdmans, 2006.

Welker, Michael. *What Happens in Holy Communion?* Translated by John Hoffmeyer. Grand Rapids: Eerdmans, 2000. Second printing 2004.

Welker, Michael, ed. *The Work of the Spirit: Academic Pneumatology and Pentecostalism.* Grand Rapids: Eerdmans, 2006.

Whitehead, Alfred North. *The Organisation of Thought, Educational and Scientific.* London: Williams & Norgate, 1917; reprint Westport, CT: Greenwood Press, 1974.

Whitehead, Alfred North. *Adventures of Ideas.* London: Collier Macmillan, 1967.

Wingert, Pat, and Martha Brant. "Studying the Baby's Brain." *Newsweek,* August 15, 2005, pp. 44-51.

Zizioulas, John. *Being as Communion: Studies in Personhood and the Church.* Crestwood, NY: St. Vladimir's Seminary Press, third printing, 1997.

A Relational Ontology Reviewed in Sociological Perspective

David Martin

The Disciplinary Background

A sociological reflection on the Trinity is odd in more than one way, beginning with its presence in a book where discourse is so largely framed by the natural sciences. That particular oddity is easily justified, however, because it draws attention to other worlds of discourse that may overlap the worlds of natural science but are differently focused on account of the exigencies of a different subject matter. In particular there are properties emerging at the socio-biological and at the social level proper relating to culture, history, human subjectivity, and spontaneity not present in the phenomena of nature. In the example I offer later, of the transparency and mutuality of musical performance, these properties are recapitulated simultaneously, given that musical performance is grounded physically in sonic and acoustic properties activated by neuro-physiological habituation "in the body" and realized in complex social interactions — dyadic, triadic, and so on.

A more substantial oddity lies in the history of the human sciences and in the very nature of their scientific intentionality. Historically the specific intentionality of the human sciences arose as part of an attempt to provide understandings of history and society less heavily weighed down by normative and teleological conceptions. Sociology set out, specifically so in Comte, to occupy the territory once held by theology, and that meant giving a naturalistic account of the role of religion in society, as well, paradoxically, as simultaneously analyzing and embodying secularization. An angle of vision generated in such a way was, and still is, disinclined to treat religious doctrines such as the Trinity as themselves candidates for the augmentation of sociological understanding, or at any rate possessed of features present by analogy and "participation" at the heart of social interaction. In the case of anthropology there were Christian origins in missionary ethnography parallel to the origins of American sociology in the "Social Gospel," but these had to be shed as part of an assertion of proper scientific credentials. Exotic doctrines in other societies might be sympathetically entertained as at least proto-sociological, but doctrines nearer home were taboo.

At the same time there are some affinities between sociological and theological concepts that go beyond questions about how far concepts deployed in social scientific enquiries have a philosophical/theological ancestry. Alienation (Marx) and anomie, that is, normlessness (Durkheim), are not straightforward characterizations of individually variable subjective experience to be measured positivistically by familiar scaling schedules. Instead they have more in common with the concept of sin, given that "sin" characterizes alienation from self and God independent of the degree to which we subjectively recognize it. Again, when sociology is characterized by Habermas as an "emancipatory project" with the goal of mutually determined communication, we are not far from a philosophical/theological notion of redemption, or, indeed, "relational ontology." Of course, all concepts like sin, alienation, and anomie are overgeneralized when it comes to specific situations, such as the civil war in Lebanon, where one first indicates background conditions and then assesses the variable influence of different factors, in particular tipping factors.

What follows now, therefore, is an imaginative journey into Christian theology by a sociologist seeking to discern analogies between disparate discourses, unimpeded by the historical and methodological inhibitions just canvassed. Sociology in a Feuerbachian mode has often discerned the heavenly in the earthly, and that necessarily includes both heavenly harmony (or transparent communication) and the demonic powers of division. The demonic is, after all, sociological territory, except that human science fails to account for the abyss of evil that opens up attendant on certain conditions of social breakdown. By contrast, mathematicians can contemplate beautiful structures of implication seemingly untainted by sin. As this volume illustrates, "corruption" is not part of the vocabulary of the natural sciences, whereas, say, for political sociology it is quite central. Corruption is allowable as a descriptive category, in spite of its moral/ theological resonances, whereas depravity is not. That marks the sociological/theological boundary.

David Martin

An Imago Dei in Human Society?

A sociologist encountering the term "relational ontology" may, if he has any theological background, suspect it has something to do with the Trinity and with the work of Colin Gunton and John Zizioulas. But he might well prefer to start with his own discipline rather than the discipline of systematics, a distant academic country of which he knows little. That means moving from the bottom up in terms of sociology rather than from the top down, and concentrating initially at least on what can be directly known, not what can only be known indirectly. A helpful sociological prolegomenon has already been written by Andrew Walker in his contribution to *The Forgotten Trinity* (1991), edited by Alasdair Heron, and that is something I need to pursue further rather than repeat. After an expert survey of different schools Andrew Walker extracts certain clues "from below" of possible relevance to Trinitarian thought. These are, that there cannot be an asocial "me" given that the socialized "me" depends on similarly socialized others, and that the necessity of language entails a relation between communion and communication. He then adds (p. 154) what might be the key text for what follows here: "How does the imago dei in human society correspond to God's community? In what sense is the church as the ecclesia the ikon of divine love? Is human personhood only realizable eschatologically?" In terms of intellectual mapping this kind of approach lies midway between the impersonal discourse of physicists and the transpersonal discourse of theologians. I shall indicate in due course how its particular scientific intentionality is focused on patterns and structures of mutual interaction between persons in a universe governed by meaning.

Clearly the incarnation as the outgoing or manifestation of God is the axis around which specifically Christian thinking has to turn. But I want to begin with the Spirit because it more easily enables me to take humanity as my frame of reference and avoid any confinement to church. Insofar as I think about the church I do so less in its extant empirical reality and more with respect to what its explicit liturgical enactments and embodiments imply about our generic human experiences of communion. This takes us back to the link between the specific enactment of "holy communion" and communication as such, hinted at in the linguistic usage whereby the priest or minister "communicates" the faithful.

Let us suppose then that the "performing art" of liturgy with respect to Holy Communion, baptism, marriage, and charismatic outpouring is an explicit institutional enactment of generic human experience in some sense available *en plein air*. All of these imitate the kenotic self-giving of Christ as expressing God's Being realized in relation and going out, from the One to the other, that is love. That at any rate is how Christians read God in their liturgical performances.

I said I wanted to begin with the Spirit, that is, with charismatic outpouring, because that more easily enables me to go beyond what is explicit in the church to what is implicit in generic human experience. I know there are problems in this approach, but I want to take it as a starting point and let the problems emerge rather than letting my foreknowledge inhibit exploration from the start. After all, in the liturgical sequence, the charismatic outpouring of the Spirit on the church is understood by reference to the prophetic promise in Joel about the outpouring of the Spirit on all flesh, meaning humanity as such. So this move is biblically based and not just a reflection of contemporary concerns with "spirituality." And since our focus is the Trinity it makes sense for me to focus on Pentecost as the feast immediately preceding and leading up to the celebration of the Trinity.

The original outpouring of the Spirit in the second chapter of Acts picked up the oekumene of the Greco-Roman world, as well as enabling all peoples to hear in their own language the generic original tongue of humanity prior to the onset of Babel. Put colloquially, people discovered in the assembly that aliens were also neighbors who "spoke their language" and shared their understanding. Cultures as linguistic communities were no longer mutually exclusive but susceptible to translation. So we are speaking of the translatability of culture through the common Spirit as both the birthday of the church and the birthday of all flesh, one humanity united and indivisible under God. I use this American language about the birthday of the USA to suggest that the birthday of the church and of restored, united humanity at Pentecost is realized in all kinds of ways beyond the specifically ecclesiastical or even explicitly religious format, notably in modern times to indicate the inclusive/exclusive communion of the nation. It is here, of course, that we encounter the problem with this kind of extra-institutional move, since nations are, like the church, not united, and like the church they have boundaries, and like the church, their unity may be malign as well as benign. On the other hand if nation and church share so many characteristics, and are often fused as well as contradictory and rivalrous versions of the sacred, it may make good sense to relate what happens in the mobilization of the church to what happens in the mobilization of the nation. In short, we can analyze both kinds of mobilization as alternative and sometimes fused outpourings of the Spirit, for example in the French Revolution, which was a kind of alternative liturgical performance of nation against church, and in the Polish movement of Solidarity where the ecclesiastical and national liturgies were fused together. Again, the differences between the national and the ecclesiastical understandings of liturgical celebration can be put on one side, for the moment. I mean, of course, the false transcendence claimed by the nation from a Christian viewpoint.

This prolegomenon should make the next steps relatively easy to articulate. The pre-eminent spiritual mobilizations of the modern era with a pan-human scope have been the Anglo-American Revolution 1642-1776, combining Christian and Enlightenment elements in concepts of Covenant and Commonwealth, and the French and Russian Revolutions based on a militant and triumphant "church of secularism." All have spawned secondary progeny with similar features, and all have generated counter-mobilizations that have in most cases called religion in aid: Ireland in relation to Britain, Eastern Europe in 1989 in relation to Russia, and Islam (with its distinctive monotheistic vocabulary) in relation to the USA and the West generally. Both the initial pan-human revolutions (which also have particular nationalist locations) and the particular mobilizations have liturgical and charismatic features in common, and like Christianity, their prototype, are prone to the same deformations.

The 2004 "Orange Revolution" in Ukraine may serve as a useful site for the kind of argument I want to make, by way of locating the universal in a dramatic particular. Up to one million people stood for two weeks in the freezing cold in the Maidan, the main square of Kiev, stimulated by television and a continuous concert. This was an entirely peaceable assembly in what could have been a confrontation with the military, as well as civil war between Ukrainian-speaking west and Russian-speaking east. In this assembly people were mobilized by processional banners and by wearing orange as their liturgical color. The television coverage (BBC 4, 15th May, 2005) suggested a more explicit religious link by cutting from the charismatic outpourings of the assembly to Ukrainians around the common table sharing the bread and wine of the Eucharist, as a kind of analogue of the self-sacrificing provision by support workers of comfort and sustenance to the thousands in the square. The assembly represented a kind of mystic marriage between people as persons, once strangers and aliens but now as one in the spirit: "I in you and thou in me."

Glossing it theologically but also in terms of real human experience, there was an "I-Thou" relationship suffusing the whole assembly. People spoke of being "born again" and of having been willing to set their faces to go to the capital and if necessary give their own precious blood for the fraternity of freedom and the rebirth of the nation. So, the explicit themes of Christianity appeared either openly or implicitly: the charismatic outpouring of Pentecost and sense of one common language of aspiration, the redemptive giving of blood, and the analogy of the "relational ontology of the Trinity" in the universal discovery of full personhood, the I-Thou relationship in its ecstasy of giving and receiving. Women gave birth in the assembly as a kind of analogy of collective rebirth, and people were married in public by way of analogy with the "mystic marriage" going on collectively all around them.

I referred earlier to the deformation such movements easily undergo, given that the appearance of the imago dei in each and everyone present becomes clouded over with the cast of sin, renewed alienation, and despair. For example, corruption and internal conflict rapidly dissipated the spirit of Ukraine's Orange Revolution. Assemblies can be malign and exclusive as well as benign and inclusive, so that the I-Thou relationship (as in Nazi Germany) turns into a descent into hell, not an ascent into heaven. That is what it means to say that full personhood is eschatological and what it means to add that the analogy of the Trinity present in the assembly is *only* an analogy and for the time being. The eternal relations of the Trinity remain as a transcendent ikon even when the heavenly city, New Jerusalem, hovers tantalizingly for a moment over the city of man.

The Sociological Approach

Thus far I have taken the sociological viewpoint for granted, as though we all know what that means and as though sociologists themselves were agreed about appropriate methods and modes of understanding. Taking the sociological viewpoint for granted is initially necessary in order to say anything at all, but at some point one needs to make clear what that involves and what decisions flow from it.

As a human science, sociology has subject matter as well as object matter. The subject matter includes a specific repertoire of motivations operating within a particular universe of cultural meanings. That specificity and that particularity are linked to an ideographic character, whereas object matter generally exhibits a nomothetic character. The distinction was made originally by Wilhelm Dilthey, and comes down to the idea that where human subjectivity and cultural particularity are concerned the nomothetic approach based on generalization and universal laws has only limited application. Generalizations do exist, for example concerning the conditions likely to generate scapegoating; but once one tries to formulate them they tend to involve specification of a spectrum of typical situations, while scapegoating as a concept turns out to be semantically multi-valent, fluid, and characterized by poorly marked boundaries. Concepts are differently inflected according to cultural and linguistic context.

In short, a subject matter rooted in subjective motives and understandings involves language rather than mathematics. Even where mathematics is deployed in the human sciences — for example, in demography and in economics — it is either tied to human subjectivity, with all that this means for the prospect of predictability, including prediction based on average tendencies, or it involves a degree of abstraction remote from actual cases. The predictions possible in such cases require a rubric based on the standard notion of "other things being equal," except that in practice the "other things" are excessively numerous, as well as conceptually interfused and overlapping. This is because one is not dealing with delimited, bounded "things" at all, but with situations. Most of the time in sociology one holistically grasps situations. This is not at all esoteric, because politicians, for example, do it all the time. You simply grasp out of your previous experience what is going on, try to give it intellectual shape, and sketch more or less likely scenarios about how matters will develop. This makes the notion of causality (in this volume promoted by Wesley Wildman) problematic in sociology because, though one can state initial conditions and trace the variable impact of different variables, one is also dealing with this or that dynamic nexus or *gestalt,* and with events originating in individual wills, motives, and imaginations. Cause easily implies asymmetry and priority, whereas social situations include mutual encounters, negotiations, and adjustments.

All this has implications for what I have said above with respect to the Trinity, understood as a kind of sign language about the divine nature, especially the relation of creator and the creator spirit to incarnation in humanity. If sociology is rooted in language — in signs, symbols, and codes that are dense, continuous, resistant to atomization, and essentially dependent on their interrelations — then it shares some characteristics with the Trinity. I mean that the sociological mode constitutes a "field" of interpenetrating implication. My "subject" shares some characteristics with our present "subject of discussion" which is the Trinity, and these are not just incidental analogues as might sometimes be the case in the physical sciences, but inherent.

In using a formulation of this kind I am voicing a viewpoint within sociology that would be contested, particularly by my more positivistic colleagues. I referred earlier to the initial decision I made before starting to write, which was to exploit the internal resonances of a semantic field. Of course, I do not as a sociologist take up any prior position on questions within or about religion itself since methodological agnosticism is of the essence of scientific intentionality. But I do exploit the semantic field of language in a way contrary to the approach of those colleagues who try to denude language of resonance and sometimes invent a special terminology. Either they invent terms or use ordinary terms with inverted commas to suggest a specific sociological take on ordinary usages.

I have now returned quite specifically to the first section of my essay because I there tried to suggest how what is liturgically explicit in the semi-bounded community of "the church" can also be used in a resonant way about generic human experience. I have also made a decision to reject the reductionist view whereby the explicit ecclesiastical language of transcendent communion enjoyed by embodied human beings is *merely* a "topped up" version of generic human experience when people come together and discover their unity of heart and mind and their Pentecostal ability to "speak each other's language." Rather than "reduction" I have, by way of methodological tactic, done the opposite. I have seen the transcendent in the immanent rather than reducing the transcendent to the immanent. If anyone wants to object to that procedure they cannot do so on scientific grounds. The objection is inherently philosophical. Translating *up* and translating down (or reducing) are tactically dependent not on scientific criteria but on philosophical ones about the primacy of the immanent.

I need to pursue further what I have so far said about the nature of a scientific intentionality when dealing with a human science that includes human subjectivity. Given limited possibilities for a mathematical rendering of the data, and the centrality of grasping holistically the logic of situations in a way in principle available to anyone, I find myself engaged qua sociologist in a conversational relationship with some other person or persons. For me what is constitutive in that relationship is my initial readiness to take seriously what the other persons have to say. After all, their language may already embody a proto-sociology or even an explicit sociology, given that we live in a sociologically permeated culture. I cannot impose a sociological translation without *first* listening properly to what my subject matter has to say about what matters to him or her. Human beings talk *back,* whereas there is not much talk back in crystallography. Thus the I-Thou or eye-to-eye relationship emerges quite centrally in my scientifically intentional scrutiny of, and conversation with, fellow humans. That is true even in economics, where fellow humans can read my predictions, other things being equal, and make things conspicuously unequal by altering course to falsify or circumvent them. Indeed, my prediction may actually be made in order for them to do just that. The rubric of contingencies accompanying any prediction based on the principle of "if this then that" expands almost minute by minute by way of constantly shifting mutual adjustments.

Real and Seeming Analogies: Music

Colleagues in the natural sciences adduce certain relationships that might be analogous to Trinitarian relations in theology. I am not equipped, to put it mildly, to assess how far these are more incidental than genuinely significant. But I want to make some comments on the nature of such analogies, and the different ways they may arise in the human compared with the natural sciences. The modus operandi seems to differ in the two cases. My colleagues in natural science are more prone to ask whether there are phenomena in the natural world that might mirror those of the Trinity. I, however, have a differently structured problematic because the person-to-person relationality present in holistically understood situations is fundamental to my scientific intentionality. After all, love and communion, along with division and alienation, are inherent in my subject matter, and insofar as there is humanity in the Godhead there is an inherent rather than an incidental overlap between sociologist and theologian. Indeed, if I may also call myself a theologian, I engage in cross-talk with myself.

Some analogies between divine and human activity can I think be put on one side. For example, the primacy in some sense of the Father in the Trinity (whereby the Son "delivers up the kingdom to the Father") cannot be translated humanly as the natural primacy of the monarch as it was in the seventeenth century, or as the natural primacy of the Holy Father. One can dismiss such obviously interested applications, which are in any case top-down rather than bottom-up.

Other analogies are very different and I shall now locate them, not in politics as in my first section, but in what seems like the very different activity of music-making. Patterns of interpersonal mutuality in the arts are rather different from the examples of heightened intersubjectivity earlier canvassed in the field of politics, though it is worth noticing that the "spirit" of the demonstrators in Kiev was in part maintained by music. Like politics and like religion, music is a collective practice and a discipline. It has strong historical links with both in terms of parades and processions, especially when heightened consciousness partly fuses religion with politics. A perfect example would be the way music provides a deeper resonance to the Remembrance Day ceremony in Whitehall. What is conspicuous about Remembrance Day is the juxtaposition of social order and precedence with the complete equality and unity of everyone in the face of sacrifice and death. This example also suggests that it might be worth exploring social analogies of precedence and order, as well as the juxtaposition of silence and music. (There is, according to Revelation 8:1, silence in heaven as well as music.) With respect to precedence and order juxtaposed with unity I have in mind the statement in the Creed "qui procedit ex patre (filioque)" and its social analogues. In sociology it is the abundance of analogies to be found, more or less loose, that is the problem, rather than any difficulty about finding them.

Music and especially musical performance offers an example of what is involved in mutual co-determination. Part of the appeal of this analogy lies in the way so many agnostics take music seriously in a way they do not take theology. They seem not to realize how close the connection is both experientially and historically. If you attend a musical performance as though invited in to share the act of communion with the performers, you are aware of their union of difference and commonality. You are also aware (and here I draw on my own experience as a performer "in concert" with others) of the relationship between neurological responses rendered automatic (determined, if you like) by practice, and the possibility of interpretative freedom. Here we encounter an analogy of the divine discipline and freedom of love. Performers are like high-wire acrobats who know precisely how, when, and where they will join hands. Their freedom is dependent on habituation, and their capacity to express it is as dependent on discipline as love is dependent on following a rule. In music the properties emerging in evolution from the physical to the biological, neurological, and cultural are simultaneously recapitulated.

Looking at them one also sees a mutual inclination of bodies derived from that total attention to the "thing in itself" one might call love, in this case love of music and love expressed in music. The physical manifestations are intakes of breath, bracings, and nods, but what transpires is closer than breathing. That total intimacy is suggested by the etymology of the word "trans-spire," and the linkages of this type provided by etymology are often profound clues to understanding. Self or person is simultaneously expressed and surpassed — an example of what Robert Bridges in *The Testament of Beauty* called "self expressed in not-self, without which no self were." Ordinary punctuated time is surpassed in an enclave of perfect musical timing dictated by a regularity rooted in breathing itself: incarnate not ex-carnate. The potential meaninglessness of "secular" time is overcome by an equivalent of the "higher time" of liturgy through a sequence based on a musical telos realized, made real, at each and every moment. Eros becomes agape without denying the body or the erotic. If there is a social analogy of the "relational ontology" of the Trinity I would find it in musical performance; and it is, of course, an analogy constantly recurrent in the Bible, poetry, and the literature of devotion.

To explore the richness of analogical implication in word and music with regard to the Trinity is quite contrary to Francis Bacon's manifesto of proper natural science in his *Novum Organum,* where language is not a portal to understanding but an idol that stands in the way of observation.

The Argument Summarized So Far

By way of recapitulation: I began with the idea of the imago dei in human society and in the generic human experience of kenotic outgoing of spirit from one to another in love. I then moved to the activation or mobilization of the spirit of communion and union in church and nation. Ecclesiastical and national mobilizations have common liturgical and charismatic features, and some mutual translatability whatever their differences in grammar. However, just as this reflects a shared imago dei, so the onset of deformation and of renewed alienation, division, and despair reflects the Fall. Indeed, all New Jerusalems setting out to restore the divine image in man re-enact the Fall, leaving Jerusalem which is "the mother of us all" still "above" and beyond. Its real presence on earth only manifests itself *hic et nunc* in the liturgical enclave as an eschatological sign.

A second part of the essay attempts to look at what is assumed by the first, given that sociology has human relations as its subject matter whereas (put crudely) the natural sciences take "matter" for their subject. That means in turn that, like religion, or at any rate the incarnation in Christianity, its generality and capacity to generalize is circumscribed by particularity, by the holistic character of the particular situation resistant to precise experimental replication, by a contingency necessary for human freedom, by the semantic depth of language both as "Word" and "Image," and by checks on mutual translatability across cultural difference. As I shall suggest later, the principle of partial translatability is of wide-ranging applicability, including the translatability of God (or his kingdom) into society.

Further Explorations:
The Double Structure and Partial Translatability

Part of the thrust of this book and therefore of this chapter is to explore possible consonances or resonances between what we understand about nature and the way Christians understand God, and that leads naturally to more personal statements of theological position. One response to that exploration found in at least one other chapter is to say that nature is the mind of God, for example in being consistent, beautiful, and entirely self-sufficient, which, so far as it goes, is at best deistic rather than Christian. It is quite a standard position. However, I do not know of anybody who suggests that *society* is the mind of God. The science of society has traditionally excluded such questions from its remit, for reasons already noted, though the sociologist is by training disposed to suspect that when natural scientists discover a consonance between what they uncover of the structures of nature and the nature of God in, say, the Trinity, that has as much to do with their particular socialization into a given religious tradition as with any objectively valid course of reasoning. In this context holding a mirror up to nature is liable to result in an image of ourselves.

There is, however, more to be said beyond this standard skeptical comment. The works of the sociological founders have varied theological implications. Thus, sociologists working within a Durkheimian tradition whereby religion and God are alike subsumed in the "conscience collective" are unlikely to make much of a Trinity which is beyond both nature and society.

Max Weber, however, has an approach that is quite open-ended and can provide stepping-stones part way across the divide between sociology and theology. Whereas conventional scientism dismisses differences between religions as just so many varieties of mistake about our historical, social, and natural worlds, Weber sees the world religions in particular as a limited set of options organized in terms of attitudes to "the world," from negative to positive, and of degrees of transcendence and immanence, that is, how far God is within and/or beyond the world. These basic attitudes generate symbol systems (I call them "tables of symbolic affinity") with profound implications for the economic, political, aesthetic, and erotic spheres of human existence.

In the specific case of Christianity a combination of negative and positive attitudes, and of transcendence and immanence, of what is created good but fallen, creates a dynamic tension between "now" and what was in the beginning and will come to be in "God's good time." We take this tension for granted, until confronted by another civilization animated (say) by a principle of natural and ethical harmony, or Stoic acceptance of the way things are. The symbol systems generated by Christianity have a double reference: eros and agape; treasures on earth contrasted with treasures in heaven; the things of God and the things of Caesar; the "powers" and the power of the Spirit; material and heavenly food. The family will be validated but also relativized through a validation of sexual abstinence and celibacy. The continuity of generation through "the fathers" and their seed will be validated but spiritually broken into, so that we are "born again" into a spiritual fraternity — "not by the will of the flesh but by the will of God."

Now I am bit by bit moving on from Weber's stepping-stones into theological deep waters. Tensions such as I have just illustrated can be suppressed by dismissing the worldly side as illusory compared with the Spirit, or by invoking a Master-slave relationship whereby a totally transcendent God (as in Job) slaps down our human questioning of his sovereign dispositions. Within Christianity the tension will sometimes move in this wholly transcendent direction through worship of the sovereign Father (and respect for his patriarchal earthly representatives), and sometimes towards outbreaks of indiscriminate immanence when the sons and daughters absorb the Father, and reverse the Fall by a dramatic re-entry into Eden. They are now once more beyond good and evil and are "as gods." These extreme swings within the overall Christian tension amount, on the one hand, to the non-translatability of God on account of his utter transcendence, and on the other, to his total translatability on account of our assumption of his prerogatives. The principle of the Trinity, based on the human incarnation of the Son (and our adoption or transfiguration as sons and daughters by grace), exemplifies a partial translatability.

When humans proclaim their own "transfiguration," the dynamic tension introduced by double-natured concepts with both a heavenly and earthly reference lapses. Eden and eschaton become one, and humanity experiences the mystical coincidence of opposites. In mainstream traditions, however, the Edenic and the eschatological remain dynamic potentials, checked by the ravages of sin, alienation, and division, so that union with Christ in the fraternal communion of each and all is by grace, or, indeed, by grace alone. The kingdom of God is held back, a latent pressure or, indeed, a lure enticing and inspiring people forward, but it has not "come on earth as it is in heaven." Thus the peace of God is "realized" only in principle, for example in sacramental symbolism, or in intermittent attempts to extend peaceable fellowship to strangers or to enemies. Such realizations remain dogged by sin. God and the perfect fraternal fellowship of the redeemed whom Christ has brought into communion with the Father of All, remain "above." If that were not so, the "temple" and the church as symbolic colonies of heaven realized in sacred spaces on earth would be abolished, as they are in the City of God, New Jerusalem. The Mass would need no *Sanctus* because all would cry *Sanctus, Sanctus, Sanctus* unceasingly. Absolution would be permanent and *Kyrie Eleison* redundant, and we would all be in a state of *Requiem Aeternam*. The *felix culpa* of Adam would no longer be operative, and change would cease.

Such a state is effectively "realized eschatology" and far from being a purely notional end-point is regularly asserted and anticipated in notions like "an end to history," the end of contradiction, and Kant's "Eternal Peace." Its theological name is "angelism," meaning that the changeful dynamic of "blessed sin" meriting "so great redemption" has been surpassed. In short, Dame Julian of Norwich was right: "Sin is behovely."

I conclude by illustrating the notion of "partial translatability," which is the key to everything just argued. The Father is not "emptied out" into humanity by the incarnation (or *kenosis*) of the Son, even though his tabernacle is now established "among men." When human beings ascend with Christ into "the bosom of the Father," they do not become so transfigured that they are "as gods," beyond good and evil (with all the horrors that entails). The vocabulary pertaining to God, such as the "glorious liberty of the sons of God," is not translatable without remainder into either liberal political freedom or radical and comprehensive liberation from oppression. In other words, God remains transcendent and is *not* dissolved in the "fiery brook" of Feuerbach. The Pentecostal unity of understanding when each and all are transpresent to each other in the communion of the Spirit, remains a *sign*, a potential constantly encountering new barriers to mutual understanding, and meeting fresh resistances, for example the reassertion of ethnic differences, as happened in the early church and in early Pentecostalism post-1906. That means that while history may be punctuated by liturgical moments when peaceful processions enter the city to occupy sacred space, as on Palm Sunday, these are always dissipated in the "divisions" of the political made manifest on Good Friday.

Palm Sunday processions into the city are both exemplary and momentary because from the moment of their inception there will be divided counsels about what practical steps follow from their success, and about who is to reap the benefits. This provides yet another illustration of the principle of partial translation, because the mutuality of I-Thou relationships runs into a coiled-up resistance, which in the Christian narrative rapidly brings about a confrontation between the hostility of "the powers" and divine humanity on Good Friday. The physical nature of power confronts the nature of spiritual power in a dramatization of the dual nature of the concept of power.

The principle of a double reference is easily assimilated to the principle of binary opposition to create a structuralist account of Christian theology that is both synchronous (that is, based on simultaneous contrasts) and diachronous (that is, based on contrasts over time). The contrasts between real city and spiritual city, real temple and spiritual temple, are complemented by contrasts over time between real manna in the wilderness and spiritual food and drink, or between Joshua crossing the Jordan into a Promised Land and Jeshua (Jesus) entering the waters of baptism to receive the "recognition" of the Spirit, or between the crossing of the Red Sea to liberty and the Easter passage through death to resurrection. In other words, Christian typology is easily rendered in structuralist terms, and so available for theological as well as sociological deployment.

The Reformation as treated by Weber can then be rendered as a partial collapse of the binary reference assisted by a partial return to major aspects of Judaism. In particular the spiritual aura or "treasure" attached to holy poverty once again reverts to the invocation of prosperity, while the link between virginity, fraternity, and resurrection becomes opaque and inconceivable. It is, after all, the Virgin Mother who both presides over the radical fraternities of the Spirit and is the temple of the Trinity, alongside her more "conservative" roles as guardian of the biological family and patroness of real cities. The spiritual fathers in God once again become real patriarchs in the biological family (and patriarchal monarchs in the family of the nation). The spiritual brotherhoods are reassimilated to natural formations, in particular unitarian brotherhoods closely related to the affirmation of ethnicity, such as the Masons, the Orange Order, and the South African *Broederbund*. The most obvious retentions of the double reference in Protestantism are found in the idea of conscience as an inviolable inner sanctum over against social consensus, and then in the idea of the spiritual journey, or pilgrim's progress to the heavenly city. Of course, that progress can also revert to a real journey to a real city, as it clearly did in the history of American colonization and of the American New Israel. (There is no space to follow through the reversion to real cities and real wars in unitarian Islam, though it is obvious enough.) What I am doing here is wondering aloud whether unitarianism, which is historically "progressive" in relation to the monarchical appropriations of the Trinity by powers that be in church and state, may not also suppress the double structure, either by fiat of pure transcendence as in Sunni Islam, or by converting eschatology into a doctrine of immanent progress, as in the "Civil Religion" of the American New Israel/New Rome.

I have been attempting to show that some modes of sociological analysis can "ground" theology while retaining their proper scientific intentionality. The underlying premise is that the properties emergent at the social level of analysis permit a range of analytical analogies and an overlap of modes of analytic understanding very significantly different from what may be available in the sciences of nature.

BIBLIOGRAPHY

Berger, Peter. *A Far Glory.* New York: Doubleday, 1992.

Berger, Peter. *A Rumour of Angels.* London: Penguin, 1969.

Burke, Kenneth. *The Rhetoric of Religion.* Berkeley: University of California Press, 1970.

Davies, Douglas. *Anthropology and Theology.* Oxford: Berg, 2002.

Flanagan, Kieran. *The Enchantment of Sociology.* London: Macmillan; New York: St. Martin's Press, 1996.

Gill, Robin. *The Social Context of Theology.* London: Mowbray, 1975.

Martin, David. *The Breaking of the Image.* Oxford: Blackwell, 1978.

Martin, David. *On Secularization.* London: Ashgate, 2005.

Martin, David. *Christian Language and Its Mutations.* London: Ashgate, 2002, chapters on music.

Martin, David. *Reflections on Sociology and Theology.* Oxford: Blackwell, 1997.

Taylor, Charles. *The Secular Age.* Cambridge, MA: Harvard University Press, 2007.

Taylor, Charles. *Sources of the Self.* Cambridge: Cambridge University Press, 1989.

Taylor, Charles. *Varieties of Religion Today.* Cambridge, MA: Harvard University Press, 2002.

Afterword: "Relational Ontology," Trinity, and Science

SARAH COAKLEY

The essays gathered in this volume of contributions from theologians and scientists present a great variety of perspectives on the central topic of "relational ontology." In this short closing section, I should like to return to some of the overarching (and unifying) themes outlined by John Polkinghorne in his Introduction, but impart to them a somewhat sharper critical gaze and a deeper historical contextualization. In effect I shall offer only two basic points of discussion and critique, but both are internally complex. Taken together, they offer some systematic choices that have to be made in charting the relation between the Trinitarian God and the ontological makeup of the physical world, such as this book proposes.

First, I shall attempt to draw out — and highlight — the differences of perspective evidenced in this volume over the central theological question of *Trinitarian* "relationality." Much hangs on this issue, not only for the constellating unity of the science and religion perspectives in the book, but also for ongoing scholarly debates about classical Christian trinitarianism, and thence for ecumenical understanding between Eastern and Western Christianity. And it may not be wholly obvious to the general reader that an internal discussion and development of ideas on this topic is going on even within the pages of this volume: between East and East, and West and West, as well as between East and West. In making the history and substance of this contemporary debate about classical trinitarianism a little more explicit, I also aim to effect a stronger ecumenical understanding — not to loosen the bonds of theological *rapprochement.* The clarification will also be of significance for the matter of how the lines of connection are to be drawn between Trinitarian relationality and forms of created relationality, as we shall see.

Second, and more briefly, I shall return once more to the very concepts of "relation" and "causation" that undergird, *philosophically,* the various efforts in this book to make fruitful connections between physics and theology. Here my efforts may seem rather more analytic than actually constructive: I propose only to lay bare some of the ambiguities in these notoriously complicated philosophical concepts. The forays made in this book between theology and physics are indeed matters of conceptual "entanglement" (though not in the technical sense utilized by physicists!). The crucial and debatable issues are what *sort* of "relation" is in question in the two fields, whether such "relation" is "causal," and — if so — in what sense of "causation" itself. Again, I do not claim to be able to resolve the differences of viewpoint evidenced in these pages, but rather to turn a brief clarificatory gaze on some of the most vexed philosophical issues that cause such divisions.

But first, to the crucial theological issue of "relationality" in the Trinity.

Relational Ontology and the Trinity

In order to clarify the current interest in "relational ontology," and to explain the differences of theological opinion present in this book, it may be illuminating to make some of the themes in the recent history of Trinitarian thinking explicit.

The broader backdrop of the views of the Trinity expressed in this book is the remarkable regeneration of Trinitarian theology that occurred, in more than one stage of development, during the twentieth century. We might talk with hindsight of three "waves" of such renewal, each involving a certain dialectical complexity of its own. In the first instance (let us call it the "late-modern" development), there was a highly creative rethinking of the Eastern Patristic heritage that occurred among Russian emigrés in Paris in the years after the Russian Revolution (Vladimir Lossky being a leading exponent, although by no means the first).[1] While Lossky newly

---

1. Sergei Bulgakov anticipated some of Lossky's themes: on this, see, among the most recent discussions of this modern Russian reclamation of the "Eastern" Patristic heritage, Aristotle Papanikolaou and George E. Demacopoulos, eds., *Orthodox Readings of Augustine* (Crestwood, NY: St. Vladimir's Seminary Press, 2008), esp. pp. 21-24 on Bulgakov; and

constructed a vision of the "Mystical Theology of the Eastern Church," wrought out of his rereading of the Greek fathers, and set it over against what he saw as the dead, rational hand of "Western scholasticism,"[2] it is not the least of the ironies of this story that influences from some modern *Western* authors were actually at the same time impinging upon him as well. He drew appreciatively, for instance, on the magisterial historical work on the Trinity of the Jesuit Théodore de Régnon, citing de Régnon's opinion that, "The Latins think of personality as a mode of nature; the Greeks think of nature as the content of the person."[3] This remark of de Régnon's has however been much misunderstood (and even more so of late, it seems). It was *not* de Régnon who suggested a disjunction between Augustine and the Cappadocians on the Trinity (since for de Régnon "Latin" meant medieval "scholastic"); and nor was it he who was responsible for the view that "East" and "West" have irreducibly disjunctive approaches to the Trinity — quite the opposite, in fact.[4] De Régnon himself was operating against the backdrop of a hardening Roman neo-scholasticism immediately after Vatican I, and was seeking, in a suitably diplomatic way, to lead Catholic theology back to the Patristic sources and to an appreciation of the *complementary* emphases that he saw in Greek, and later Latin scholastic, theologies. But for Lossky's purposes de Régnon's pedagogic attempts at generalization (in the course of a very long

---

Paul L. Gavrilyuk, "The Reception of Dionysius in Twentieth-Century Eastern Orthodoxy," in *Re-Thinking Dionysius the Areopagite*, ed. Sarah Coakley and Charles M. Stang (Oxford: Wiley-Blackwell, 2009), chap. 12, and esp. pp. 179-82 on Bulgakov.

2. Vladimir Lossky, *The Mystical Theology of the Eastern Church* (orig. 1944; ET London and Cambridge: James Clarke, 1957), see esp. chaps. 1-3. For Lossky's attempt to mark off "Eastern" mystical theology as utterly distinct from its "Western" forms, even given the shared resource of the Pseudo-Dionysius, see Rowan Williams, "Lossky, the *Via Negativa* and the Foundations of Theology," in *Wrestling with Angels: Conversations in Modern Theology*, ed. Mike Higton (London: SCM Press, 2007), chap. 1.

3. Lossky, *Mystical Theology,* p. 58, citing de Régnon's *Études de théologie positive sur la St. Trinité*, vol. 1 (Paris: Victor Retaux, 1892), p. 433.

4. On de Régnon and some current misunderstandings about him, see Kristin Hennessy, "An Answer to de Régnon's Accusers: Why We Should Not Speak of 'His' Paradigm," *Harvard Theological Review* 100 (2007): 179-97, esp. 196 for her conclusions. Hennessy comments incisively on an important earlier article by Michel Barnes, "De Régnon Reconsidered," *Augustinian Studies* 26 (1995): 51-79, which had already highlighted Lossky's reliance on (and partial distortion of) de Régnon's position; but not — unfortunately — without inadvertently precipitating a spate of further false readings of de Régnon's views. De Régnon is emphatically not responsible for a disjunctive reading of "Eastern" and "Western" trinitarianisms, as Hennessy elegantly shows.

and complicated historical study) were used to instigate his own new rhetorical *disjunction* between "Eastern" trinitarianism and "Western" trinitarianism; and this was a proposal much less irenically motivated than was de Régnon's original intent. As stated by Lossky, the Greeks "start from the concrete" (i.e., the *hypostasis*),[5] whereas "For the West, the relations diversified the primordial unity."[6] "Relationality" and "personhood" — themes at the heart of classical Patristic trinitarianism — had become a newly polemical matter in Lossky's account.[7]

Simultaneously in Europe, however, another — parallel — renewal of trinitarianism had been occurring in the work of the great Protestant (Reformed) thinker, Karl Barth. Rather than going back first to writings of the Greek fathers, as Lossky did, Barth had made the doctrine of the Trinity the authoritative *"theologoumenon"* of the first volume of his *Church Dogmatics* as a hallmark of his turn away from any rational or experiential grounding of theology, and a return to the sheer "givenness" of biblical revelation.[8] In both Lossky and Barth, however — different as they were in their starting-points — there was a shared, but implicit, concern to loose Trinitarian thinking from any vulnerability to critique from secular philosophy or science, and thereby to evade the metaphysical roadblock that had seemingly been constructed impassibly by Kant against all doctrinal speculation about God-in-Godself. There are interesting ironies in the fact that the debates in this current book can climb on the shoulders of Lossky and Barth but with no remaining squeamishness about a science/theology accord. That in itself is a sign of the passage into a "postmodernity" no longer constrained by one, Enlightenment paradigm of philosophy.

The third towering figure in the first wave of the Trinitarian revival was the Jesuit theologian Karl Rahner. The strong influence of Barth on

5. Lossky, *Mystical Theology*, p. 56.

6. Lossky, *Mystical Theology*, p. 58.

7. Quite how novel this polemically disjunctive reading was is now made clear in George E. Demacopoulos and Aristotle Papanikolaou, "Augustine and the Orthodox: 'The West' in the East," in Papanikolaou and Demacopoulos, eds., *Orthodox Readings of Augustine*, pp. 11-40. If they are right, Lossky's urge to paint the views of the "East" as wholly different from those of the West was deeply bound up with the nationalist sensibilities of the "neo-Patristic" school, and their need to sustain a sense of theological distinctiveness during exile in the West following the Russian Revolution.

8. Karl Barth, *Die Kirchliche Dogmatik I: Die Lehre vom Wort Gottes* 1 (Zürich: Evangelischer Verlag A.G., 1932); ET *Church Dogmatics I/1: The Doctrine of the Word of God* (Edinburgh: T. & T. Clark, 1936), esp. pp. 1-47.

him led to his own enunciation of the famed principle that "the immanent Trinity *is* the economic Trinity."[9] That is: the Christian life of discipleship in interaction with the divine Trinitarian life simply *is* an encounter with the "immanent" Trinity. It was therefore a fundamental mistake — according to Rahner and many others who echoed him — to divide the immanent and the economic, as much Western scholastic theology had done, by prioritizing the discussion of the *de deo uno,* and dislocating it from the *de deo trino.*[10] This ploy had rendered the immanent Trinity otiose from the point of view of Christian "experience," Rahner claimed, and made it further vulnerable in terms of philosophical defense. Less marked than Barth, therefore, by any antipathy to philosophy or human "experience" as such, and indeed strongly drawn to aspects of the Greek Patristic tradition himself,[11] Rahner's trinitarianism might be read as straddling the differences between Lossky's and Barth's, were it not for one significant feature of the new "East/West" division that was becoming particularly contentious. Whereas Lossky majored in his insistence on the irreducible basicality of the "persons" in the Trinity, Barth and Rahner were both nervous about calling the *hypostases* "persons" at all, given the bag and baggage (both individualized and psychologized) that had accrued to the term "person" in the modern West. Barth, then, favored talk of "modes of being" over "person"; and Rahner too underscored the same problems, but stopped short — in deference to churchly authority — of actually changing the term "person."[12] Yet the very anxiety voiced by Barth and Rahner was actually what was to animate the second phase of Trinitarian renewal, indeed to become its watchword — a move against modern "individualism." It is again ironic, in hindsight, that the same move was to produce a trend in "social trinitarianism" of which both Barth and Rahner would themselves have been highly suspicious.

So it is against the background of this first wave of twentieth-century Trinitarian renewal that we must place the significance of John Zizioulas's

---

9. Karl Rahner, *The Trinity* (Tunbridge Wells: Burns & Oates, 1970), p. 23.

10. See Rahner, *The Trinity,* pp. 15-21. A similar criticism is made by Jürgen Moltmann, *The Trinity and the Kingdom of God* (London: SCM Press, 1981), pp. 16-20, although Moltmann goes on to offer critical remarks about Rahner's account of the unity in the Trinity (pp. 144-48).

11. As is implicitly evident in *The Trinity,* but also in Rahner's treatment of the Trinity in his "systematic" volume, *Foundations of Christian Faith* (New York: Crossroad, 1993), chap. 4, with its explicit criticism of Augustine (see p. 135).

12. See Rahner, *The Trinity,* pp. 106-9.

work, which — while still much influenced by Lossky — took Trinitarian reflection into a new turn, a second wave of significant renewal and imaginative influence. Whereas the unspoken enemy of the first wave had been Enlightenment resistance to theological metaphysics in general, and to ramified doctrinal speculation in particular, the new, and explicit, bogeyman in the second wave was now modernity's "turn to the subject," and in particular its anthropological emphasis on individualism and atomism.[13] By bringing Patristic Trinitarian thought creatively into connection with *ecclesiology,* Zizioulas could extend Lossky's emphasis on the significance of the perfect relations of the Trinitarian "persons," but now — with a new polemical twist of Zizioulas's own — pronounce the persons' "relationality" to be *more fundamental* than their individualization.[14] As in God, so in the church: "communion" must be seen as the basic reality, and individualized notions of personhood merely derivative. It is an interesting hermeneutical question as to what influenced Zizioulas most in this particular turn, which was to prove wildly popular amongst Western systematic theologians for at least a generation. Zizioulas argued (as he does again in this book) that the prioritizing of "personhood" *as understood in relation* (the key Greek terms are *hypostasis* and *schesis*) can already be demonstrated from the writings of the late fourth-century Cappadocian fathers, and that this position can be clearly demarcated from an Augustinian prioritization of (monadic) "substance."[15] But it should be noted that this reading of the Cappadocians (and indeed of Augustine) has not gone without important critique;[16] and it is even riposted — albeit diplo-

13. Moltmann's form of "social trinitarianism" — perilously close to tritheism at times — was animated by a similar reaction to modern "subjectivity": see, e.g., *The Trinity and the Kingdom of God,* pp. 13-16.

14. Lossky, in contrast, had seen "relationality" as both individualizing *and* uniting: see *Mystical Theology,* p. 58. See Aristotle Papanikolaou, *Being with God: Trinity, Apophaticism, and Divine-Human Communion* (Notre Dame: University of Notre Dame Press, 2006), chaps. 3-4, for a comparison of Lossky and Zizioulas on this point.

15. See John D. Zizioulas, *Being in Communion* (Crestwood, NY: St. Vladimir's Seminary Press, 1997), esp. pp. 40-42, 105-7.

16. The most salient hermeneutical issue is whether the Cappadocian fathers ever argued for a disjunctive *choice* between the prioritizing of "person" or "substance": see Sarah Coakley, ed., *Re-Thinking Gregory of Nyssa* (Oxford: Blackwell, 2003), with relevant discussion in chap. 1 (Sarah Coakley), chap. 2 (Lewis Ayres), and chap. 7 (Lucian Turcescu). The further issue is whether the Cappadocian and Augustinian readings of the Trinity are as significantly different from one another as Zizioulas claims: for an important recent discussion that resists Zizioulas's views, see Lewis Ayres, *Nicaea and Its Legacy* (Oxford: Oxford Univer-

matically so — in this volume by a fellow Orthodox bishop, Kallistos Ware.[17] The more fascinating question then is whether other, perhaps even modern "Western," influences or concerns have to some degree propelled Zizioulas's vision of the priority of "relationality,"[18] just as Lossky too was covertly influenced by Western paradigms. Zizioulas strongly denies this, and has repeated the denial emphatically of late;[19] but there is an ongoing debate on that point which lies just below the surface of this book's text. At least one critic has suggested that Zizioulas's stress on relational "personhood" owes as much to certain (minority, reactive) strands in modern Western philosophy as it does to the original Cappadocian exposition of *hypostasis*.[20]

The influence of Zizioulas on a wide range of eager Western admirers has led to a veritable regeneration of Trinitarian thinking, with many authors strangely given to a form of self-flagellation about their own "Western" heritage.[21] Whereas Lossky had utilized Western authors in his original insistence on the superiority of the Eastern trinitarianism, now Western writers took up the cudgels *against* the trinitarianism of their own tradition (Augustine and Aquinas, *par excellence*) under the explicit influence of an Eastern prelate and theologian — John Zizioulas. Augustine

---

sity Press, 2004), chaps. 14, 15; and the critical debate on this topic in Sarah Coakley, ed., *The God of Nicaea: Disputed Questions in Patristic Trinitarianism*, special issue of the *Harvard Theological Review* 100 (2007): esp. 141-71 (Lewis Ayres in debate with John Behr and Khaled Anatolios).

17. Herein lies the "East/East" tension within this volume.

18. See Alan Brown's somewhat intemperate discussion in Douglas H. Knight, ed., *The Theology of John Zizioulas* (London: Ashgate, 2007), chap. 2, esp. pp. 41-45.

19. See John D. Zizioulas, *Communion and Otherness: Further Studies in Personhood and the Church*, ed. Paul McPartlan (London: T. & T. Clark, 2006), esp. chap. 4, "Appendix," pp. 171-77.

20. So Lucian Turcescu (see n. 16 above), to whom Zizioulas has now responded in *Communion and Otherness*. It should be pointed out that even if Turcescu's genealogy could be substantiated, it would not invalidate the force of Zizioulas's stance *in se*.

21. I think here of Trinitarian systematicians such as Colin Gunton, Catherine LaCugna, Miroslav Volf, and Stanley Grenz, all of whom have recently exhibited a tendency for the preferential treatment either of "Greek" models of the Trinity in general, or for Zizioulas's in particular. Note that we should be careful to distinguish Zizioulas's position, and Zizioulas's influence, from the more clearly tritheistic tendency of the work of Moltmann, against which Karen Kilby has memorably inveighed: "Perichoresis and Projection: Problems with Social Doctrines of the Trinity," *New Blackfriars* 81 (2000): 432-45. It should be stressed that Moltmann's position is more appropriately dubbed "social trinitarianism" than is Zizioulas's, although they are often considered together.

was declared by the late Colin Gunton, for instance, to be ultimately responsible for the later, baleful, subjectivist moves of Descartes;[22] and from the perspective of a convinced Zizioulas devotee the only Western writer to escape critique was Richard of St. Victor, who was read by Gunton precisely in this "social" mode.[23] Meanwhile, however, Zizioulas's ideas about "relationality" had also inspired a response from scientists — notably John Polkinghorne, as represented in this volume — that had been much less easy or obvious to effect in the first wave of Trinitarian renewal, given Barth's antipathy to any form of non-biblical "foundationalism," and his concomitant resistance to any easy *rapprochement* with secular science.[24] It is in the context of this second "wave" of twentieth-century Trinitarian revival, then, that the central themes of this current book, and the editorial framing, must be read. It is this wave that has distinctively and importantly informed John Polkinghorne's work for some time, and it has thereby also inspired the vision of the *connection* between divine "relationality" and relationality in the physical universe that lies at the heart of this volume. According to this view there is a natural and significant correlation between intra-divine relationality of this Trinitarian form and the relationality that physicists may glimpse, in a variety of ways, in the basic structures of the created universe.

But it must be noted that a "third wave" of such Trinitarian renewal, one in some important ways reactive to the second, is already in progress, and it is — in a somewhat muted, but significant, way — already present as a contrapuntal voice in this book.[25] As hinted above, this third wave has returned to the Patristic (and scholastic) sources with a concern to question the polemical disjunctions between "East" and "West" that character-

22. See Colin E. Gunton, "Augustine, the Trinity and the Theological Crisis of the West," *Scottish Journal of Theology* 43 (1990): 33-58; later in *The Promise of Trinitarian Theology* (Edinburgh: T. & T. Clark, 1991), chap. 3.

23. See Colin Gunton, "The One, the Three and the Many: An Inaugural Lecture in the Chair of Christian Doctrine" (King's College, London, 1985), in which Richard of St. Victor is read as "preceding" the relational understanding of personhood found in John Macmurray and as being the only classical author in the West approaching such a "relational" view.

24. It is notable that John Polkinghorne can now talk, quite unembarrassedly, in his Introduction to this volume of science as the "foundation," and theology or philosophy as the upper structures, of a discourse shared between them. Such a metaphor would doubtless have been anathema to Barth.

25. See especially the contribution of Lewis Ayres, but also — as already intimated — some strands in Kallistos Ware's essay.

ized Lossky's re-imagining of Christian doctrinal history in the aftermath of the Russian revolution, and which were then taken forward, in somewhat different form, into the work of Zizioulas. This questioning has by no means been univocal;[26] but at least the following aspects of it should be highlighted, for it profoundly affects how we are to read the relation of Trinitarian ontology and physical ontology in the ongoing dialogue between theology and physics evidenced in this book.

First, this "third-wave" reaction has been concerned to question the thesis of an early "East/West" division in fourth- to fifth-century trinitarianism, and instead to stress the remarkable extent to which "pro-Nicene"[27] theologians concurred on basic Trinitarian principles in this crucial transition period of doctrinal deepening and reflection. Second, then, this wave of Trinitarian thought has returned to the texts of the Cappadocian fathers themselves,[28] their contemporaries and immediate forebears writing in Greek, and their Western receptors (including Augustine), to read their Trinitarian arguments afresh, and without the constricting hermeneutical clamp of a presumed East/West disjunction. Third, this has allowed a reconsideration of the question basic to this book, *viz.*, how the issue of "relationality" features in the texts of these various authors: Is it *more* fundamental than individualized "personhood" in any of them (as Zizioulas claims of the "Eastern" writers), or is it *simultaneously constitutive* of such "personhood," and if so, how is this simultaneity to be construed and expressed? Fourth, and finally, it has asked how these same classic Patristic authors were to conceive of what we may call the third-order level of "relation" at stake in this book: the relation *between* relationality-in-God (the Trinity), on the one hand, and relationality-in-the-physical-world, on the other. That is: How did the Greek Patristic writers of this formative period

26. Cf., e.g., the views of Kallistos Ware, John Behr (from the Orthodox side) and — *inter alia* — Rowan Williams, Lewis Ayres, Michel Barnes, and myself (on the Anglican and Roman Catholic side). The special issue of *Harvard Theological Review* on *The God of Nicaea: Disputed Questions in Patristic Trinitarianism* (see n. 16) provides a useful introduction to this new "wave" of discussion, including some evidence of internal disagreement within it. It should be added that Yves Congar, OP, already anticipated several elements of the "third wave" in his magisterial *I Believe in the Holy Spirit* (New York: Crossroad, 1997).

27. A term not coined by Lewis Ayres, but made his catchword in *Nicaea and Its Legacy*.

28. It is important, however, as this new wave of writing also stresses, to realize that the block characterization of the "Cappadocian fathers" as a unit was only concocted in the nineteenth century. On this point see Joseph T. Lienhard, SJ, "Augustine of Hippo, Basil of Caesarea, and Gregory Nazianzen," in Papanikolaou and Demacopoulos, eds., *Orthodox Readings of Augustine*, pp. 81-99, esp. 81-82.

signal the unspeakable transcendence of the divine *over against* the created order, and were their "apophatic" moves really of a different order (as Lossky claimed) from the similar insistences of Augustine that all analogies for the Trinity ultimately fail?[29] Further, and finally, what should we then make of the much later Western scholastic reflection on this third-order relation, and its significance for clarifying the possibility of an "analogy of being" between these two orders? Was such a notion devised only at the cost of a simultaneous loss of a true "apophatic" sensibility (as Lossky and his intellectual descendents had again charged against "the West")?[30]

The effect of this re-questioning of doctrinal paradigms of East/West "division" (an idea that we now see was introduced, and reinforced, quite newly in the course of the twentieth century)[31] is not, in my own view, to obliterate the important differences of *emphasis* between many Patristic and scholastic Trinitarian authors, both East and West. But it is to highlight that the broad brushstrokes of "East/West" disjunction that have served the textbooks pedagogically for a century and more, are now radically up for review. And clearly we cannot begin to draw conclusions about the "relation" of the Trinitarian God to "relations" in the physical world unless we get clear about these systematic and hermeneutical choices, just outlined. *If* Zizioulas is right and God is in some sense *more* "relational" than individualized in the "East," and God's creation, made in his image, can thus be seen — without any major noetic slippage caused by the gap of divine transcendence — to mirror that "relationality," then the central intuition of this book stands, along with the presumption that a so-called "Eastern" approach to the Trinity is a superior one to that of the "West." But if any of the axioms just mentioned are questioned, then a more chastened, or at least more complicated, argument has to be mounted for the

---

29. A point Lossky himself did not acknowledge, but is especially stressed by Augustine in Book XV of *De trinitate,* as he reviews the various analogies he has earlier utilized, but stresses the remaining — and ultimately incomprehensible — difference between God and the human mind: *De trinitate* XV, 11-13.

30. See Lossky, *The Mystical Theology,* chap. 2, and the insightful discussion in the essay by Rowan Williams mentioned above (n. 2). Here we should note, however, the importance of rereadings of the Dionysian influence on Aquinas that have occurred in the last generation of Thomas-scholarship, and which strongly reemphasize the apophatic dimensions of Aquinas's thought: see, by way of résumé of this trend, David Burrell and Isabelle Moulin, "Albert, Aquinas, and Dionysius," in Coakley and Stang, eds., *Re-Thinking Dionysius the Areopagite,* chap. 7.

31. See esp. again Papanikolaou and Demacopoulos, eds., *Orthodox Readings of Augustine,* pp. 11-40.

third-order relation of Trinitarian and physical relationality, one perhaps in which it might be acknowledged that "Eastern" and "Western" traditions of Trinitarian theology (in all their acknowledged internal variety) have something to learn from one another, and to go on learning, as pressing contemporary issues of science and religion continue to be debated. That is why the argument I have so far mounted should not be perceived as anti-ecumenical in spirit; on the contrary, it is a spur to more intense, and mutually appreciative, ecumenical endeavor.

In sum: the moment of the "postmodern" is one in which theologians long unaccustomed to conversing with scientists are beginning to regain the courage to do so. But for a number of generations since the Enlightenment many of them, especially Protestants, have been regrettably ill-trained in this regard — given the "liberal" rejection of realist ontology, on the one hand, and the reactive Barthian aversion to engagement with the "secular," on the other. Now, the serious reconsideration of premodern options in theological metaphysics (including, in this book, Trinitarian visions of "relational ontology") signals the end of a mandatory Enlightenment clamp on speculative metaphysics about the divine. To be sure, secularists and pragmatists of various stripes naturally continue to be severely skeptical about such an undertaking: the new postmodern situation certainly does not mean that *anything goes* philosophically. And reflection on the nature of God-as-Trinity continues to be hotly debated by philosophical theologians, as we have indicated; the hypothesis that "relationality" is ontologically *more basic* than "hypostatic" individualization is one such topic of intense debate and disagreement, not only between the so-called "East" and "West," as we have now seen, but between hermeneutical factions and exponents within and between each of these supposedly disjunctive categories. I have myself indicated some skepticism that a *choice* between Trinitarian "hypostatization" and "relationality" (in terms of ontological priority) is either desirable theologically, or indeed mandated by our authoritative Patristic sources. These notions stand and fall together, and must be seen as mutually inflecting one another. Only then can we proceed — in a non-polemical manner — to a sustained reflection on what such Trinitarian ontology has implied, in classic Christian traditions, for the notion of creation and for theological anthropology.

Philosophical Problems of "Relation" and "Causation"

But this debate about the Trinity presumes that we can also make *philosophical* sense of the key analytic terms utilized in this volume. Let me now end, therefore, with a brief correlative set of comments about the central philosophical categories of "relation" and "causation," which prove to be the key ones for the intuition running through this book that there is a fundamental "holistic connectivity" (as the editor puts it) in the universe. What exactly does this mean, and how does it depend on a clarification of the concepts of "relation" and "cause"?

John Polkinghorne remarks in his Introduction that, "The history of twentieth-century physics can be read as the story of the discovery of *many levels* of intrinsic relationality present in the structure of the universe" (my emphasis); and he also stresses in the opening to his own chapter that there are not only many such "levels," but equally many different *types* of relationality — from "simple juxtaposition" through to a metaphysical, Trinitarian relationality in the Godhead. His supposition in the Introduction is that, given the bewildering range of such notions of "relationality," we should think of them as in degrees of "cousinly connection" — perhaps rather in the spirit of Wittgensteinian "family resemblance." This is a useful starting-point; but unfortunately the insight does not, in and of itself, help us to navigate, or critically interpret, the rather bewildering range of notions of "relationality" at play in this book, or indeed beyond it. Perhaps just a few critical remarks on this problem may be helpful in furthering future debate. I suggest four basic points, outlined in the following paragraphs:

The Complexity of Analytic Debates about "Relation"

In his essay, Wesley Wildman (who attempts the most sustained analytical account of categories of "relationality" in this volume) asserts, rather than strictly argues, that "relation" is best understood as "causality." He does not tell us why he feels free to make this assumption; presumably it is because the five different "relational ontologies" of the sort he then outlines are of particular interest to religionists and theological metaphysicians, and seemingly share this assumption, in one way or another. But it should be stressed immediately that making this presumption (that "relation" = "cause") closes off some very significant debates that have animated the discussion of "relation" in analytic philosophy in the last generation or so.

First, the most technical discussions of the topic of "relation" in recent analytic philosophy have focused on the *logical* analysis of "relation" simply as a "two-or-more-place property," as exemplified in set theory. Various sorts of "relation" can thereby be usefully distinguished (e.g., "reflexive," "transitive," "symmetrical," "asymmetrical," "anti-symmetrical," etc.), while entirely bracketing deeper philosophical questions about the very nature of "causality," or of whether "relation" therefore implies it. Further, this kind of set-theory analysis can also be highly fruitful in logic and semantics without necessarily tangling with the deeper philosophical problem of so-called "internal" and "external" relations, that is, the question of what relations are "essential" properties of an entity, *e.* (If a relation is "internal" to *e*, it means that, if it were not present or taken away, *e* would no longer be *e*; if it is "external," it does not have that "essential" characteristic for *e.* An example might be: it is a relation "internal" to the cathedral town Ely that it is northeast of Cambridge; but it is a relation only "external" to my bicycle that it is also currently northeast of Cambridge, in Ely.) This latter debate about the differentiation of external and internal relations has had a fascinating modern history, arising from the difficulties in trying to defend Aristotle's original distinction between "essence" and "accidents": the distinction seems obviously commonsensical, and yet becomes curiously elusive when one attempts to batten it down.

Underneath both the logical/semantic and the external/internal debates on "relation," however, is another — and one might say even more fundamental — layer of metaphysical choice, to which this book arguably jumps a little too quickly; here is the old divergence between nominalists and idealists about whether the very notion of "relation" implies "universals" of which particulars are mere exemplifications. In other words: Are "relations" ontologically *real?* Most of the contributors to this book, it should be noted, exemplify a clear Platonic bias on this fundamental issue (doubtless on account of their Christian, Trinitarian commitments), and some tilt also towards what Richard Rorty has called the "extreme" position of assuming that *all* "relations" are "internal" to entities (since everything is "related" intrinsically to everything else in some presumed form of monism or radical idealism). This position may be naturally attractive if one is already committed to a particular form of Christian theism strongly influenced by Plato or Leibniz (or indeed to certain forms of Indian monist metaphysics, as Wildman points out); but it must be said that to the majority of contemporary analytic philosophers, and indeed to some Christian philosophers also, this supposition may seem a straightforwardly dead option. (As one has recently remarked, quite flat-footedly, "Although such doctrines have some historical importance [in, e.g., Plato and Bradley], *they have disappeared.*")[32] This is not, of course, to say that these — dogmatic! — secular philosophers are right; but only to comment that a lot of heavy lifting is required by "Trinitarian ontologists" if they are to make their metaphysical views on "relation" both analytically precise, and also defensible in the current Western philosophical climate.

In sum: not only is it not obvious that all "relationality" *is* "causal," but there is a thicket of anterior philosophical issues about the very meaning and significance of "relation" that has to be cleared away before one can get to the big metaphysical decisions to which this book alluringly invites us.

The Problems of "Causation"

Second, even if it could be argued successfully — as Wildman proposes — that all "relationality" *is* causal, it would hardly be a blow for instant philosophical clarification of our topic. For the very notion of "causality" is itself such a multi-valent — and contested — term philosophically, that a great deal of work remains to be done, here also, in sorting out what theories of causality would apply with even pragmatic force or efficacy in any particular realm of science and theology.

For instance, if causation is simply reducible to observed constant conjunction (as was Hume's view, on most readings of him),[33] there would be little to support the ontological claims about "relation" and "cause" made by many participants in this volume. So-called "counterfactual" accounts of causation, which have tended to dominate in recent analytic literature as new variants on Hume (crudely put: an event E *counterfactually* depends on another circumstance C in a way that if C had not happened, E would not have either), are not going to aid the ontological bias of this volume any better. In short, the "reductionist" drift of most theories of causality in recent analytic philosophy is a high hurdle that "relational ontologists" are going to have to scale to give their theories some credibility in the current philosophical climate.

---

32. Steven J. Wagner, "Relation," in *The Cambridge Dictionary of Philosophy*, ed. Robert Audi (Cambridge: Cambridge University Press, 1995), pp. 688-90, at 690 (my emphasis).

33. A counter-reading has been mounted by Galen Strawson, *The Secret Connexion: Causation, Realism, and David Hume* (Oxford: Clarendon Press, 1989), who argues for traces of a "realistic" account of cause in Hume after all. This remains a minority view on Hume, however.

Sarah Coakley

But perhaps more importantly, the quite different nature of *divine* causality (and thus divine "relation" to the physical world) is, as Thomas Aquinas saw more clearly than many others since, a *sui generis* matter peculiarly hard to grasp in its transcendent uniqueness.[34] Even if we set aside that divine complication initially (precisely as *sui generis*), we shall not find much agreement among contemporary philosophers about what constitutes "causality" elsewhere, within the created universe, and especially as evident in empirical science. I would myself be inclined to follow here the recent arguments of the philosopher of science Ned Hall that, in the arena of so-called "causes," we are dealing with a *variety* of ways of attempting to capture what is at stake in particular debates about "cause," with different definitions proving themselves pragmatically fruitful in different empirical and scientific realms of discussion.[35] If this is right, then we either may be hunting the Snark in expecting the reduction of "relation" to "cause" to lead to a simplification of our theological theme, or else — as I believe likely — we are letting ourselves in for a much more complex analytic task of classifying forms of "relation" (causal or otherwise) than this exploratory volume has been able to attempt.

The Question of the Analogy and Disanalogy Between Divine and Created "Relationality"

It follows that, if the "relation" of the Trinitarian God to the physical universe is *sui generis* and conceptually hard to grasp, as Aquinas insisted, then we should beware of expectations of straightforward "mirrorings" of such relationality in the physical universe. In one sense "relationality" is, in a truistic and trivial sense, all around us (if by that we mean some vague intuition of connectedness); but the conceptual task of marshalling and analyzing different forms of such relationality is formidable, and not easily constrained into consistent patterns directly redolent of "God." At the very

34. A fine explication of this point in relation to current debates about science and religion (which often fail to grasp its full significance) can be found in William E. Carroll, "Divine Agency, Contemporary Physics, and the Autonomy of Nature," *Heythrop Journal* 49 (2008): 582-602.

35. Ned Hall provides a fine survey of the current debates and options in the philosophical theory of causation in his essay "Causation," in *The Oxford Handbook of Contemporary Philosophy*, ed. Frank Jackson and Michael Smith (Oxford: Oxford University Press, 2005), pp. 505-33.

least, to *participate* in divine, Trinitarian "relationality" must surely involve some radical reworking — indeed purgation — of the fallen creation's use and understanding of relation, a reworking such as glimpsed by Paul in his "proto-Trinitarian" vision of the cosmos and its ends (Romans 8).

Why Three in Relation?

Finally, we must end with an intriguing question about ontological "threeness" in God that remains somewhat underexplored in this book. What all Christians agree upon, both "East" and "West," is that "hypostatic" relationality in God is not merely binary but — distinctively, and irreducibly — threefold. A sustained argument for the necessity of the *third* in God's internal relationality is not however given in this book: it is assumed, seemingly on ecclesial authority. But if physics and theology are to indicate some intrinsic connection between their theoretical and speculative realms, then the *specialness* of threefold relationality is the particular challenge still to be explained and defended. As more than one contributor to this book will have it, Peirce's philosophical notion of "thirdness" is doubtless suggestive here, for all its own elusiveness. But much more work needs to be done than could be undertaken in this particular volume to explain why *triadic* ontological relationality, as such, is normative for Christians,[36] and what this means for the future of the important physics/theology accord already so creatively fostered in this volume. We must be grateful, indeed, for the visionary set of metaphysical possibilities that have been opened up for reflection in these pages.

---

36. I have made my own attempt to mount an initial argument for the necessity of the divine "third" in "Why Three? Some Further Reflections on the Origins of the Doctrine of the Trinity," in *The Making and Remaking of Christian Doctrine*, ed. Sarah Coakley and David A. Pailin (Oxford: Oxford University Press, 1993), pp. 29-56.

Contributors

John Charlton Polkinghorne, KBE, FRS, the former president of Queens' College, Cambridge, and the winner of the 2002 Templeton Prize, has been a leading figure in the dialogue of science and religion for more than two decades. He resigned his professorship of mathematical physics at Cambridge University to take up a new vocation in midlife and was ordained a priest in the Church of England in 1982. A Fellow of the Royal Society, he was knighted by Queen Elizabeth II in 1997. In addition to an extensive body of writing on theoretical elementary particle physics, including most recently *Quantum Theory: A Very Short Introduction* (2002), he is the editor or co-editor of four books, the co-author (with Michael Welker) of *Faith in the Living God: A Dialogue* (2001), and the author of nineteen other books on the interrelationship of science and theology, including *Belief in God in an Age of Science* (1998), a volume composed of his Terry Lectures at Yale University, *Science and Theology* (1998), *Faith, Science and Understanding* (2000), *Traffic in Truth: Exchanges between Theology and Science* (2001), *The God of Hope and the End of the World* (2002), *Living with Hope* (2003), *Science and the Trinity: The Christian Encounter with Reality* (2004), *Exploring Reality: The Intertwining of Science and Religion* (2005), *Quantum Physics and Theology: An Unexpected Kinship* (2007), *Theology in the Context of Science* (2008), and *Questions of Truth: Fifty-one Responses to Questions about God, Science, and Belief* (2008). His autobiography, *From Physicist to Priest*, was published by SPCK in 2007.

Lewis Ayres is Bede Professor of Catholic Theology at Durham University. He was formerly an associate professor of historical theology at the

Candler School of Theology and in the Graduate Division of Religion at Emory University and earlier taught at Duke University Divinity School and Trinity College, Dublin. He is the author of *Nicaea and Its Legacy: An Approach to Fourth-Century Trinitarian Theology* (2004) and *Augustine and the Trinity* (forthcoming from Cambridge University Press). He is also the co-editor of four books, including (with Andrew Louth and Frances Young) *The Cambridge History of Early Christian Literature* (2004) and (with Vincent Twomey) *The Mystery of the Holy Trinity in the Fathers of the Church* (2007). He is presently editing three volumes: *The Trinity Reader* for Blackwell, (with Mark DelCogliano) *Works on the Spirit: Athanasius and Didymus* for St. Vladimir's Seminary Press, and (with his wife Medi Ann Volpe) the *Oxford Handbook of Catholic Theology,* in addition to writing *Early Christianity: An Introduction* for Cambridge University Press and *The Practice of Christian Doctrine: A Catholic Essay* for Blackwell.

Jeffrey Bub is Distinguished University Professor in the Department of Philosophy and the Institute for Physical Science and Technology at the University of Maryland. He has held appointments at Yale and the University of Western Ontario. He has published numerous articles in scientific and scholarly journals on the conceptual foundations of quantum mechanics and is the author of two books: *The Interpretation of Quantum Mechanics* (1974) and *Interpreting the Quantum World* (1997 and 1999), which won the Lakatos Award in 1998 for providing a unified reconstruction and systematic assessment of quantum mechanics. His current research is focused on foundational questions arising in the field of quantum information and computation.

Sarah Coakley is the Norris-Hulse Professor of Divinity at Cambridge University and was previously Mallinckrodt Professor of Divinity at Harvard Divinity School. Her books include: *Christ Without Absolutes: A Study of the Christology of Ernst Troeltsch* (1988), *Powers and Submissions: Spirituality, Philosophy and Gender* (2001), (editor) *Religion and the Body* (1997), (editor) *Re-Thinking Gregory of Nyssa* (2002), and three collaborative volumes specifically on the interface of science and religion, (co-editor with Kay Shelemay) *Pain and Its Transformations* (2007), (editor) *Spiritual Healing: Science, Meaning and Discernment* (forthcoming from Eerdmans), and (co-editor with Martin A. Nowak) *Evolution, Games and God: The Principle of Cooperation* (forthcoming from Harvard University Press). She is at work on a four-volume systematic theology to be published by Cambridge University Press. The first volume will appear as *God, Sexuality and the Self: An Essay "On the Trinity."* Dr. Coakley is an Anglican priest in the diocese of Ely.

Michael Heller is a professor of philosophy at the Pontifical Academy of Theology in Cracow, Poland, and an adjunct member of the staff of the Vatican Observatory. A Roman Catholic priest, who won the Templeton Prize in 2008, he is the founder and director of the Copernicus Center for Interdisciplinary Studies in Cracow. He is the author of more than twenty books, including *Is Physics an Art?* (1998), *Creative Tension* (2003), and *Some Mathematical Physics for Philosophers* (2005).

Panos A. Ligomenides is professor emeritus of electrical engineering and computer science at the University of Maryland and a life member of the Academy of Athens. He formerly taught at Stanford University, the University of California at Los Angeles, and San Jose and Santa Clara universities as well as working as a research scientist at IBM. Throughout his career, he has been a technical advisor to private companies and public agencies in the United States and in Greece. He is the author of seven technical books and of *The Apricot's Peel* (2002), a study of the ontological and metaphysical implications of recent discoveries in physics and information theory, which was published in Greek.

David Martin is a professor emeritus of sociology at the London School of Economics and Political Science. A Fellow of the British Academy, he formerly held the Elizabeth Scurlock Professorship of Human Values at Southern Methodist University. The editor or co-editor of eleven books, he is the author of eighteen others, including *Pacifism: An Historical and Sociological Study* (1965), *A General Theory of Secularization* (1979), *Tongues of Fire: Conservative Protestantism in Latin America* (1990), *Does Christianity Cause War?* (1997), *Pentecostalism: The World Their Parish* (2002), and *On Secularization: Notes Towards a Revised General Theory* (2005).

Argyris Nicolaidis is an associate professor of theoretical physics at the University of Thessaloniki. He is the recipient of the Empirikion Prize for the Natural Sciences. The co-organizer of international conferences on science, philosophy, and religion and of the 2002-2004 "Cosmos in Science and Religion" project at Thessaloniki, he is the author of a book on elementary particles published in Greek in addition to numerous scientific papers.

Contributors

Kallistos of Diokleia (Timothy Ware) was the Spalding Lecturer in Eastern Orthodox Studies at Oxford University for thirty-five years until his retirement. Ordained to the priesthood in 1966, he took monastic vows at the Monastery of St. John the Theologian in Patmos, Greece, and remains a member of that community. In 1982, he was consecrated titular Bishop of Diokleia, the first Englishman to become a bishop within the Orthodox Church since the eleventh century, and in 2007, he was elevated to titular Metropolitan of Diokleia. Long active in the work of Christian unity, he is the co-translator of two Orthodox service books and of *The Philokalia*, a collection of texts written between the fourth and fifteenth centuries by Orthodox spiritual masters. He is the author of four books, including *The Orthodox Church* (1963; revised edition 1993), and *The Inner Kingdom* (2000), the first of six volumes of his collected works.

Michael Welker is professor and chair of systematic theology in the Theological Faculty of the University of Heidelberg and director of the Research Center for International and Interdisciplinary Theology (FIIT). A member of the Heidelberg Academy and the Finnish Academy of Science and Letters, he is an ordained minister in the *Evangelische Kirche der Pfalz* (Protestant Church of the Palatinate). The more than thirty books he has written or edited include: *God the Spirit* (1992 and 1994), *What Happens in Holy Communion?* (2000), (edited with John Polkinghorne) *The End of the World and the Ends of God: Science and Theology on Eschatology* (2000), (with John Polkinghorne) *Faith in the Living God: A Dialogue* (2001), (edited with Ted Peters and Robert John Russell) *Resurrection: Theological and Scientific Assessments* (2002), (with Wallace M. Alston) *Reformed Theology: Identity and Ecumenicity* (vol. 1 2003, vol. 2 2006), (editor) *The Work of the Spirit: Pneumatology and Pentecostalism* (2006), and *Theological Profiles: Schleiermacher — Barth — Bonhoeffer — Moltmann* (2009).

Wesley J. Wildman is an associate professor in the Department of Philosophy, Theology, and Ethics at the Boston University School of Theology. He is author of *Fidelity with Plausibility: Modest Christologies in the Twentieth Century* (1998) and *Science and Religious Anthropology* (2009). He is co-editor (with W. Mark Richardson) of *Religion and Science: History, Method, Dialogue* (1996), and (with Niels Gregersen and Nancy Howell under chief editor J. Wentzel van Huyssteen) of the two-volume *Encyclopedia of Science and Religion* (2003).

Contributors

Anton Zeilinger is professor of physics at the University of Vienna and co-director of the Institute of Quantum Optics and Quantum Information of the Austrian Academy of Sciences. He previously held professorships at Innsbruck University, the Technical University of Vienna, and the Massachusetts Institute of Technology. He is the recipient, among other honors, of the King Faisal Prize of Science, the German Order of Merit, and the Isaac Newton Medal of the British Institute of Physics. In addition to publishing numerous scientific papers, he is co-editor (with Dirk Bouwmeester and Artur Ekert) of *The Physics of Quantum Information* (2000) and (with Chiara Macchiavello and G. Massimo Palma) of *Quantum Computation and Quantum Information Theory* (2001) and the author of *Einstein's Schleier* (2003) and *Einstein's Spuk* (2005).

John D. Zizioulas is a Greek Orthodox bishop and theologian. He was professor of systematic theology at the University of Glasgow for fourteen years and, subsequently, at King's College, University of London, and the University of Thessaloniki until his recent retirement. As Metropolitan of Pergamon, he represents the Ecumenical Patriarchate of Constantinople on international church bodies and has led theological dialogue with the Roman Catholic Church and the Anglican Communion. He is the former chair of the Academy of Athens. His *Being as Communion* (1985) has been highly influential among Western scholars seeking to recover a view of Christian community as more than a conglomeration of individuals, and he is also the author of *Eucharist, Bishop, Church* (1965, 1990, and 2001), *Communion and Otherness: Further Studies in Personhood and the Church* (2007), *Remembering the Future: An Eschatological Ontology* (2009), and *Lectures in Christian Dogmatics* (2009).

Index

Agapastic evolution, 102
Agape, 102, 106, 163
Algebra, noncommutative, 48-49, 50-51
Amphilochius of Iconium, 147, 148
Analogy and relational ontology: Burrell's account of God's distinction from the world, 139-40; Cappadocians and "uni-personal" Trinitarian analogies, 118, 120; and divine interaction/participation with creation, 138-42; "dualities" and cosmological theories, 99; music and divine/human activity, 176-78; Neoplatonic accounts of participation, 140; and process metaphysics, 133-34; question of analogy/disanalogy between divine and created "relationality," 198-99; question of ontological or analogical connection between the divine and world, 153-57; relational Trinitarian ontologies, 11-12, 118, 120, 131-34, 138-42, 153-57, 198-99; Sokolowski's distinction between Creator and creation, 139; theological concepts and analogy, 11-12; Zizioulas's distinction between person and relation, 133
Anancastic evolution, 102
Anderson, Philip, 2

Anglo-American Revolution, 172-73
Anthropic cosmological principle, 85-86, 99, 155-56
Apophatic theology, 12, 24
Aquinas, Thomas, 117, 198
Aristotle, 59, 64, 146-47
Aspect, Alain, 78
Athanasius of Alexandria, 114, 115
Atomism, vii, 2, 57, 75
Augustine, St., 190-91; differences between Cappadocians' perspectives and, 119-21, 186-87; *Filioque* doctrine, 120; "firmament" image, 136; ontological priority of substance over relation, 147-48; "Trinity of love" and relational character of Trinity, 118-21, 122; "uni-personal" analogies, 118, 119, 120; on unity of the Trinity, 144
Ayres, Lewis, ix, 130-45, 200-201

Bacon, Francis, 178
Baptism, 109-11
Barbour, Julian, 43
Barrow, John, 81-82
Barth, Karl: and God as communion/relational being, 108; Protestant renewal of Trinitarianism, 187-88, 191; and Rahner's trinitarianism, 188
Basil the Great, St., 114, 133

Bell, John, 20-21, 35, 36, 78, 97
Berdyaev, Nikolai, 123
Bohm, David: entanglement and quantum potential, 77-79; and holistic wholeness of the relational world, 77; and implicate-order metaphysics, 65-66; and "no cloning" principle, 28
Bohr, Niels: and epistemological nature of reality to which quantum mechanics refers, 35; quantum complementarity and Copenhagen interpretation, 17-18, 20; quarrel with Einstein over quantum entanglement, 15-18, 20, 35, 77-78
Bondi, Hermann, 16
Bose statistics, 4
Bridges, Robert, 178
Bub, Jeffrey, vii, 15-31, 201
Buber, Martin, 125-26
Buddhism: and all relations as internal, 60; and *anatta*, 64; and causal theories of relations, 64-65; compassion and non-attachment, 64; doctrine of *pratītya-samutpāda*, 57, 64-65; and entanglement in quantum physics, 65; and relations, 56
Bulgakov, Sergei, 123, 185
Burrell, David, 139-40
"Butterfly effect," 7

Cantorian infinities, 99-100
Cantor's theorem, 100
Cappadocian fathers and Trinitarian theology: Basil the Great, 114, 133; causation and intra-Trinitarian relationships, 115-16, 150; contrasting to Western/Latin approach of Augustine, 119-21, 186-87; debate over substance and personhood, 147, 148-50; divine hypostases, 117-18, 148, 150; divine unity and *koinonia* of the three divine subjects, 114-18; Gregory of Nazianzus, 107-8, 114-15, 116, 118, 120, 122; Gregory of Nyssa, 105, 114-15, 116, 117, 118; and the Holy Spirit, 115; interrelationship of Trinity, 114-18;

koinonia/love paradigm, 125; Lossky and "the de Régnon paradigm," 119-20, 186-87; and Maximus the Confessor, 105, 150-52, 154-55; and *perichoresis*, 117; and relational nature, 95; "social" interpretations of the Trinity, 116-17; and twentieth-century Trinitarian revival/renewal, 186-87, 192; "uni-personal" analogies, 118, 120; Zizioulas and prioritizing of personhood, 189-90. *See also* Patristic Trinitarian thought and relational ontology
Causation-based relational metaphysics (and causal theory of relations), x, 7-9, 55-73; ascertaining whether relations are ontologically real or linguistic attributions, 58-59; bottom-up and top-down, 9, 63; Buddhist *pratītya-samutpāda* metaphysics, 57, 64-65; and chaos theory/unpredictability, 8-9; and commonsense "hitting" views of causation, 60, 67, 69; and communion with God, 69-70; and contentious philosophical issues surrounding relations, 58-61; criteria for an adequate causal theory of relations, 62-63; five examples of causal theories of relation, 63-66; and fundamental physics, 67-68; and God-world relation in Trinitarian theology, 56, 57; idealist philosophers, 58, 59; illustrating the causal theory of relations, 67-71; and implicate-order metaphysics, 65-66; nominalist/non-nominalist empiricist approaches, 58, 60; operationalizing in imagination-forming traditions, 58; and participation metaphysics, 64, 69, 70; and Patristic Trinitarian theology, 70, 115-16, 150; and phenomenological analysis, 61; philosophical problems of relations and causation, 55-58, 185, 194-99; practical consequences of a philosophical understanding of relations, 57-58, 71; predictions based on

causal relations, 75; and process metaphysics, 65, 68-70; quantum entanglement, 62, 65, 67-68; quantum physics and predictions/unpredictability, 8-9, 33, 36, 37-38, 78, 79; questions of ontological priority of substance over relation, 59; and relational ontology, 61-66; relations in theology, 69-70; relations in the world of experience, 68-69; relations that a causal theory cannot explain, 70-71; and semiosis metaphysics, 65, 66, 69, 70; and sociological approaches, 174; specifying what relations are ontologically primary, 59-60; theistic philosophers, 58-59; theological ramifications, 61-62; theories of relation that pay no attention to causation, 60-61; the varieties of everyday relations, 55; and worldviews, 57

Chaos theory, 7, 8-9

Children's mental development and complexity of "relation," 159-62

Church's theorem, 42, 54

Coakley, Sarah, ix-x, 184-99, 201-2

Communion, God as: and Barth, 108; and causation-based metaphysics, 69-70; Gregory of Nyssa, 114-15; Patristic Trinitarian theology and relationality, 107-9; Zizioulas and "Being as Communion," 12-13, 108

Complex systems (non-linear systems), 98

Confessions (Augustine), 136, 137

Copenhagen interpretation, 17-18, 20

Copernicus, Nicolaus, 17

Cosmic effects, 10-11

Cosmic microwave background (CMB) data, 98-99

Cosmology, 98-99; and "anthropic principle," 85-86, 99, 155-56; and "dualities" (analogies) between disparate theories, 99; inflationary expansion, 98-99; Mach's principle and cosmic frame of reference, 10-11; possibility

of random dynamics and "guided randomness," 99; quantum fluctuations in the inflaton field, 98-99

Creation and relations, 93-106; agape as the relational mode of existence, 106; analogy and divine participation with creation, 138-42; Cappadocians and relational nature, 95; the Creator's relationality reflected/embodied in creation, 95; different kinds of relationality in nature, 1; hierarchical proposals regarding nature, 93-94; and hypostasis, 95, 96-97; and interpersonal Trinitarian creativity, 123-24; and modern science, 96-101; nature and evolutionary change, 104; nature as cosmos (Greek Ionians/paganist model), 93; nature as inert (Descartes/humanist model), 93; and Patristic Greek tradition, 104-6, 153-54; Peircean paradigm and semiosis metaphysics, 65, 95, 101-3, 106; Peirce's three modes of evolutionary development, 101-2; personhood in relation to creation, 153-54; and quantum mechanics, 97-98; relation and essence, 104-5; relativity theories and spacetime, 96-97; and Trinitarian theology, 56, 57, 109, 123-24; Zizioulas's interaction model and relationality principle, 94

Critique of Pure Reason (Kant), 161

Dalibard, Jean, 78

De Broglie, Louis, 65-66

Decoherence solutions and quantum measurement, 29

De Deo uno (Augustine), 148

Democritus's atomistic theory, 2, 75

De Régnon, Théodore, 119-20, 186-87

Descartes, René, 93-94, 191

De Sitter, Wilhelm, 45

Dilthey, Wilhelm, 174

Dionysius the Areopagite, St., 105, 124, 150, 151

Dirac, Paul, 3

Durkheim, Émile, 169, 179

Einstein, Albert: and Copenhagen interpretation, 17-18, 20; Einsteinian closed universe and initial conditions/boundary conditions, 44; groundbreaking 1905 papers, 32; and Mach's Principle, 41, 43-45; quantum entanglement and "ideal of the detached observer," 15-18; quantum theory and EPR effect, 6-7, 18-20, 35, 78-79; quarrel with Bohr over quantum entanglement, 15-18, 20, 35, 77-78; relativity theories and local inertia/local inertial properties, 44; relativity theories and spacetime, 4-5, 96-97; on religion and science, 91; and self-contained theory of the universe, 41, 44, 53-54; and Spinoza's God, 53-54, 81; and "spooky" action at a distance, 6, 35
Electromagnetism, 3, 5
Eliot, T. S., 127
Emergence, 10
Entanglement. *See* Quantum entanglement
EPR (Einstein-Podolsky-Rosen) effect, 6-7, 18-20, 35, 78-79
Eros, 124, 150, 163
Ether, 3
Eucharist, 111
Evagrius, 154
Evolution, creative, 83-86; agapastic evolution, 102; anancastic evolution, 102; and the "anthropic principle," 85-86, 99, 155-56; greenhouse-Earth and humanity as intrinsic evolutionary value, 84-86; and human consciousness, 85; nature and morphogenesis, 86; Peirce's three modes of evolutionary development, 95, 101-2; tychastic evolution, 102; and undivided wholeness, 80
Exploring Reality (Polkinghorne), 152

Faraday, Michael, 3, 5, 151-52

Fermi statistics (and "exclusion principle"), 4
Feuerbach, Ludwig, 181
Feynman, Richard, 15-16
Filioque, 120
"Firmament," 136-37
Florensky, Pavel, 115, 123, 127
Folk theories of relational ontology, 57, 67-68
The Forgotten Trinity (ed. Heron), 169
Forster, E. M., 107, 128
French Revolution, 172-73
Friedman, Alexander, 4-5
Fyodorov, Nikolai, 127

Galileo Galilei, 5
Geometrodynamics, 46-47
Geometry, noncommutative, 48-49
Gödel's theorem, 42, 54, 100-101
Grand Unified Theory (GUT), 5
Gravity, 3, 4, 5
Greenberger-Horne-Zeilinger (GHZ) experiment, 21-24, 97
Gregory of Nazianzus, St., 107-8, 114-15, 116, 118, 120, 122
Gregory of Nyssa, St., 105, 114-15, 116, 117, 118, 133
Gregory of Sinai, St., 118
Gregory Palamas, St., 105, 117-18, 154
Grenz, Stanley, 190
"Guided randomness," 99
Gunton, Colin, 170, 190, 191

Habermas, Jürgen, 169
Hall, Ned, 198
Hart, David Bentley, 120
Hartle, James, 88
Hartshorne, Charles, 155
Hegel, G. W. F., 58
Heidegger, Martin, 61, 104
Heisenberg, Werner, 8, 17-18, 38, 78, 97
Heisenberg's uncertainty principle, 8, 38, 78, 97
Heller, Michael, vii, 41-54, 202
Heron, Alasdair, 170
Hoffmann, Martin, 160

Holistic worldviews: and a "divine organizing principle," 80; and implicate-order metaphysics, 65-66; reconciling coexistence of diversity and wholeness, 89; and twentieth-century scientific discoveries, 77, 80-82, 89

Holographically encoded reality, 77, 80-81

Holy Spirit: Cappadocians and interrelationship of Trinity, 115; and divine-human relations, 164-66; and imago dei in human society, 170-72; and Pentecost, 171; and spiritual mobilization of nations, 171-73, 178; and Trinitarian orientation of baptism, 110-11; and Trinitarian relationship of interpersonal love, 113

Hubble, Edwin, 5

Hume, David, 58, 197

Husserl, Edmund, 61

"Ideal of the detached observer," 15-18, 20

Ignatius of Antioch, St., 125

Imago dei in human society, 170-73, 178

Implicate-order metaphysics, 65-66

Incarnation and Trinitarian theology, 109

Inflationary expansion, 98-99

Instrumentalism, 17

Irenaeus, 151

Islam, 183

"I-Thou" relations, 157, 162, 172-73

James, William, 58

John, Gospel of, 125, 163

John Chrysostom, St., 111

John of Damascus, St., 108, 118

Johnson, Elizabeth, 130

Julian of Norwich, 181

Jung, C. G., 126

Kant, Immanuel, 161, 181, 187

Kilby, Karen, 190

Koinonia, 114-18, 125

Krishnamurti, J., 66

LaCugna, Catherine, 190

Leibniz, Gottfried, 41, 196

Lemaître, Georges, 4-5

Lense, Josef, 45

Levinas, E., 104

Lewis, C. S., 127

Lewis, Gilbert N., 32

Ligomenides, Panos A., viii, 74-92, 202

Logos, 105-6, 150-52, 154-55

Lorentz, H. A., 27-28

Lorentz transformations, 16, 96

Lossky, Vladimir: and Barth's Trinitarianism, 187, 188; and first wave of Trinitarian revival/renewal, 185-87; and Rahner's Trinitarianism, 188; and "the de Régnon paradigm," 119-20, 186-87; and Zizioulas, 189, 190

Love: agape, 102, 103, 106; Augustine's "Trinity of love," 118-21, 122; differentiating between *eros, agape,* and *philia,* 163; as example of reciprocal interpersonal relations, 162-64; as fundamental stance involving the totality of our human personhood, 113; God's love and freedom of love, 124; God's love and mutual joy, 124; Gospel of John, 163; infinite/finite, 113-14; and *koinonia*/love paradigm of the Cappadocians, 125; mutual love, 113-14, 121-22, 124; parental love, 163; and reciprocal co-enhancement, 163-64; Richard of St. Victor and analogy of triadic love, 121-23; Russian religious thought and Trinitarian love paradigm, 123; self-love, 121; shared love, 122-23; and Trinitarian creativity, 123-24; and Trinitarian interrelationship, 113-14

Mach, Ernst, 10

Mach's Principle (MP), 10-11, 33, 41-42, 43-47, 52-53; and question of foundations, 43; and relativistic physics, 43-46; and Wheeler's geometrodynamics, 46-47

Macmurray, John, 125-27

Index

Marion, Jean-Luc, 134
Martin, David, ix, 168-83, 202
Marx, Karl, 169
Maximus the Confessor, 105, 124, 150-52, 154-55
Maxwell, James Clerk, 3, 5
Mechanism. *See* Reductionism and mechanism
Merleau-Ponty, Maurice, 61
Mermin, D., 97-98
Mind of God. *See* Scientific knowledge as a bridge to the mind of God
Minkowski spacetime, 16
Modalism, 13
Moltmann, Jürgen, 190
Music: and analogy between divine and human activity, 176-78; and mutual co-determination, 177; and time, 178

Nature. *See* Creation and relations
Nelson, Charles, 159
Neoplatonism, 64, 140
Newton, Isaac, 3, 41. *See also* Physics, classical (Newtonian)
Nicene-Constantinopolitan Creed, 108
Nicetas Stethatos, 118
Nicolaidis, Argyris, viii, 93-106, 202
Nietzsche, Friedrich, 93-94
"No cloning" principle of quantum mechanics, 26-30
Noncommutative spaces and fundamental physics, 47-51, 52-54; and MP formulations, 52-53; noncommutative algebra, 48-49, 50-51; noncommutative geometry, 48-49; philosophical importance for relational ontologies, 52-54; and process ontology, 52; and self-closed/self-contained universe, 53-54; Tomita-Takesaki theorem, 50-51; and unification of dynamics and probability, 49-51, 53; and unified theories, 47-48, 49-51, 53; von Neumann algebra, 50-51
Nonlocality/nonlocalizability: Bell's theorem and quantum entanglement, 78; and Bohm's quantum potential,

79; and EPR effect, 6-7, 18-20, 35, 78-79
Nygren, Anders, 163

Oersted, Hans Christian, 5
On the Holy Spirit (Basil the Great), 114
On the Trinity (Augustine), 118
On the Trinity (Richard of St. Victor), 121
"Orange Revolution" in Ukraine (2004), 172-73
"The Organisation of Thought" (Whitehead), 158-59
Origen, 154
Osiander, Andreas, 17

Pagels, Heinz, 88
Panentheism, 53-54
Partial "inaccessibility" of quantum information, 26
Partial translatability and the Trinity, 180-82
Participation metaphysics, 64, 69, 70
Pascal, Blaise, 10
Patristic Trinitarian thought and relational ontology, 104-6, 107-29, 185-94; Athanasius, 114, 115; Augustine's "Trinity of love," 118-21, 122; baptism, 109-11; Basil the Great, 114, 133; and causal metaphysics, 70, 115-16, 150; contrasting the Eastern/Greek approach and the Western/Latin approach, 119-21, 135, 186-87; debate over substance and personhood, 147-50, 152; and Dionysius the Areopagite, 105, 124, 150, 151; divine hypostases, 117-18, 148, 150; and *eros*, 150; God as communion, 107-9; God as mutual, interpersonal love, 113-14; God's love and freedom of love, 124; God's love and mutual joy, 124; Greek (Eastern) tradition, 104-6, 119-21, 135, 185-87; Gregory of Nazianzus, 107-8, 114-15, 116, 118, 120, 122; Gregory of Nyssa, 105, 114-15, 116, 117, 118, 133; Gregory Palamas, 105, 117-18, 154;

and Holy Spirit, 113, 115; the human person as icon of the Trinity, 125-28; *koinonia*, 114-18, 125; *logos* and *tropos*, 105, 150-52, 154-55; and Lossky, 119-20, 185-87; Maximus, 105, 150-51, 154-55; notion of consubstantiality *(homoousios)*, 114; and ontological priority of substance over relation, 59, 146-48; and onto-theology in Western tradition, 135; outlines of a Trinitarian anthropology, 125-28; perichoretic trinitarian relations, 1, 13, 70, 117; personalistic ontology based on freedom and nondeterminism, 152-53; personhood in relation to creation, 153-54; and physical world, 123-24, 192-93; and physics, 151-53, 191; prayer, 111-12; question of ontological or analogical connection between the divine and the world, 153-57; relation and essence, 104-5; Richard of St. Victor and analogy of triadic love, 121-23; Russian thought and "trinity of love," 123; sacraments, 110-11; salvation history, 109-12; "social" interpretations of Trinity, 116-17; time *(telos)* and goal or purpose, 151; Trinitarian creativity/doctrine of creation, 123-24; and "uni-personal" analogies, 118, 119, 120. *See also* Cappadocian fathers and Trinitarian theology; Trinitarian theology and relational ontology

Pauli, Wolfgang, 15, 16-18

Peirce, Charles Sanders: contributions and influence, 101; cosmological model, 102; semiosis metaphysics, 65, 95, 101-3, 106; three modes of evolutionary development, 95, 101-2; and triadic relations, 103, 106, 199

Pentecost, 110, 171, 181-82

Perichoresis, 1, 13, 70, 117

Personhood and Trinitarian theology, 107-29, 133, 146-50, 152-56, 189-90, 192; Cappadocians, 147, 148-50; debates over ontological priority of sub-

stance/relation, 59, 146-50, 152; dialogue between theology and physics over creation and personhood, 152-56; and God as mutual love, 113-14; human person as icon of the Trinity, 125-28; personhood, freedom, and non-determinism, 152-53; process thought and personalization of the world, 155; and Trinitarian anthropology, 125-28

Philia, 163

Photons, 4, 24-25, 32-33

Physics, classical (Newtonian): fields, 3; gravity, 3; and "ideal of the detached observer," 16-18; implications of EPR effect and entanglement, 7; and "no cloning" principle in quantum mechanics, 27, 28-29; spacetime and inertial frames, 16, 27

Physics and relationality, 1-11; causal connections, 7-9; cosmic effects, 10-11; eighteenth-century atomism, 2; emergence, 10; freedom and non-determinism, 152-53; and inadequacy of reductionistic methodology, vii, 2-11, 77; Mach's Principle, 10-11, 33, 41-42, 43-47, 52-53; and noncommutative model, 47-51, 52-54; and nonlocalizability (EPR effect), 6-7, 18-20, 35, 78-79; particles and fields, 3-4; and self-contained theories of the universe, 41-54; space and time, 4-5; twentieth-century discoveries of intrinsic relationality, vii, 42, 195; unified theories, 5, 47-48, 49-51, 53; what physics can teach about metaphysical and theological matters, x. *See also* Quantum entanglement

Planck level/Planck threshold, 47, 49

Platonism, 64, 105, 140, 141, 196-97

Plotinus, 147

Podolsky, Boris, 6-7, 18-20, 35, 78-79

Polkinghorne, John, vii-x, 1-14, 152, 191, 195, 200

Porphyry, 147

Index

Position measurement/momentum measurement, 19, 38

Pratītya-samutpāda metaphysics (dependent co-origination), 57, 64-65

Prayer, 111-12

Prigogine, Ilya, 152

Process metaphysics: analogy and relational Trinitarian ontology, 133-34; and causation-based relational metaphysics, 65, 68-70; linking divine and personhood, 155; and noncommutative model, 52; and the onto-theological critique, 135; prehension and concrescence, 65

Protestantism, 182-83, 194

Quantum chromodynamics, 2

Quantum complementarity, 17-18, 20, 38

Quantum computation, 21

Quantum cryptography, 21

Quantum entanglement, 15-31; Bell's reconsideration of, 20-21, 35, 36, 78; Bohm's quantum potential, 77-79; and Buddhist *pratītya-samutpāda* metaphysics, 65; and causation-based relational metaphysics, 62, 65, 67-68; and commonsense "hitting" views of causation, 67; conceptual implications, 36-40; Copenhagen interpretation, 17-18, 20; distinction between reality and information, 39; Einstein v. Bohr quarrel, 15-18, 20, 77-78; and epistemological reality, 35, 38-40; EPR argument and nonlocalizability, 6-7, 18-20, 35, 78-79; example of entangled "quantum dice," 35-36; experimenter's role, 33-34, 38; and folk versions of relational ontology, 67-68; Heisenberg's uncertainty principle, 8, 38, 78, 97; and hypostasis, 24; the "ideal of the detached observer," 15-18, 24; and information-theoretic ideas, 21, 29, 30; "no cloning" principle, 26-30; non-classical features of entangled states, 21-24; ongoing debate over, 20-21; ontological/epistemological interpretations, 32-40; position measurement/momentum measurement, 19, 38; and predictions about probability of future events, 8-9, 33, 36, 37-38, 78, 79; problem of intelligibility, 15-16; and quantum information, 24-30; and quantum teleportation, 24-26, 35-37; "remote steering" and "sinister" consequences, 20, 24; Schrödinger and, 19-20, 21, 24

Quantum information (communication), 21, 24-30; and comparision of relativity theory with quantum mechanics, 26-30; new research on application of information-theoretic ideas, 21; and "no cloning" principle, 27-29; and partial "inaccessibility," 26; quantum teleportation, 24-26, 35-37; "qubits" and differences from classical information, 25-26; Shannon's theory of information, 25, 28

Quantum mechanics/physics, 97-98; Bell's inequalities and Greenberg-Horne-Zeilinger equalities, 97; and EPR effect, 6-7, 18-20, 35, 78-79; and "exclusion principle," 4; field theory and quantum particles, 3-4; foundational debate, 34, 43; Heisenberg's uncertainty principle, 8, 38, 78, 97; and holistic worldviews, 77; and the measurement problem, 19, 38; ontological/epistemological interpretations, 32-40; and statistics that govern/constrain behavior of particles, 3-4; unpredictability, 8-9, 33, 36, 37-38, 78, 79. *See also* Quantum entanglement

Quantum teleportation, 24-26, 35-37

Rahner, Karl, 148, 187-88

Reductionism and mechanism, 2-11, 75-76, 77; and atomism, vii, 2, 57, 75; and causation, 8; problems with, vii, 2-11, 77; and a "theory of everything," 76

Relational ontology and causation. *See* Causation-based relational metaphysics (and causal theory of relations)

Relational ontology and science/physics. *See* Physics and relationality; Quantum entanglement

Relational ontology and sociology. *See* Sociological perspectives and relational ontology

Relational ontology and Trinitarian theology. *See* Trinitarian theology and relational ontology

Relations and complexity, 157-67; and children's mental development, 159-62; and continuum of self-awareness, 161-62; defining the inner complexity of a relation, 158-62; and divine-human relations, 164-66; the dynamics of reciprocal, interactive, personal relations, 162-64; and intersubjective "I-Thou relations," 157, 162; Kant on transcendental apperception, 161; and love, 162-64; self-perceptions and familiarity with oneself, 159-62; "subject-object-relation" conceptions, 157; two self-referential "reference points" (subject and object), 157-58; visual awareness of perceptions, 160-61; Whitehead on the organization of thought, 158-59

Relations/relationality, defining, x, 1, 55-58, 132, 146, 158-62

Relativity theories, 3-4; comparing the light postulate to "no cloning" principle of quantum mechanics, 26-30; and foundational debate in quantum physics, 34; general relativity and equivalence principle, 34; general relativity and Lense-Thirring effect, 45; general relativity and Mach's Principle, 44-46; general relativity and quantum theory, 47-48; general relativity and spacetime, 97; and holistic worldviews, 77; and spacetime, 4-5, 16, 27, 96-97; special relativity, 7, 16, 27, 34, 96-97

Resurrection, 110

Richard of St. Victor, 121-23, 191

Roger, Gérard, 78

Rorty, Richard, 196

Rosen, Nathan, 6-7, 18-20, 35, 78-79

Russell, Bertrand, 101

Russian Revolution, 172-73

Sacraments, 110-11

Salam, Abdus, 5

Salvation history, 109-12

Schrödinger, Erwin, 15, 19-20, 24, 36

Science and the Trinity (Polkinghorne), 152

Scientific knowledge as a bridge to the mind of God, 74-92; and "anthropic principle," 85-86, 99, 155-56; and causal relationships, 74-75; concept of an "emerging auto-germinating universe," 82; concepts of "organization" or "depth," 82; and creative evolution, 80; defining "existence," 86-87; and "fields"/"fields of force," 80, 83, 87; God and notion of "divinity," 89; the greenhouse-Earth, 84-86; holistic worldviews, 77, 80-82, 89; and intrinsic evolutionary values, 83-86; and "locality"/"non-locality," 79, 83; "mind of God" and world-manifesting "stream," 80-81; and non-random nature of many systems, 82-83; and "order," 83; the peculiarities of our relational world, 74-83; and physical laws of nature, 87-88; "physical phenomena" and the flow of time, 74; quantum entanglement and Bohm's quantum potential, 77-79; reconciling diversity and wholeness, 89; and reductionistic/mechanistic worldview, 75-76, 77; science and spirituality, 86-92; scientific cerebration and the insightful experience of "sacred," 91-92; social sciences/natural sciences and the mind

of God, 179; undivided wholeness and idea of "divine organizing principle," 80-82; and the world as "algorithmically compressible," 82-83
Self-contained theories of the universe, 41-54; and noncommutative spaces, 53-54; and panentheism, 53-54
Semiotic metaphysics: and causal relations, 65, 66, 69, 70; and Peirce, 65, 95, 101-3, 106; and perichoretic Trinitarian relations, 70
Shannon, Claude E., 25, 28
Sociological perspectives and relational ontology, 168-83; affinities between sociological and theological concepts, 168-69, 179-80; the discipline of sociology/human sciences, 168-69; double nature/double reference and binary opposition in theology, 180, 182-83; Durkheimian tradition, 179; and Holy Spirit, 170-72; and imago dei in human society, 170-73, 178; language, subjectivity, and predictions, 174-76; liturgical performance, 170-71; music and analogies between divine and human activity, 176-78; nomothetic character of sociological subject matter, 173-74, 178-79; pan-human spiritual mobilizations of the modern era, 171-73, 178; problematic notion of causality, 174; and the semantic field, 175; social sciences/natural sciences and the Mind of God, 179; the sociological approach, 173-76, 178-79; sociology and the demonic/corruption, 169; sociology's shared characteristics with the Trinity, 174-75; the specific intentionality in the human sciences, 168-69, 175-76; theological implications of sociology, 179-80; Walker's sociological approach to relational ontology, 170; Weberian tradition, 179-80
Sokolowski, Robert, 139
Spinoza, Benedict, 53-54, 81
Stengers, Isabelle, 152

String theory, 5, 103
Substantivist ontology, 55, 58, 66

Tarski's theorem, 42, 54
Tertullian, 147
Theodoret of Cyrrhus, 118
Theoleptos of Philadelphia, 118
Theoria, 136-37
"Theory of everything" (TOE), 76
Thirring, Hans, 45
"Threeness," 199
To Ablabius (Gregory of Nyssa), 117
Tomita-Takesaki theorem, 50-51
Transfiguration, 110
Trinitarian theology and relational ontology, 1, 12-13, 130-45, 146-56; and analogy, 11-12, 118, 120, 131-34, 138-42, 153-57, 198-99; and causality, 132, 150; and commitments to earlier persuasive ontologies, 138; dialogue between theology and physics, 152-56; differing Eastern/Western perspectives, 184, 185-94; and dimension of transcendence, 155; Dionysius the Areopagite, 105, 124, 150, 151; and *eros*, 150; and eschatology, 155, 181; and heresies, 13; immanent Trinity/economic Trinity, 188; and onto-theology in Western tradition, 134-35; and partial translatability of the Trinity, 180-82; and personhood, 107-29, 133, 146-50, 152-56, 189-90, 192; the "postmodern" moment, 194; problems/flaws in arguments, 130-35; and reflection on modes of unity and plurality, 144-45; reflection on relationships between divine communion and ontology, 138-40; theological reflection on divine creation (physical universe), 11-13, 136-37; *theoria*, 136-37; and Trinitarian accounts of divine action, 141-42; twentieth-century renewal/revival, 185-94. *See also* Cappadocian fathers and Trinitarian theology; Patristic

Trinitarian thought and relational ontology

Tritheism, 13

Turing's theorem, 42, 54

Twentieth-century renewal of Trinitarianism, 185-94

Tychastic evolution, 102

Unified theories, 5; dynamics and probability, 49-51, 53; general relativity and quantum theory, 47-48; and noncommutative regimes, 47-48, 49-51; "theory of everything" (TOE), 76

Unitarianism, 183

Unpredictability, quantum, 8-9, 33, 36, 37-38, 78, 79

Voiculescu, Dan V., 51

Volf, Miroslav, 130, 190

Voltaire, 86

Von Balthasar, Hans Urs, 151

Von Neumann algebra, 50-51

Walker, Andrew, 170

Ware, Timothy (Kallistos of Diokleia), ix, 107-29, 203

Weber, Max, 179-80, 182

Weinandy, Thomas G., 134

Weinberg, Steven, 5

Welker, Michael, ix, 157-67, 203

Wheeler, John Archibald, 46-47

Whitehead, Alfred North: on the organization of thought, 158-59; on parental love as model for mature love, 163; process metaphysics and causation-based relations, 65, 68-69; process ontology/metaphysics, 52, 65, 68-69

Wildman, Wesley J., viii, 55-73, 132, 195, 197, 203

William of Ockham, 58

Williams, Charles, 126

Wittgenstein, Ludwig, 56

Zeilinger, Anton, vii, 32-40, 204

Zizioulas, John D., ix, 114, 146-56, 170, 204; arguments for Trinitarian relational ontology, 130-31, 133; and "Being as Communion," 12-13, 108; and divine/human personhood, 133, 189-90; influence on scientists/physicists, 191; influence on Western theologians, 190-91; and Lossky, 189, 190; and participation metaphysics, 64; and relationality principle, 94-95; and second wave of Trinitarian revival/renewal, 188-91